American Popular Music

Comprehensive Index

American Popular Music

Blues
Classical
Country
Folk
Jazz
Rhythm & Blues, Rap, and Hip-Hop
Rock and Roll

General Editor: Richard Carlin

American Popular Music

Comprehensive Index

Facts On File
An imprint of Infobase Publishing

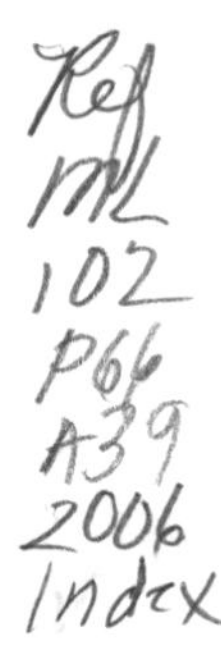

American Popular Music: Comprehensive Index

Facts On File, Inc.
An imprint of Infobase Publishing
132 West 31st Street
New York NY 10001

Cataloging-in-Publication data for this book is on file with the Library of Congress.

ISBN: 0-8160-6516-0

Facts On File books are available at special discounts when purchased in bulk quantities for businesses, associations, institutions, or sales promotions. Please call our Special Sales Department in New York at (212) 967-8800 or (800) 322-8755.

You can find Facts On File on the World Wide Web at http://www.factsonfile.com

Text design by James Scotto-Lavino
Cover design by Nora Wertz

Printed in the United States of America

VB FOF 10 9 8 7 6 5 4 3 2

This book is printed on acid-free paper.

Preface

American popular music reflects the rich cultural diversity of the American people. From classical to folk to jazz, America has contributed a rich legacy of musical styles to the world over its two-plus centuries of existence. The rich cross-fertilization of cultures—African-American, Hispanic, Asian, and European—has resulted in one of the unique musical mixtures in the world.

American Popular Music celebrates this great diversity by presenting to the student, researcher, and individual enthusiast a wealth of information on each musical style in an easily accessible format. The subjects covered are:

Blues
Classical music
Country
Folk music
Jazz
Rock and Roll
Rhythm and Blues, Rap, and Hip-Hop

Each volume presents key information on performers, musical genres, famous compositions, musical instruments, media, and centers of musical activity. The volumes conclude with a chronology, recommended listening, and a complete bibliography or list of sources for further study.

How do we define popular music? Literally, any music that attracts a reasonably large audience is "popular" (as opposed to "unpopular"). Over the past few decades, however, as the study of popular music has grown, the term has come to have specific meanings. While some might exclude certain genres covered in this series—American classical music leaps to mind—we felt that it was important to represent the range of musical styles that have been popular in the United States over its entire history. New scholarship has brought to light the interplay among genres that previously were felt to be unrelated—such as the influence of folk forms on classical music, opera's influence on jazz, or the blues' influence on country—so that to truly understand each musical style, it is important to be conversant with at least some aspects of all.

These volumes are intended to be introductory, not comprehensive. Any "A to Z" work is by its very nature selective; it's impossible to include *every* figure, *every* song, or *every* key event. For most users, we hope the selections made here will be more than adequate, giving information on the key composers and performers who shaped each style, while also introducing some lesser-known figures who are worthy of study. The Editorial Board and other outside advisers played a key role in reviewing the entry lists for completeness.

All encyclopedia authors also face the rather daunting task of separating fact from fiction when writing short biographies of performers and composers. Even birth and death dates can be "up for grabs," as artists have been known to subtract years from their lives in their official biographies. "Official" records are often unavailable, particularly for earlier artists who may have been born at home, or for those whose family histories themselves are shrouded in mystery. We have attempted

to draw on the latest research and most reliable sources whenever possible, and have also pointed out when key facts are in dispute. And, for many popular performers, the myth can be as important as the reality when it comes to their lives, so we have tried to honor both in writing about their achievements.

Popular music reflects the concerns of the artists who create it and their audience. Each era of our country's history has spawned a variety of popular music styles, and these styles in turn have grown over the decades as new performers and new times have arisen. These volumes try to place the music into its context, acknowledging that the way music is performed and its effect on the greater society is as important as the music itself. We've also tried to highlight the many interchanges between styles and performers, because one of the unique—and important—aspects of American cultural life is the way that various people have come together to create a new culture out of the interplay of their original practices and beliefs.

Race, class, culture, and sex have played roles in the development of American popular music. Regrettably, the playing field has not always been level for performers from different backgrounds, particularly when it comes to the business aspects of the industry: paying royalties, honoring copyrights, and the general treatment of artists. Some figures have been forgotten or ignored who deserved greater attention; the marketplace can be ruthless, and its agents—music publishers, record producers, concert promoters—have and undoubtedly will continue to take advantage of the musicians trying to bring their unique voices to market. These volumes attempt to address many of these issues as they have affected the development of individual musicians' careers as well as from the larger perspective of the growth of popular music. The reader is encouraged to delve further into these topics by referring to the bibliographies in each volume.

Popular music can be a slave itself to crass commercialism, as well as a bevy of hangers-on, fellow travelers, and others who seek only to make a quick buck by following easy-to-identify trends. While we bemoan the lack of new visionary artists today like Bessie Smith, Miles Davis, Pauline Oliveros, or Bob Dylan, it's important to remember that when they first came on the scene the vast majority of popular performers were journeymen musicians at best. Popular music will always include many second-, third-, and fourth-tier performers; some will offer one or two recordings or performances that will have a lasting impact, while many will be celebrated during their 15 minutes of fame, but most will be forgotten. In separating the wheat from the chaff, it is understandably easier for our writers working on earlier styles where the passing of time has helped sort out the important from the just popular. However, all the contributors have tried to supply some distance, giving greatest weight to the true artists, while acknowledging that popular figures who are less talented can nonetheless have a great impact on the genre during their performing career—no matter how brief it might be.

All in all, the range, depth, and quality of popular musical styles that have developed in the United States over its lifetime is truly amazing. These styles could not have arisen anywhere else, but are the unique products of the mixing of cultures, geography, technology, and sheer luck that helped disseminate each style. Who could have forecast the music of Bill Monroe before he assembled his first great bluegrass band? Or predicted the melding of gospel, rhythm and blues, and popular music achieved by Aretha Franklin during her reign as "Queen of Soul"? The tinkering of classical composer John Cage—who admitted to having no talent for creating melodies—was a truly American response to new technologies, a new environment, and a new role for music in our lives. And Patti Smith's particular take on poetry, the punk-rock movement, and the difficulties faced by a woman who leads a rock band make her music particularly compelling and original—and unpredictable to those who dismissed the original rock records as mere "teenage fluff."

We hope that the volumes in this series will open your eyes, minds, and, most important, your ears to a world of musical styles. Some may be familiar, others more obscure, but all are worthy. With today's proliferation of sound on the Web, finding even the most obscure recording is becoming increasingly simple. We urge you to read deeply but also to put these books down to listen. Come to your own conclusions. American popular music is a rich world, one open to many different interpretations. We hope these volumes serve as your windows to these many compelling worlds.

Richard Carlin,
General Editor

Index

Individual volumes in the American Popular Music series are identified by the following codes:
BL = *Blues*
CL = *Classical*
CO = *Country*
FO = *Folk*
JA = *Jazz*
RR = *Rock and Roll*
RB = *Rhythm and Blues, Rap, and Hip-Hop*

Page numbers in **bold** indicate main entries; page numbers in *italic* indicate photographs.

A

AABA form JA: **1,** 19, 23
AAB form JA: **1**
AACM. *See* Association for the Advancement of Creative Musicians
Aaliyah RB: 79, 258
Abas, Matyas CL: 163
Abbey, Henry CL: 154, 155
Abbruzzese, Dave RR: 168
ABC radio network CL: 239; CO: 142
Abdul, Paula RB: **1,** 223
Aberbach, Julian BL: 47
Abercrombie, John JA: **1,** 80, 124, 154, 224
Abner, Ewart RB: 239
Above the Law RB: **1–2**
Abrahams, Roger BL: 53
Abrams, Miriam CL: 241
Abrams, Muhal Richard JA: **1–2,** *2,* 7, 46, 122, 197
Abramson, Herb BL: 9, 121, 179; RB: **2,** 83
Abravenel, Maurice CL: *1,* **1–2,** 2, 231
Abravenel Hall CL: 1, **2,** 231
Abshire, Nathan CO: 29; FO: **1,** 2, 11, 27
Academy of St.-Martin-in-the-Fields CL: 24, 148
Acadia FO: 27
a cappella FO: 42, 154; RB: **2,** 78–79, 205–206, 226
accent JA: **2,** 91, 192
accordions FO: **1–2**
AC/DC RR: 106
Ace, Johnny BL: 158, 181; RB: **2,** 203
Aces, The BL: 148–149, 241
"Achy Breaky Heart" CO: **1,** 49
acid jazz JA: xxv, **2–3,** 252*t;* RB: **2–3**
acid tests RR: 93
Ackley, Bruce JA: 166
acoustic bass. *See* double bass
acoustic guitar BL: *1,* **1–4,** *2, 4;* RR: 99
"Act Naturally" CO: **1,** 45, 62, 156; RR: 44
Acuff, Roy CO: **1–2,** *2*
  Bailes Brothers CO: 9; FO: 10
  "Little" Jimmy Dickens CO: 57
  Dobro CO: 60; FO: 54
  Grand Ole Opry CO: 87
  Bobby Hebb RB: 120
  Melba Montgomery CO: 142
  record labels CO: 170
  Fred and Wesley Rose CO: 179
  "Wabash Cannonball" CO: 209
  "Wreck on the Highway" CO: 221
Acuff-Rose Publishing
  Boudleaux and Felice Bryant CO: 26
  Everly Brothers CO: 70
  Nashville sound CO: 147
  record labels CO: 170
  Fred Rose CO: 179
  Aaron Tippin CO: 199
Acuna, Alex JA: 15
AD RB: **3**
Adagio for Strings (Samuel Barber) CL: **2,** 17

Adams, Claus CL: **2**
Adams, Faye RB: **3**
Adams, John CL: **2–3, 168–169,** 197, 198, 251
Adams, Johnny BL: 238
Adams, Oleta RB: **3–4**
Adams, Pepper JA: **3,** 19
ADC Band RB: **4**
Adcock, Eddie FO: 11, 43–44
Adderley, Cannonball JA: **3,** RB: 257, 275
  Miles Davis JA: 49
  Barry Harris JA: 86
  Coleman Hawkins JA: 87
  Kind of Blue JA: 113
  Yusef Lateef JA: 121
  Nancy Wilson JA: 218
  Joe Zawinul JA: 223
Adegbolola, Gay BL: 187
Adkins, Trace CO: **2,** 99
Adler, Kurt Herbert CL: **3,** 198
Adler, Larry BL: 194
Adler, Lou RR: 146, 152
Adler, Peter Herman CL: **3–4**
Adler, Samuel CL: **4**
Aeolian Hall (New York City) CL: 188; JA: 213
Aerosmith RR: **1–3,** *2*
AFM. *See* American Federation of Musicians
Africa BL: xv. *See also* South African jazz
  banjo BL: 13; JA: 9
  blind musicians and singers BL: 19
  Richard Bona JA: 20
  Abbey Lincoln JA: 123
  Alan Lomax BL: 118
  Lloyd Price BL: 165
  "Wimoweh" FO: 215–216
Afrocentricity RB: 192, 223, 235, 287
Afro-Cuban music. *See* Latin and Afro-Cuban jazz
Afros, The RB: **4**
Aftertones of Infinity (Joseph Schwantner) CL: **4**
AG. *See* Showbiz and AG
AIDS CL: 138; RR: 193
Air Music (Ned Rorem) CL: **4**
Akeman, David. *See* Stringbean
Akiyoshi, Toshiko JA: **3–4,** *4,* 103
Alabama (state). *See* FAME Studio; Muscle Shoals, Alabama
Alabama (vocal group) CO: **3,** 144, 203
Aladdin Records RB: **4**
Albeneri Trio CL: **4–5,** 16, 123, 200
Albert, Stephen CL: **5**
Albert E. Brumley Music Company CO: 26; FO: 22
Albert Hall (London, England) RR: 78
Albertson, Chris BL: 194
Albin, Peter RR: 122
Albion Band FO: 40, 102, 117
Albrecht, Charles CL: **5**
Alderman, Tony FO: 97
Alexakis, Art RR: 99
Alexander, Arthur RB: 115, 189
Alexander, Honey BL: 163
Alexander, Texas BL: **4,** 40, 45, 66, 81, 96
Alexander, Van JA: 70
Alexander's Daybreakers CO: 20
Alger, Pat FO: **2**
Ali, Bardu BL: 155
Ali, Rashied JA: 41, 46
Alias, Don JA: 15
aliases BL: **5,** 72, 77
Alice in Chains RR: 98
Alice Tully Hall CL: **5,** 7, 14, 48, 112, 228
Alkan, Valentin CL: 136
Alka-Seltzer CO: 148
Allan, Buddy CO: 155
Allan, Davie, and the Arrows RR: 116
Allcock, Martin FO: 64
Allen, Annisteen RB: **4–5,** 183
Allen, Austin FO: 3, 4
Allen, Duane CO: 153
Allen, Henry "Red" BL: 165
Allen, Jules Verne FO: **2**
Allen, Lee FO: 3, 4; RB: 21; RR: 58
Allen, Lewis BL: 76
Allen, Marshall JA: 190
Allen, O. K. FO: 123
Allen, Paul BL: 75; RR: 110–111
Allen, Red FO: **2–3,** 61, 83, 153, 154
Allen, Rex CO: **3**
Allen, Richard BL: 244
Allen, Rosalie CO: 22
Allen, Steve RR: 180
Allen, Terry FO: **3**
Allen Brothers FO: **3–4,** 179
Aller, Eleanor CL: **5,** 105, 209, 210
Alligator Records BL: **5,** 51–52, 85
Allison, Jerry RR: 68, 111–114
Allison, Luther BL: **5,** *6*
Allison, Mose BL: **6,** 138, 237
Allman, Duane BL: **6,** 41; RR: 3–5
Allman, Gregg BL: 6; RR: 3–6
Allman Brothers Band, The BL: **6;** RR: **3–6**
  blues rock RR: 29
  instrumental rock RR: 116
  "Statesboro Blues" BL: 206
  "Stormy Monday" BL: 207
  Derek Trucks BL: 222
Allman Joys RR: 4
"All My Ex's Live in Texas" CO: **3**

"All My Rowdy Friends (Have Settled Down)" CO: **3,** 217
all-women orchestras JA: 47, 53, 99. *See also* women in jazz
Almanac House FO: 212
Almanac Singers, The BL: 168; FO: 87, 168, 182, 212, 214
Alomar, Carlos RB: 269
ALP (American Labor Party) BL: 168
Alpert, Herb RB: 178
Alsop, Marin CL: **5–6,** 41
Alsup, Tommy CO: 101
ALT RB: **5**
Altamont festival RR: 206, 210
Altan FO: **4**
alt-country CO: 24, 245; FO: 137, 215; RR: 210
alternative rock RR: xx, **6–8,** 97–99
Altman, Robert CO: 126
alto saxophone. *See* saxophone; *specific alto players*
Altschul, Barry JA: 22, 41, 42
"Always Late (With Your Kisses)" CO: **3–4**
Amahl and the Night Visitors (Gian Carlo Menotti) CL: xxv–xxvi, 4, **6,** 152, 200
ambient techno RB: 254, 260
Ambrose, Bert JA: 25
Amburgey, Bertha CO: 33
Amburgey, Opal CO: 33
Amburgey Sisters CO: 33
Ament, Jeff RR: 167
Americana RR: 210
American Bach Soloists CL: **6**
American Bandstand
  Bobby Darin RR: 51
  Four Seasons RR: 86
  Righteous Brothers, The RR: 205
  Silhouettes, The RB: 239
  Simon and Garfunkel RR: 217
  Phil Spector RR: 222
  Ritchie Valens RR: 239
American Beauty (Grateful Dead) CO: 45; RR: 95, 211
American Brass Quintet CL: **6–7,** 203
American Composers Forum CL: **7,** 134
American Composers Orchestra CL: **7,** 13, 23, 65, 224
American Federation of Musicians (AFM) BL: 178–179
American Festival Overture (William Schuman) CL: **7**
American Folklife Center FO: 5
American Guild of Artists and Composers BL: 218
American Indians. *See* Native Americans
An American in Paris (George Gershwin) CL: **7,** 87
American Jazz Museum (Kansas City, Missouri) JA: **4**
American Jazz Music (Wilder Hobson) JA: **4**
American Labor Party (ALP) BL: 168
American Music (journal) CL: **7**
American Music Center CL: **7,** 22, 143, 227, 237
American Society of Composers, Authors and Publishers (ASCAP) CL: 102; BL: 72, 145
American Songbag, The (Carl Sandburg collection) FO: viii, 180, 189
American String Quartet CL: **7–8**
American Symphony Orchestra CL: **8,** 35, 203, 217
American Symphony Orchestra League CL: 2, **8**
Ammons, Albert BL: 27, 96, 114
Ammons, Gene JA: 188
Amnesty International RR: 235
amplification BL: xxii–xxiii, 73, 87, 116
Anastasio, Trey RR: 53, 118
Ancient Voices of Children (George Crumb) CL: **8**
Andersen, Arild JA: 185
Anderson, Debra RB: 245, 246
Anderson, Eric FO: **4**
Anderson, Ian RR: 184
Anderson, Ivie JA: *5,* **5,** 99
Anderson, John CO: **4,** 195; FO: 80
Anderson, Jon RR: 184
Anderson, June CL: *8,* **8–9**
Anderson, Laurie CL: **9;** RB: 162
Anderson, Liz CO: 4
Anderson, Lynn CO: **4,** 43, 44, 180
Anderson, Marian CL: **9–10,** *10*
Anderson, Michael FO: 43
Anderson, Pete FO: 69
Anderson, Pink BL: **6–7,** 213
Anderson, Reid JA: 9
Anderson, Signe Toly RR: 119
Anderson, "Whispering" Bill CO: **4,** *157*
  Jan Howard CO: 105
  Roger Miller CO: 140
  Connie Smith CO: 187
  "Still" CO: 192
  Lee Ann Womack CO: 219
And His Mother Called Him Bill (Duke Ellington) JA: **4–5,** 189
Andrew, Sam BL: 100; RR: 122
Andrews, Lee, and the Hearts RB: **5**
Andrews, Tom FO: 15

Andrews Sisters BL: 28; CO: 162, 203
Anglin, Jack CO: 212
Angola Penitentiary (Louisiana) BL: 112, 244; FO: 123, 127
Animals, The BL: **7,** 245; RR: **8–9,** 28, 152
Anita Kerr Singers CO: 147
Anka, Paul FO: 79
Annan, Kofi CL: 153
Ann Arbor, Michigan BL: 19
Ann Arbor Blues and Jazz Festival BL: 123, 269
Ansermet, Ernest JA: 12
Antek, Samuel CL: 163
Antes, John CL: **11**
Antheil, George CL: **11–12,** 16
Anthony, Eddie BL: 61, 82
antiwar movement. *See* Vietnam War
Antoinette RB: **5–6**
Antone, Clifford BL: 207, 216
Antone's (nightclub, Austin, Texas) BL: 12, 25, 113, 207–208
Antony and Cleopatra (Barber) CL: 18, 155
Apollo's Fire CL: **12**
Apollo Theater (Harlem)
  DJ Hollywood RB: 63
  Drifters, The RB: 72
  John Hammond, Sr. BL: 71
  Eddie Kendricks RB: 151
  Stephanie Mills RB: 184
  New York City BL: 152
  Bessie Smith JA: 183
  Joe Tex RB: 256
  Sister Rosetta Tharpe BL: 217
  Sarah Vaughn JA: 205
Apollo Theater Amateur Night RB: 49, 51, 89, 115
Appalachian Spring (Aaron Copeland) CL: **12,** 57, 147
Appel, Mike RR: 224
A&R (artists and repertoire) CO: 5–6
Archer, Frederick CL: 179
Archive of American Folk Song, The FO: ix, **4–5,** 96, 113, 127
Archive of Folk Culture FO: 5
Arc Music BL: xxi, 39
Ardoin, Alphonse "Bois Sec" FO: 5
Ardoin, Amédée FO: 1, 5
Ardoin, Chris FO: 5
Ardoin, Lawrence "Black" FO: 5
Ardoin, Sean FO: 5
Ardoin Family FO: **5**
Area Code 615 CO: 136
Areas, José "Chepito" RR: 213
Argento, Dominick CL: **12, 82,** 134
Arhoolie Records BL: **7,** 35, 145. *See also* Strachwitz, Chris
Arkansas BL: xix, **7**. *See also* Helena, Arkansas
Arkie the Arkansas Woodchopper FO: **5**
Arm, Theodore CL: 221
Armadillo World Headquarters BL: 216
Armstrong, Floyd FO: 6
Armstrong, Frankie FO: **5–6,** 131
Armstrong, Howard BL: **7–8,** 62, 125, 208
Armstrong, Lil Hardin. *See* Hardin, Lil
Armstrong, Lloyd FO: 6
Armstrong, Louis BL: xviii, **8;** JA: xxiii, **5–6**
  Sid Catlett JA: 30
  in Chicago JA: xxiii
  Chicago jazz JA: 32
  Cozy Cole RB: 46
  cornet JA: 43
  "Dipper Mouth Blues" JA: 52
  Baby Dodds JA: 53
  Johnny Dodds JA: 54
  Fats Domino RR: 59
  Roy Eldridge JA: 59
  European jazz JA: 64
  Ella Fitzgerald JA: 70
  Dexter Gordon JA: 77
  Lionel Hampton JA: 81
  Lil Hardin JA: 84
  Lil Hardin and JA: xxx
  "Heebie Jeebies" JA: **88–89**
  Fletcher Henderson JA: 89
  Earl "Fatha" Hines JA: 91
  Billie Holiday JA: 91
  Hot Five and Hot Seven JA: **94**
  Alberta Hunter BL: 83
  Japanese jazz JA: 103
  jazz BL: 92
  jazz firsts JA: 116
  Lonnie Johnson BL: 96; RB: 144
  Freddie Keppard JA: 113
  Hugh Masekela JA: 129
  Lizzie Miles BL: 135
  Charles Mingus JA: 136
  New Orleans BL: 121
  New Orleans jazz JA: 143
  Newport Jazz Festival JA: 144
  King Oliver JA: 147, 148
  Kid Ory JA: 150
  Ralph Peer BL: 158
  Ma Rainey BL: 177; JA: 161
  recordings of early jazz JA: 162
  Don Redman JA: 163
  Jimmie Rodgers BL: 184; CO: 177
  "St. Louis Blues" JA: 187

saxophone, trombone, trumpet, and clarinet BL: 189
scat singing JA: 171
Artie Shaw JA: 175
"Singin' the Blues" JA: 182
Bessie Smith BL: 194; JA: 183
Stuff Smith JA: 184
Jack Teagarden JA: 195
"Trouble in Mind" BL: 222
Fats Waller JA: 210
Mary Lou Williams JA: 215
Armstrong Twins FO: **6**
Arnold, Billy Boy BL: 73
Arnold, Blind Man BL: 18, 78
Arnold, Eddy CO: **4–5**
"Bouquet of Roses" CO: 19
Boudleaux and Felice Bryant CO: 26
"Cattle Call" CO: 36
Cowboy Copas CO: 43
Jimmy Driftwood CO: 63
Grand Ole Opry CO: 87
Rex Griffin CO: 89
Jordanaires CO: 112
Pee Wee King CO: 117
"Make the World Go Away" CO: 131
Arnold, Jerome BL: 33
Arnold, Kokomo BL: **8**
"Dust My Broom" BL: 55
"How Long, How Long Blues" BL: 82
protest songs BL: 167
slide guitar BL: 193
"Sweet Home Chicago" BL: 210
Peetie Wheatstraw BL: 241
Arno Pres CL: 76
arrangement JA: **6**
arranger JA: **6**
Arrested Development RB: 238
Arrington, Charles FO: 86
Art Ensemble of Chicago JA: **6–7,** 7, 20–21, 69, 137
Arthur, Emry CO: 107; FO: **6**
Arthur, Henry FO: 6
Arthur, Sam FO: 6
Arthur Godfrey Show CO: 14, 116
Art of Noise, The RB: 125
ASCAP. *See* American Society of Composers, Authors and Publishers
Asch, Moses (Moe) BL: **8–9;** FO: **7.** *See also* Folkways Records
Broadside magazine FO: 19
Folkways Records BL: 64
Lead Belly FO: 123
Brownie McGhee BL: 129
New York City BL: 153
Sandy Paton FO: 155
recording FO: 163–164
record labels BL: 180; CO: 170
Sing Out! magazine FO: 186
Harry Smith FO: 189
Hobart Smith FO: 190
Asch, Sholem FO: 7
Asher, Peter FO: 200
Asher, Tony RR: 16
Asheville, North Carolina FO: 128–129, 138, 142, 195
Ashford, Bill BL: 184
Ashford, Nick RB: 6
Ashford & Simpson RB: **6**
Ash Grove club (Los Angeles) BL: 35, 213; FO: 115
Ashley, Enoch FO: 7
Ashley, Robert CL: **12–13**
Ashley, Tom (Clarence) FO: **7–8,** 29, 170, 190, 211
Asleep at the Wheel CO: **5,** 214; FO: 77, 213
Aspen Music Festival and School CL: **13**
Association, The RR: 176
Association for the Advancement of Creative Musicians (AACM) JA: **7**
Muhal Richard Abrams JA: 1–2
Lester Bowie JA: 20
Anthony Braxton JA: 21
Leroy Jenkins JA: 107
George Lewis JA: 122
Roscoe Mitchell JA: 137
Astaire, Fred CL: 86
Astbury, Ian RR: 64
Atcher, Bob FO: **8**
Athens, Georgia RR: 201
"A-Tisket A-Tasket" JA: **7,** 70, 212
Atkins, Chet CO: xviii, **5–6,** *6*
Suzy Bogguss CO: 18
"Cowboy" Jack Clement CO: 38
Floyd Cramer CO: 47
Everly Brothers CO: 70
Everly Brothers, The RR: 77
Don Gibson CO: 81
Grand Ole Opry CO: 87
guitar CO: 90
Bobby Hebb RB: 120
Waylon Jennings CO: 110
Jordanaires CO: 112
Grady Martin CO: 134
Jimmy Murphy FO: 144
Nashville sound CO: 147, 148
Elvis Presley RB: 210; RR: 181
record labels CO: 168
Jerry Reed CO: 171
Merle Travis CO: 200
Dottie West CO: 213
Atkins, Juan RB: **6,** 95

Atlanta, Georgia BL: **9**
Atlanta Symphony Orchestra CL: **13,** 208, 212
Atlantic Records BL: **9**. *See also* Abramson, Herb; Dowd, Tom; Ertegun, Ahmet; Ertegun, Nesuhi; Wexler, Jerry
 jump blues and rhythm and blues BL: 101
 Memphis BL: 132
 Muscle Shoals RB: 189
 music business BL: 147–148
 New York City BL: 153
 record labels BL: 179, 180
Atlantic Starr RB: **6**
atonality CL: 36, 171, 203, 233
Auer, Leopold CL: 74, 100, 245
Auger, Brian RR: 127, 251
Augusta, Georgia BL: 142
Auldridge, Mike FO: 183
Aung San Suu Kyi RR: 237
Austin, Dallas RB: 186, 259
Austin, Gene CO: 104; FO: 168
Austin, Lonnie FO: 159
Austin, Lovie BL: **9–10,** 54, 161; JA: **7**
Austin, Texas BL: 25–26, **216**
Austin, William CL: **13**
Australia CO: 47; RR: 157
Austria JA: 126–127, 223; RR: 157
autoharp CO: **6,** 34; FO: 18, 37, 181
Autori, Franco CL: 39
Autry, Gene CO: **7,** *7*
 "Back in the Saddle Again" CO: 9
 Johnny Bond CO: 19
 cowboy songs CO: 46
 Fats Domino RR: 59
 Duke of Paducah, The CO: 65
 Don Edwards CO: 67–68
 guitar CO: 90
 Bill Haley and His Comets RR: 101
 Stuart Hamblen CO: 93
 Haywire Mac FO: 94
 Pee Wee King CO: 117
 Roy Rogers CO: 179
 Fred Rose CO: 179
 "Rudolph, the Red-Nosed Reindeer" CO: 182
 "Tumbling Tumbleweeds" CO: 204
 yodeling CO: 224
Avakian, George JA: 158
Avalon, Mississippi BL: 83, **137;** FO: 101, 102
Avalon Ballroom RR: 122
avant-garde JA: xxiv, **7**. *See also* free jazz/free improvisation
Avery Fisher Hall CL: 8, **14,** 164
Avory, Mick RR: 128
Avshalomov, Daniel CL: 8
Ax, Emanuel CL: **14,** 214
Axton, Charles "Packy" RB: 175
Axton, Estelle BL: 131, 180; RB: 175, 246
Axton, Hoyt FO: **8,** 208
Axton, Mae Boren FO: 8
Ayres, Frederic CL: **14**
Azara (John Knowles Paine) CL: **14**
Azor, Hurby "Luv Bug" RB: 5, 152, 159, 233, 234
Azteca RB: 237

B

Babbitt, Milton CL: **15,** 55, 138, 149, 197
Babbs, Ken RR: 249
"Baby, Please Don't Go" BL: **11,** 243
Babyface RB: 223. *See also* Reid, L. A. and Babyface
Bach, Johann Sebastian CL: xxi, 43, 173, 205, **218**
Bach, P. D. Q. (Peter Schickele) CL: 134, 199, 200
Bacharach, Burt RB: 274
Bachman, Maria CL: 134
Bachman, Randy RR: 253
"Back in the Saddle Again" CO: 7, **9**
"Backwater Blues" BL: **11**
Backwoods Band, The FO: 97
Bacon, Ernst CL: **15**
Bacon Fat BL: 163, 194
Bad Boy Records RB: **7**
Badfinger RR: 177
Bad Plus, The JA: **9**
Bad Religion RR: 189
Badrena, Manolo JA: 15, 223
Baez, Joan FO: ix, **9,** 34, 76, 81, 82
bagpipes FO: **9–10,** 34–35; JA: 85–86
Bailes, Homer Abraham, Jr. CO: 9
Bailes, Johnnie CO: 9; FO: 10
Bailes, Kyle CO: 9
Bailes, Walter Butler CO: 9; FO: 10, 197
Bailes Brothers, The CO: **9,** 123; FO: **10**
Bailey, DeFord CO: **9–10**
 Grand Ole Opry CO: 86
 harmonica BL: 72; FO: 90, 92
 Hay, George D. CO: 97
 railroad songs CO: 166
Bailey, Mildred BL: 238; JA: 211
Bailey, Philip RB: **7,** 77
Bain, Aly FO: 18, 75
Baker, Anita RB: **7–8**
Baker, Chet JA: **9,** 75, 80, 142, 172
Baker, Etta BL: **11;** FO: **10–11,** 36

Baker, Ginger BL: 41, 46; RR: 40, 45, 68
Baker, Hylda JA: 14
Baker, Janet CL: 82, 184
Baker, Kenny CO: 141; FO: **11,** 81, 122
Baker, LaVern RB: **8**
Baker, Madelon RB: 203
Baker, Mickey BL: 55; RB: 119, 228
Baker, Ray CO: 10
Baker, Shorty JA: 215
Bakersfield Sound CO: **10**
  Tommy Collins CO: 41
  country rock RR: 44
  Merle Haggard CO: 91–92
  Wade Hayes CO: 97
  Ferlin Husky CO: 106
  Bonnie Owens CO: 155
  Buck Owens CO: 155–156
Balanchine, George JA: 172
Baldknobbers, The CO: 22
Baldry, Long John BL: **11,** 108
Balfa, Dewey FO: 11–12
Balfa, Harry FO: 11
Balfa, Nelda FO: 12
Balfa, Rodney FO: 11, 12
Balfa, Will FO: 11, 12
Balfa Brothers, The CO: 29; FO: 1, **11–12,** 27, 170, 180
Balfa Toujours FO: 12
Bali (Henry Eichheim) CL: **15**
Balin, Marty RR: 119–121, 206
Ball, E. C. and Orna FO: **12**
Ball, Marcia BL: **11–12,** 207
Ball, Orna FO: 12
Ball, Wilbur CO: 31
Ballad of Baby Doe, The (Douglas S. Moore) CL: **15**
"Ball and Chain" BL: 100, 219–220; RR: 123
Ballard, Glen RR: 53
Ballard, Hank, and the Midnighters RB: **8–9,** *9*
ballet CL: 29–30
Ballet méchanique (George Antheil) CL: 11, **16**
ballrooms JA: 170–171
Balsam, Artur CL: 5, **16,** 83, 130, 174
Balsley, Phil CO: 192
Baltimore Symphony Orchestra CL: **16–17**
Bambaataaa, Afrika RB: **9–10,** 109, 162, 259
Banchetto Musicale. *See* Boston Baroque
Band, The RR: **11–13,** *12*
  Bob Dylan RR: 71
  Albert Grossman FO: 83–84
  Louisiana Red BL: 121
  rock festivals RR: 207
  roots rock RR: 211
Band, The (2nd album) RR: 12–13, 211
Band of Gypsys RB: 183; RR: 109–110
Bandy, Moe CO: **10–11,** 99
Bangs, Lester RR: **13–14**
banjo BL: xviii, xxii, *12,* **12–14,** *14;* JA: xxvi, **9**
banjo (five-string) CO: *11,* **11–12;** FO: **12–13,** *13*
Banks, Darrell RB: **10**
Bankston, Dick BL: **14**
Bannon, R. C. CO: 133
Banton, Buju RB: **10**
Barbata, John RR: 120
Barbecue Bob BL: 9, **15,** 77, 142, 240
Barber, Chris BL: 108
Barber, John JA: 15
Barber, Samuel CL: ix, xxv, **17–18**
  Adagio for Strings CL: **2**
  Marin Alsop CL: 6
  John Browning CL: 39
  Raya Garbousova CL: 85
  Gian Carlo Menotti CL: 152
  Metropolitan Opera CL: 155
  NBC Symphony Orchestra CL: 162
  Daniel Pinkham CL: 178
  recommended listening CL: 250
  Thomas Schippers CL: 200
  Vanessa CL: **233**
Barbieri, Gato JA: 1, **9–10,** 31, 97
Barbirolli, Sir John CL: **18,** 190
Barbour, Ross BL: 137
Bard Music Festival CL: **18–19,** 35
Bare, Bobby CO: viii, **12,** 55, 56, 105, 198
Barenberg, Russ FO: 42, 55
Barenboim, Daniel CL: **19,** 50
Barere, Simon CL: **19–20**
Barge, Gene "Daddy G" RB: 22
Barili, Alfredo CL: **20**
baritone saxophone JA: 3, 141–142, 187, 191
Bar-Kays RB: **10**
Barker, Blue Lu BL: 15
Barker, Danny BL: **15**
Barker, Horton FO: 155
Barnes, Clive CL: 74
Barnes, J. J. RB: **10–11**
Barnes, James "B. J." RB: 205
Barnet, Charlie JA: 93, 117, 196; RB: 124
Barnum, P. T. CL: 139
Barrand, Tony. *See* Roberts, John and Tony Barrand
barrelhouse BL: 208–209
Barrett, Aston and Carlton RB: 175
Barrett, Emma JA: **10**
Barrett, Richard RB: 38, 105; RR: 90

Barrett, Syd BL: 7; RR: 172
Barron, Kenny JA: 30
Barron Wilkins' Club JA: 85
Barrow, Keith RB: **11**
Barry, Garrett FO: 35
Barry, Jeff RB: 20, 62, 142; RR: 34, 91, 223
Barry, Joe CO: 51
Barry, Len RB: 200
Barth, Bill BL: 90
Bartholomew, Dave RB: 64, 165; RR: 57–59
Bartók, Béla CL: 70, 129
Barton, Lou Ann BL: 12, 185, 207, 228
Barzin, Leon CL: **20**
Basehead RB: **11**
Basho, Robbie FO: 63
Basie, Count JA: **10,** *11*
  Tony Bennett JA: 13
  Carnegie Hall JA: 28
  comping JA: 41
  Roy Eldridge JA: 60
  Ella Fitzgerald JA: 70
  Billie Holiday JA: 91
  Helen Humes BL: 83
  JATP JA: 106
  jazz and the blues BL: 92
  James P. Johnson JA: 107
  Quincy Jones JA: 110
  Thad Jones JA: 110
  Kansas City jazz JA: 111
  Bennie Moten JA: 141
  Oscar Peterson JA: 153
  recordings of early jazz JA: 162
  Don Redman JA: 163
  Jimmy Rushing BL: 186
  Savoy Ballroom JA: 171
  Clark Terry JA: 196
  Sir Charles Thompson JA: 197
  Big Joe Turner BL: 223
  Joe Williams BL: 244
  Shadow Wilson JA: 218
  Lester Young JA: 220
bass BL: 53, 86–87; RR: **14–15,** 153. *See also* double bass; electric bass
bass and drums BL: **15–16**
Bassett, Leslie CL: *20,* **20–21**
bass fiddle. *See* double bass
bass guitar JA: **10–11**. *See also* electric bass
Bastin, Bruce BL: **16,** 121
Bate, Alcyone CO: 12
Bate, Buster CO: 12
Bate, Dr. Humphrey BL: 72; CO: 9, **12,** 86; FO: 92
Bates, Deacon L. J. (Blind Lemon Jefferson) BL: 77
Baton Rouge, Louisiana BL: 69, 115, 151
Battin, Skip FO: 25; RR: 37
Battiste, Harold RB: **11–12**
Battle, Kathleen CL: **21**
Battlefield Band FO: **13**
"Battle of New Orleans, The" CO: **13,** 63, 104
Batts, Will BL: 207
Baucom, Terry CO: 186
Bauer, Harold CL: **21,** 23, 209
Bauer, Marion CL: 7, 15, **21–22**
Bauer, Ross CL: **22**
Bauzá, Mario JA: xxiv, **11,** 125
Bavan, Yolande JA: 120
Baxter, J. R., Jr. CO: 85
Baxter, Jeff "Skunk" RR: 226
Bay Psalm Book CL: xx, **22**
BBC
  Ivy Benson JA: 13, 14
  Dubliners FO: 55
  Seamus Ennis FO: 61
  Archie Fisher FO: 68
  A. L. Lloyd FO: 126
  Ewan MacColl FO: 131
  Tommy Smith JA: 185
B-Boy Records RB: **12**
b-boys RB: 121
Beach, Amy CL: 22, **22–23**
Beach, John Parsons CL: **23**
Beach Boys RR: **15–18,** *17,* 25, 176, 208, 229–230
Beale Street (Memphis) BL: 105, 132, 241
Beale Streeters, The RB: 2, 19
Beale Street Sheiks BL: 206–207
Bean Blossom festival FO: 80, 197
Beard, Frank BL: 255
Beaser, Robert CL: 7, **23**
Beasler, Norma Jean. *See* Norma Jean
Beasley, Walter BL: 240
Beastie Boys RB: 4, **12–13,** 55
Beatles, The RB: ix; RR: **18–22,** *20. See also* Harrison, George; Lennon, John; McCartney, Paul; Starr, Ringo
  "Act Naturally" CO: 1
  Beach Boys RR: 16
  Chuck Berry RR: 25
  British invasion RR: 32, 33
  Byrds RR: 35
  Fats Domino RR: 59
  Donovan RR: 60
  Electric Light Orchestra RR: 75, 76
  folk-rock FO: 71
  Four Seasons RR: 86
  girl groups RR: 91
  Buddy Holly RR: 114
  instrumental rock RR: 116
  Little Richard RR: 142
  Monkees RR: 149
  Motown RR: 152
  Oasis RR: 163
  Roy Orbison RR: 165
  Carl Perkins BL: 158; CO: 162; RR: 169

power pop RR: 176
Elvis Presley RR: 179
Billy Preston RB: 211
progressive rock RR: 183
Rolling Stones RR: 209
Del Shannon RR: 216
Shirelles RR: 217
Phil Spector RR: 221, 223
Vee-Jay Records BL: 180; RB: 271
Beats by the Pound RB: 167, 178
Beaucoups of Blues (Ringo Starr) CO: 45, 62, 94
Beauford, Carter RR: 52
Beaulieu, Priscilla RR: 181
Beausoleil CO: 29, 61; FO: **14,** 27
Beaux Arts Trio CL: **23,** 93
Beaver, Landon FO: 96
bebop JA: xxiv, xxxii, **11–12,** 84, 252*t*. *See also* Minton's Playhouse; *specific musicians*
Bechet, Sidney JA: **12**
clarinet JA: 33
cutting contest JA: 45
European jazz JA: 63–64
Alberta Hunter BL: 83
Steve Lacy JA: 119
"Maple Leaf Rag" JA: 127
Kid Ory JA: 150
saxophone JA: 171
Beck, Jeff
Donovan RR: 60
Jan Hammer JA: 81
instrumental rock RR: 116
Led Zeppelin RR: 134, 136
Yardbirds, The BL: 247; RR: 251, 253
Beck, Johann H. CL: **23**
Becker, John J. CL: **23–24**
Becker, Walter RR: 226–228
Beckett, Barry RB: 115, 189
Beecham, Sir Thomas CL: 106–107, 204
Beecher, Frank "Fanny" RR: 104
Beefeaters, The FO: 71
Bee Gees, The RB: **13–14**
Beethoven, Ludwig von CL: viii, xxi, 129, 194, 221
Begle, Howell BL: 31, 147–148
Begley, Brendan FO: 18
"Behind Closed Doors" CO: **13,** 173
Beiderbecke, Leon "Bix" JA: **12,** *13*
Jimmy Dorsey JA: 55
Geoff Muldaur BL: 142
Artie Shaw JA: 175
"Singin' the Blues" JA: **182**
Frankie Trumbauer JA: 199
Joe Venuti JA: 206
Paul Whiteman JA: 214
Beinhorn, Michael JA: 165
Belafonte, Harry FO: ix, **14**
Chad Mitchell Trio FO: 30
Civil Rights movement FO: 33
Hugh Masekela RB: 178
Diane Reeves JA: 163
Malvina Reynolds FO: 169
Sonny Terry BL: 215
young black country blues artists BL: 248–249
Beland, John CO: 75
Belcher, Supply CL: **24**
Belew, Adrian RR: 232
Bell, Aaron JA: 98
Bell, Al CO: 136; RB: 245
Bell, Archie, and the Drells RB: **14**
Bell, Bobby FO: 80
Bell, Carey BL: **16,** 73
Bell, Delia FO: 80
Bell, Derek FO: 33
Bell, Joshua CL: *24,* **24**
Bell, Lurie BL: 16, 26
Bell, May FO: 3
Bell, Robert RB: 47, 156
Bell, Thom RB: **15,** 281
Bell, William RB: **15,** 247
Bellamy, David CO: 13
Bellamy, Howard CO: 13
Bellamy Brothers CO: **13**
Bell Biv DeVoe RB: 194
Below, Fred BL: 16, **16,** 39, 149, 241
Belvin, Jesse RB: 278
"Be My Baby" RR: 91, 223
Benford, Mac FO: 96, 97
Benitez, Jellybean RB: 173
Benjamin, Andre "Dre" RB: 201
Bennett, Richard Rodney CL: 129
Bennett, Robert Russell CL: **24–25**
Bennett, Sheldon FO: 96
Bennett, Tony CO: 26, 40, 217; JA: **12–13,** 123
Bennett, Veronica (Ronnie) RB: 229; RR: 223
Benson, Al RB: 92, 93
Benson, George RB: **15–16,** 243
Benson, Ivy JA: **13–14**
Benson, Ray CO: 5
Bensusan, Pierre BL: 223
Benton, Brook RB: *16,* **16,** 275
Bentonia, Mississippi BL: 90, **137,** 155
Berg, Alban CL: 78, 130
Berge, Paul CL: 108
Berger, Arthur CL: **25,** 142, 207, 238
Bergmann, Carl CL: **25–26**
Bergsma, William CL: **26,** 89, 186, 199–200
Berigan, Bunny JA: 55
Berklee College of Music JA: **14**

Berkshire Music Center CL: 124, 154. *See also* Tanglewood Music Center
Berlin, Irving BL: 176; FO: 202
Berlin, Steve FO: 97
Berline, Byron FO: **14–15,** *15*
  Gene Clark FO: 36
  Country Gazette FO: 43
  Dan Crary FO: 46
  Dillards FO: 52
  Flying Burrito Brothers CO: 75
  John Hartford FO: 92
  Nickel Creek CO: 150
Berlin Philharmonic CL: 128, 153
Berlin Wall RR: 175
Berlioz, Hector CL: 23
Berman, Boris CL: **26**
Bernstein, Leonard CL: xxvi, **26–28,** *27*
  Marin Alsop CL: 5–6
  Marc Blitzstein CL: 31
  Schuyler Chapin CL: 48
  James DePreist CL: 67
  Irving Fine CL: 78
  Horacio Gutiérrez CL: 95
  Alan Hovhaness CL: 108
  Janis Ian FO: 105
  Joseph Kalichstein CL: 123
  Kennedy Center for the Performing Arts CL: 125
  Young Uck Kim CL: 126
  Yo-Yo Ma CL: 145
  Mass CL: **149–150**
  Peter Mennin CL: 151
  Dimitri Mitropoulos CL: 158
  New York Philharmonic Orchestra CL: 165
  Seiji Ozawa CL: 171
  Shulamit Ran CL: 186
  recommended listening CL: 250
  Fritz Reiner CL: 187
  Roger Sessions CL: 206
  Harold Shapero CL: 207
  Virgil Thomson CL: 224
  Bruno Walter CL: 236
  André Watts CL: 236
Berry, Bill RR: 201–203
Berry, Chu (tenor saxophone) JA: 27
Berry, Chuck BL: **16;** RB: **16–17;** RR: *23,* **23–25**
  Beach Boys RR: 16
  Fred Below BL: 16
  Chess Records BL: 39
  Johnnie Johnson BL: 94; RB: 143
  Carl Perkins CO: 162
  Rolling Stones, The RR: 209
  St. Louis, Missouri BL: 140
Berry, Richard RB: 138
Bertelsmann CO: 168
Best, Pete RR: 18, 19
Bethel, New York RR: 247
Bethune, Thomas (Blind Tom) CL: **28–29,** *29*
Better Days BL: 33
Betts, Dickey BL: 6, 222; RR: 4–6
Bevan, Bev RR: 76, 77
Beverly Hillbillies CO: 16, 74, 134
BG The Prince of Rap RB: **17**
Bibb, Eric BL: **16–17,** 251
Bibb, Leon BL: 16, 249, 251
"Big Bad John" CO: **13–14,** 55
big band BL: 28, 92; JA: **14,** 192, 196. *See also* swing; *specific bands and bandleaders*
Big Bill Blues (Broonzy & Bruynoghe) BL: 29; FO: 21
Big Bopper, The CO: 52; RR: 113
Big Brother and the Holding Company BL: 99–100; RR: 122–124, 151
Big Jeff and Tootsie FO: 133
Big Maceo BL: **17,** 52, 212; RB: 253
Big Maybelle BL: **17;** RB: **17–18**
Big Road Blues (David Evans) BL: 18, 60, 99
Bigsby, Paul CO: 200; FO: 142
Big Star RR: 177
Big Three Trio, The RB: 63
Big Youth RB: **18**
Bihari Brothers BL: 35
Bikel, Theodore FO: **15**
Billboard magazine BL: xx; CO: vii–viii, 19, 48; JA: 31; RR: 178
Billings, Bud and Joe FO: 129
Billings, William CL: viii, xxi, **29,** 162, 163
Billops, Quincy, Jr. RB: 201
Billy the Kid (Aaron Copland) CL: viii, **29–30**
Biloxi, Mississippi BL: 252
Bilson, Malcolm CL: **30**
Bing, Sir Rudolf CL: 10, **30,** 44, 155
Binkley, Amos FO: 15
Binkley, Gale FO: 15, 16
Binkley Brothers Dixie Clodhoppers FO: **15–16**
Birchfield, Sonny FO: 154
"Birdland" JA: **15,** 126, 208
Birdland (nightclub) JA: **14–15,** 147, 157
Birdsong, Cindy RB: 161, 256
Birmingham, Alabama BL: 49, 161, 185, 195
Birmingham, England RB: 112–113
Birth of the Cool (Miles Davis—Gil Evans) JA: **15,** 42, 49, 67, 141, 172

Bishop, Elvin BL: **17,** 20, 33, 233
Bitches Brew (Miles Davis) JA: **15–16**
  Billy Cobham JA: 35
  Chick Corea JA: 42
  Miles Davis JA: 49
  Jack DeJohnette JA: 51
  fusion JA: 72
  Dave Holland JA: 92
  John McLaughlin JA: 131
  Wayne Shorter JA: 178
  Joe Zawinul JA: 223
Bivins, Edward RB: 174
Bivins, Michael RB: 24, 194
Black, Bill BL: 209; RB: 209; RR: 179, 205
Black, Clint CO: **14,** 217
Black, Karen FO: 146
Black, Mary FO: 50
Black & Blue (Broadway revue) RB: 8, 29
"Black and Tan Fantasy" JA: **16**
"Black Bottom Stomp" JA: **16**
Blackbyrds, The RB: 32
Black Crowes RR: 136
"Black Magic Woman" BL: 63; RR: 213
Blackman, Cindy JA: **16**
Blackmon, Larry RB: 25, 34
black-owned record labels BL: **17**
"Black Patti." *See* Jones, Sissieretta
Black Radical MK II RB: **18**
Black Sabbath RR: 106
"Black Snake Moan" BL: 144, 206
Blackstock, Narvel CO: 137
Blackstreet RB: 194
Blackwell, Chris RB: 133, 175; RR: 200–201
Blackwell, Ed JA: **16–17,** *17, 37*
  Don Cherry JA: 31, 32
  Anthony Cox JA: 44
  Free Jazz (Ornette Coleman) JA: 71
  Charlie Haden JA: 79
Blackwell, Francis "Scrapper" BL: **17**
  Leroy Carr BL: 36
  Indianapolis, Indiana BL: 86
  piano BL: 161
  "Sweet Home Chicago" BL: 210
Blackwell, Otis CO: 34; RB: 49, 247; RR: 86, 181
Blackwell, Robert A. "Bumps" RB: **18,** 169; RR: 141, 142
Blackwood, Cecil CO: 14, 15
Blackwood, Doyle CO: 14
Blackwood, James, Jr. CO: 15
Blackwood, James, Sr. CO: 14, 15
Blackwood, Mark CO: 15
Blackwood, R. W. CO: 14
Blackwood, Roy CO: 14
Blackwood Brothers CO: **14–15,** 86
Blaine, Hal RR: 68
Blair, J. H. FO: 213
Blair, Ron RR: 177
Blake, Blind BL: **18**
  acoustic guitar BL: 1
  blues lyrics BL: 23
  Chicago BL: 40
  Detroit BL: 52
  Papa Charlie Jackson BL: 89
  protest songs BL: 167
  Charley Spand BL: 205
  Jesse (Babyface) Thomas BL: 219
Blake, Eubie BL: 137, 152, 162, 201
Blake, Nancy FO: 16
Blake, Norman CO: 45; FO: **16,** 93
Blake, William RR: 62
Blakey, Art JA: **17–18.** *See also* Jazz Messengers
  Cindy Blackman JA: 16
  Clifford Brown JA: 23
  Donald Byrd JA: 26; RB: 31
  Stanley Clarke JA: 34
  Kenny Garrett JA: 73
  Freddie Hubbard JA: 95
  Japanese jazz JA: 103
  Keith Jarrett JA: 104
  Chuck Mangione JA: 125
  Wynton Marsalis CL: 148; JA: 127
  Moanin' JA: **137–138**
  Lee Morgan JA: 140
  Courtney Pine JA: 155
  Sonny Rollins JA: 165
  Wayne Shorter JA: 178
  Horace Silver JA: 179, 180
  Jimmy Smith JA: 183
  Mary Lou Williams JA: 215
  Steve Williamson JA: 217
Bland, Bobby "Blue" BL: **18,** 131, 157, 207; RB: 2, **18–19**
Bland, James BL: 136; FO: 79, 140
Blank, Les FO: 196
Blanton, Jimmy JA: **18,** 137, 154, 193
Blenders, The RB: **19**
Blesh, Rudi BL: 76, 219
Bley, Carla JA: **18**
  avant-garde JA: 7
  Gary Burton JA: 26
  Charlie Haden JA: 79
  Steve Lacy JA: 119
  Michael Mantler JA: 126–127
  Pharoah Sanders JA: 170
  Andy Sheppard JA: 177
  Steve Swallow JA: 191, 192
Bley, Paul JA: 72, 191, 224
Blige, Mary J. RB: **19–20,** *20,* 195
Blind Faith RR: 40, 46, 114

blind musicians and singers BL: **18–19,** 44, 57, 78
Blind Pig Records BL: **19**
Blind Tom. *See* Bethune, Thomas
Bliss, Anthony CL: **30**
Blitz, Paul CL: 108
Blitzstein, Marc CL: **30–31,** 160; FO: 100
Bloch, Ernest CL: *31,* **31**
  George Antheil CL: 11
  Cleveland Institute of Music CL: 52
  Quincy Porter CL: 182
  San Francisco Conservatory of Music CL: 198
  Roger Sessions CL: 206
  Randall Thompson CL: 224
Bloch, Ray JA: 109
Block, Rory BL: **19–20,** 82, 153, 251
Blomstedt, Herbert CL: 199
Blondie RR: **25–28,** *26*
Blood, Sweat, and Tears JA: 22, 90
"Blood Count" JA: 4, 189
Blood on the Fields (Wynton Marsalis) CL: **31;** JA: 217
Bloods and Crips RB: **20**
Bloom, Bobby RB: **20**
Bloom, Luka FO: 141
Bloomfield, Michael BL: **20**
  "Baby, Please Don't Go" BL: 11
  Elvin Bishop BL: 17
  Paul Butterfield BL: 33
  Bob Dylan BL: 55
  guitar RR: 100
  Bob Koester BL: 108
  Mark Naftalin BL: 151
  vocal styles BL: 233
  Joe Louis Walker BL: 235
  Muddy Waters BL: 239
Blossom Music Center CL: **31–32,** *32,* 52
Blossoms, The RB: **20–21,** 52
Blount, Herman "Sonny." *See* Sun Ra
Blow, Kurtis RB: **21,** 122
"Blowin' in the Wind" FO: 57, 157; RR: 70–71
Blue Belles, The RB: 161
Bluebird sound (Bluebird beat) BL: 15, 41, 87, 212, 238, 239
Blue Cheer RR: 42
blue-eyed soul RB: 218, 225–226, 244
bluegrass CO: xvii, 11–12, **15–16,** 72, 86, 170–171. *See also* progressive bluegrass; *specific artists*
Bluegrass Alliance FO: 46, 146
Blue Grass Boys, The CO: 73, 141, 194; FO: 137
bluegrass gospel FO: 196–197
"Blue Moon of Kentucky" CO: **16;** RR: 179, 205
"Blue Moon" progression RR: 65, 175
blue note BL: 91; JA: **18**
Blue Ridge Duo, The FO: 168
Blue Ridge Playboys CO: 51
Blue Rose Band, The FO: 68, 125
blues BL: 1–276; JA: **19;** RR: ix. *See also specific artists*
  AAB form JA: **1**
  12-bar structure JA: **200**
Blues and Roots (Charles Mingus) JA: **19**
Blues and the Abstract Truth, The (Oliver Nelson) JA: **19**
Bluesbreakers, The BL: 127
Blues Brothers, The (movie) BL: 142, 210
blues festivals BL: xvi, 26, 191, 269
Blues Foundation BL: 269
Blues Heaven Foundation, Inc. BL: 40, 53; RB: 63
Blues Incorporated BL: 108
Blue Sky Boys CO: *17,* **17–18,** 132, 212; FO: 126, 133
Blues & Legends Hall of Fame Museum BL: 139
blues lyrics BL: ix, xviii, **20–25,** 248
Blues Project, The BL: **25,** 153; RR: 29, 152
blues revival BL: xvi, xx, **25–26,** 179–180, 249–250, 253. *See also* folk-blues revival
blues rock BL: viii, xvi; RR: xx, **28–29**
Blues Serenaders BL: 9
"Blue Suede Shoes" BL: 158; RR: 169, 205
Blues Walk of Fame BL: 138
Blue Train (John Coltrane) JA: **19**
Blue Velvet Band, The FO: 114, 176
blue yodels BL: 184, 232. *See also* yodeling
Blume, David FO: 95
Blumenfeld, Felix CL: 106
Blumenfeld, Roy BL: 25
BMI. *See* Broadcast Music International
Boaz, Edgar FO: 173
Bob B. Soxx & the Blue Jeans RB: 21
Bobbettes, The RB: **21–22**
Bob & Earl RB: 54
Bobo, Willie RR: 213
Bockris, Victor RR: 242
Bo Diddley beat BL: 52; RR: 54–55

"Body and Soul" JA: **19,** 87, 88
Boehm flute FO: 69, 70
Bofill, Angela JA: 16
Bogan, Lucille BL: 185
Bogan, Ted BL: 8, 208
Boggs, Dock BL: 13; FO: 7, **16–17,** *17,* 181
Bogguss, Suzy CO: 6, **18,** *18,* 99; FO: 82
Boghetti, Giuseppe CL: 9
Bog Trotters Band, The FO: 210
"Bohemian Rhapsody" RR: 191, 193
Bok, Gordon FO: **17,** 155
Bok, Mary Curtis CL: 17, 62
Boland, Francy JA: 34
Bolcom, William CL: 6, *32,* **32–33,** 227–229
Bolden, Buddy JA: xxvi, **19–20**
  cutting contest JA: 45
  double bass JA: 56
  jazz firsts JA: 116
  Freddie Keppard JA: 112
  New Orleans jazz JA: 143
  use of string bass in band JA: xxii
Bolet, Jorge CL: **33**
Bolger, Brian FO: 140
Bolick, Bill and Earl CO: 17–18
Bolin, Tommy BL: 253, 255
Bolton, Mississippi BL: 228
Bomb Squad, The RB: 103, 130
Bona, Richard JA: **20,** 152
Bond, Graham RR: 45
Bond, Johnny CO: **19,** 58, 105, 175
Bonds, Gary "U.S." RB: *22,* **22;** RR: 225
Bonfire, Mars RR: 228
Bonham, Jason RR: 136
Bonham, John BL: 113; RR: 60, 68, 133, 136, 137
Bonnie and Clyde (movie) CO: 16, 74, 76
Bono (Bono Vox) FO: 35; RR: 166, 235–237
Bono, Sonny RB: 11
Bonoff, Karla FO: 90
Bonsall, Joe CO: 153
Boogie Down Productions RB: 12, 157
boogie-woogie BL: **26–28;** JA: **20**
Boogie Woogie Trio BL: 114
Book Binder, Roy BL: **28**
Booker, James BL: **28,** 54
Booker T. & the MGs RB: *23,* **23–24**
  instrumental rock RR: 116
  Albert King BL: 104; RB: 153
  Memphis BL: 132
  Monterey Pop Festival RR: 152
  Wilson Pickett RB: 207
  Otis Redding RB: 220
  Stax Records BL: 180; RB: 247
Boom Boom Room (San Francisco) BL: 35
Boone, Debby CO: **19**
Boone, Pat RB: 168; RR: 58, 141, 180
Boone, Steve BL: 122
Boone County Jamboree CO: 43, 112, 169, 200
Boone Creek CO: 81, 186; FO: 55
Boosey & Hawkes CL: **33**
bop. *See* bebop
border radio CO: 34, 83; FO: 158, 180
Borge, Victor CL: **33**
Born in the U.S.A. (Bruce Springsteen) RR: 223, 225
"Born to Be Wild" RR: 105, 228
Borowski, Felix CL: **34**
Bortnick, Avi JA: 173
bossa nova JA: **20,** 74, 75, 107, 117
Boston Baroque CL: **34**
Boston Camerata CL: **34**
Boston Composers String Quartet CL: **34**
Boston Pops Orchestra CL: **34,** 77–78, 131, 140, 240
Boston Symphony Orchestra CL: xxiii–xxiv, **35**
  Harold Bauer CL: 21
  Amy Beach CL: 22
  Ernest Bloch CL: 31
  Boston Pops Orchestra CL: 34
  Nadia Boulanger CL: 36
  Concerto for Orchestra CL: 55
  Aaron Copland CL: 56–57
  Henry Eichheim CL: 73
  Harold Farberman CL: 75
  Lukas Foss CL: 81
  Heinrich Gebhard CL: 86
  Charles T. Griffes CL: 94
  Edward Burlingame Hill CL: 103
  Franz Kneisel CL: 127
  Serge Koussevitzky CL: 128, 129
  William Kroll CL: 130
  Jacob Lateiner CL: 134
  Erich Leinsdorf CL: 135
  James Levine CL: 136
  Peter Lieberson CL: 138
  Lilacs (George Walker) CL: 138
  Charles Martin Loeffler CL: 141
  Dimitri Mitropoulos CL: 157
  Pierre Monteux CL: 158
  Carl Muck CL: 160

Boston Symphony Orchestra (*continued*)
Charles Munch CL: 160
Kent Nagano CL: 161
New England Conservatory of Music CL: 162
Seiji Ozawa CL: 171–172
Walter Piston CL: 178–179
Ruth Posselt CL: 182
Peter Serkin CL: 205
Roger Sessions CL: 206
Robert Spano CL: 212
William Steinberg CL: 214
Symphony Hall CL: **218**
Tanglewood Music Center CL: 221
Michael Tilson Thomas CL: 223
Efrem Zimbalist CL: 245
"Both Sides Now" FO: 39, 140; RR: 220
Bothy Band, The FO: **17–18,** 24, 158
Botstein, Leon CL: 8, 19, **35**
bottleneck guitar BL: 2, 193, 231–232. *See also* slide guitar
Bouchillon, Chris BL: 232; FO: 128
Boulanger, Nadia CL: ix, **35–36**
Daniel Barenboim CL: 19
Leslie Bassett CL: 21
Marion Bauer CL: 22
Robert Russell Bennett CL: 24–25
Arthur Berger CL: 25
Marc Blitzstein CL: 30
Elliott Carter CL: 46
Schuyler Chapin CL: 48
Paul Chihara CL: 50
Aaron Copland CL: 56
David Diamond CL: 68
Irving Fine CL: 78
Ross Lee Finney CL: 78
Philip Glass CL: 89
Roy Harris CL: 99
Andrew Imbrie CL: 111
John Kirkpatrick CL: 126
Ralph Kirkpatrick CL: 127
Gail Kubik CL: 131
Douglas Moore CL: 159
Daniel Pinkham CL: 178
Walter Piston CL: 178
Harold Shapero CL: 207
Virgil Thomson CL: 224
Lester Trimble CL: 227
Boulez, Pierre CL: **36**
Cleveland Orchestra CL: 52
New York Philharmonic Orchestra CL: 164
David Tudor CL: 228
Ellen Taafe Zwilich CL: 246
"Bouquet of Roses" CO: **19**
"Bourgeois Blues" BL: **28–29,** 112, 168
Bourke, Ciaran FO: 55
Bowden, Al RB: 192
Bowen, Jimmy CO: **19–20,** 169
Bowers, Bryan CO: 6; FO: **18**
Bowie, David RR: **29–32,** *30*
Chic RB: 41
Gil Evans JA: 68
glam rock RR: 91
Motown RR: 153
new wave RR: 159
David Sanborn JA: 169
Luther Vandross RB: 269
Stevie Ray Vaughan BL: 228
Bowie, Lester JA: 6, **20–21**
Bowles, Paul CL: **36**
Bowman, Charlie FO: 97
Boxcar Willie CO: **20**
Box of Frogs RR: 253
Boyce, Tommy RR: 150, 151
Boyd, Bill CO: **20–21,** 191
Boyd, Eddie BL: **29**
Boyd, Jim CO: 20, 21
Boyd, Joe FO: 64; RR: 202
Boyd, John CO: 21
Boyd, Patti RR: 40
Boy George RR: 157
"A Boy Named Sue" CO: **21,** 35
Boys of the Lough FO: **18,** 75
Boyz II Men RB: **24,** 213
Bracey, Ishmon BL: xix, **29,** 125, 128, 228, 230
Brackeen, Joanne JA: 17, **21**
Bracken, Jimmy RB: 270
Bracken, Vivian and James BL: 180
Braddock, Bobby CO: 197
Bradford, Perry BL: xxi, 46, 162, 243; JA: 184
Bradley, Harold CO: 21
Bradley, Jan RB: **24**
Bradley, Owen CO: xviii, **21**
Patsy Cline CO: 39
Jack Greene CO: 88
"I Fall to Pieces" CO: 107
k. d. lang CO: 121
Brenda Lee CO: 121
Loretta Lynn CO: 127
Moon Mullican CO: 145
Nashville sound CO: 147
Jimmy "C" Newman CO: 150; FO: 148
record labels CO: 169
Conway Twitty CO: 206
Bradshaw, Tiny RB: 89
Brady, Paul FO: **18–19,** 107, 112, 141, 158
Braggs, Al "TNT" BL: 109
Brailowsky, Alexander CL: **36–37**
Braithwaite, Junior RB: 175
Bramlett, Bekka RR: 84
Brand, Dollar. *See* Ibrahim, Abdullah
Brand, Oscar FO: **19**
Brandenburg Ensemble CL: **37,** 201, 205

Brand Nubian RB: 110
Brandy RB: 186
Branscombe, Gena CL: **37**
Branson, Missouri CO: **21–22**
Moe Bandy CO: 11
Boxcar Willie CO: 20
Albert E. Brumley FO: 22
Roy Clark CO: 38
David Allan Coe CO: 40
Gatlin Brothers CO: 79
Mickey Gilley CO: 82
Barbara Mandrell CO: 133
Johnny Paycheck CO: 159
Ray Price CO: 163
Sons of the Pioneers CO: 189
Mel Tillis CO: 199
Conway Twitty CO: 206
Faron Young CO: 225
Brant, Henry CL: *37,* **37–38,** 111, 129
brass JA: **21,** 142. *See also specific brass instruments, e.g.:* trumpet
brass bands JA: 143, 221
Brass Fantasy JA: 21
Brass Monkey FO: 30, 117
Braun, Edgar CL: 198
Braxton, Anthony JA: **21–22**
AACM JA: 7
avant-garde JA: 7
Ed Blackwell JA: 16
Conference of the Birds JA: 41
Chick Corea JA: 42
Marilyn Crispell JA: 44
Andrew Cyrille JA: 46
Dave Holland JA: 92
Leroy Jenkins JA: 107
George Lewis JA: 122
third stream jazz JA: 197
Brazil JA: 20, 75, 107, 126
Brazos Valley Boys CO: 197
Bread and Roses FO: 66
break JA: **22**
break dancing RB: 121
Breakfast Special FO: 204
B-Real RB: 52
Brecht, Bertholt FO: 6
Brecker, Michael JA: 20, 22, **22,** 134, 180, 216
Brecker, Randy JA: 20, **22,** 180
Brecker Brothers (band) JA: 169
Brennan, Ciaran FO: 35
Brennan, Maire FO: 35
Brennan, Noel FO: 35
Brennan, Pol FO: 35
Brenston, Jackie BL: 223; RB: **24–25,** 262; RR: 170
Breuning, Fred FO: 173
Brewster, Margie FO: 197
Brewster Brothers, The FO: 195
Brian May Band RR: 193
bridge JA: **23**
Bridgewater, Dee Dee JA: **23**
Brigati, Eddie RB: 218; RR: 199
Briggs, Billy FO: 96
Brill Building RB: 50, 106; RR: 91, 175
Brilliant Corners (Thelonious Monk) JA: **23**
"Bring It on Home" RB: 219; RR: 134
Briskin, Elias CL: 179
Bristol, Johnny RB: 248
Bristol recording sessions CO: 167, 177, 190; FO: 163, 166, 193
Bristow, George Frederick CL: **38**
British invasion RB: ix; RR: x, xix–xx, **32–34**
Animals RR: **8–9**
Beatles RR: 20
blues rock RR: 29
classic rock RR: 41
Bo Diddley RR: 55
folk rock RR: 84
garage rock RR: 89
girl groups RB: 106; RR: 91
guitar RR: 100
Buddy Holly RR: 114
John Lee Hooker RB: 124
keyboards RR: 126
Kinks RR: 128
power pop RR: 176
psychedelic rock RR: 185
Rolling Stones RR: 209
roots rock RR: 211
Vee-Jay Records RB: 271
British Isles CO: 72. *See also specific countries*
Boys of the Lough FO: 18
Martin Carthy FO: 30
fiddle FO: 66
Bert Jansch FO: 109
John Kirkpatrick FO: 117
John Renbourn FO: 167
Britt, Elton CO: **22**
Broadcast Music International (BMI)
Bo Diddley RR: 56
"Gentle on My Mind" CO: 80
Vince Gill CO: 81
harmonica BL: 72
music business and the blues BL: 145
Righteous Brothers, The RR: 204
Fred Rose CO: 179
Broadside magazine FO: **19,** 31, 57, 156
Broadway CL: xxiv
LaVern Baker RB: 8
Danny Barker BL: 15
Robert Russell Bennett CL: 25
Leonard Bernstein CL: 27
Theodore Bikel FO: 15
Marc Blitzstein CL: 30
Victor Borge CL: 33

Broadway (*continued*)
Ruth Brown BL: 31; RB: 29
Harry Chapin FO: 31
Guy Davis BL: 51
Mac Davis CO: 54
Ronnie Dyson RB: 75
Duke Ellington JA: 61
Gatlin Brothers CO: 79
George Gershwin CL: 86
Morton Gould CL: 92
Lena Horne JA: 93–94; RB: 124
Cisco Houston FO: 100
Glenn Jones RB: 145
Sissieretta Jones CL: 119
Louis Jordan BL: 100
Taj Mahal BL: 124
Reba McEntire CO: 138
Brownie McGhee BL: 129
Roger Miller CO: 140
Stephanie Mills RB: 184
Melba Moore RB: 188
Gary Morris CO: 144
music business BL: 145–146
Kenny Neal BL: 151
K. T. Oslin CO: 154
Red Clay Ramblers FO: 165
social history BL: 201
Amii Stewart RB: 248
Sonny Terry BL: 215
Ethel Waters BL: 238
Josh White BL: 242
Brockman, Polk BL: 212; CO: 33, 123, 167
Bromberg, David FO: **19–20,** *20,* 37
Bronson, Art JA: 219
Bronson, Bernard FO: 189
Bronx, New York RB: 121; RR: 56
Brook, Charles FO: 53
Brooklyn Academy of Music CL: 9, **38**
Brooklyn Philharmonic Orchestra CL: **38,** 81, 212
Brooks, Arthur and Richard RB: 30
Brooks, Carrie CO: 37
Brooks, Charles RB: 34
Brooks, Garth CO: **22–23,** *23*
Jimmy Bowen CO: 20
"Friends in Low Places" CO: 78
Scott Hendricks CO: 99
George Jones CO: 111
Trisha Yearwood CO: 223
Brooks, Harvey BL: 20; JA: 15
Brooks, Leon Eric "Kix" CO: 23, 151
Brooks, Lonnie BL: **29,** 236, 240
Brooks, Patricia CL: **38**
Brooks and Dunn CO: **23–24,** 64, 113
Broonzy, Big Bill BL: xix, **29;** FO: **20–21**
acoustic guitar BL: 3, 4
Bumble Bee Slim BL: 32
censorship BL: 37
Chicago BL: 40, 41
Blind John Davis BL: 49
electric guitar BL: 58
Jazz Gillum BL: 68
"Key to the Highway" BL: 104
Alan Lomax BL: 118
Tommy McClennan BL: 127
Lester Melrose BL: 130, 131
Memphis Minnie BL: 133
protest songs BL: 167, 168, 170
saxophone, trombone, trumpet, and clarinet BL: 189
Charley Spand BL: 205
Sunnyland Slim BL: 209
talent scouts BL: 211
Eddie "Cleanhead" Vinson BL: 228
vocal styles BL: 231
Washboard Sam BL: 238
Sonny Boy Williamson I RB: 279
Brotherhood of Breath JA: 187
Brother J RB: 287
Brothers Johnson RB: **25**
Broughton, Mary Selena CL: 93–94
Brower, Cecil CO: 24
Brower, Frank FO: 139
Brown, Alison CO: 117–118
Brown, Bobby RB: **25,** 194, 223
Brown, Bonnie CO: 25
Brown, Charles BL: **30;** RB: **25**
Johnny Moore's Three Blazers RB: 143
jump blues and rhythm and blues BL: 101
Los Angeles, California BL: 35
rhythm and blues combos BL: 182
vocal styles BL: 231
Brown, Chuck, and the Soul Searchers RB: **25–26**
Brown, Clarence "Gatemouth" BL: **30,** *30,* 62, 158; RB: **26**
Brown, Clifford JA: **23–24,** 81, 165, 211
Brown, David RR: 213
Brown, Durwood CO: 25
Brown, Earle CL: 23, **38–39,** *39*
Brown, Ella Maxine CO: 25
Brown, Errol RB: 124, 125
Brown, Foxy RB: **26**
Brown, Gerald RB: 237
Brown, Iona CL: 141
Brown, James BL: xxiii, **31;** RB: **26–27,** *27*
Afrika Bambaataaa RB: 10
funk RB: 98
King Records BL: 107

Lonnie Mack BL: 123
Elvis Presley RR: 180
David Sanborn JA: 169
social history and the blues BL: 203
Fred Wesley & the J.B.'s RB: 276
Paul Williams RB: 279
Brown, Jim RB: 97
Brown, Jim Ed CO: 25, 44
Brown, "Junior" CO: **24**
Brown, Les FO: 83
Brown, Milton CO: **24–25,** 51, 214, 218; FO: 134, 213
Brown, Norma CO: 25
Brown, Pete RR: 45
Brown, Peter RB: **27**
Brown, Raphael (Tweety) RB: 195
Brown, Ray JA: **24,** 153
Brown, Roy BL: 74; RB: **27–28;** RR: 180
Brown, Ruth BL: 9, **31,** 147–148; RB: 8, *28,* **28–29**
Brown, Tony CO: 27, 37, 40, 84, 169
Brown, Walter BL: 130
Brown, Willie BL: **31**
acoustic guitar BL: 3
"Crossroads Blues" BL: 47
Son House BL: 82
Robert Johnson BL: 97
Tommy Johnson BL: 99
Charley Patton BL: 157
Walls, Mississippi BL: 140
Brown, Willie, Jr. RB: 261
Browne, Jackson BL: 228; FO: 178; RR: 221
Browne, Tom RB: **29**
Browning, John CL: **39**
Brownlee, John CL: 147
Browns, The CO: 6, **25**
Brown's Bar (Detroit) BL: 52
Brown's Ferry Four CO: 56, 112, 200
Brownsville Station BL: 107
Brozman, Bob BL: *31,* **31–32,** *32,* 193; FO: *21,* **21–22**
Brubeck, Dave BL: 186; JA: **24–25,** 117, 130, 144, 197
Bruce, Ed and Patsy CO: 131
Bruce, Jack
Eric Clapton RR: 39, 40
Cream BL: 46; RR: 45
Alexis Korner BL: 108
John Mayall BL: 127
John McLaughlin JA: 131
Bruce, Michael RR: 43
Bruckner, Anton CL: 192
Bruford, Bill RR: 69, 184
Brumley, Al, Jr. CO: 26, 86; FO: 22
Brumley, Albert E. CO: **25–26;** FO: **22**
Brumley, Tom CO: 10, 26; FO: 22
Brun, Philipe JA: **25,** 64
Bruner, Cliff CO: 24, 51, 144, 202
Bruning, Dale BL: 183
Brunning, Bob RR: 81
Bruynoghe, Yannick BL: 29; FO: 21
Bryan, James FO: 16, 28
Bryant, Anita CO: 155
Bryant, Boudleaux and Felice CO: **26–27,** 27, 70, 99; RR: 78
Bryant, Jimmy CO: 145
Bryant, Ray JA: 25
Bryson, (Robert) Peabo RB: **29,** 291
Buchanan, Elwood JA: 48
Buchanan, James CL: 29
Buchanan, Roy BL: **32;** RR: 116
Buchla synthesizer JA: 192
Buck, Deborah CL: 134
Buck, Peter RR: 201, 202
Buckeyes, The RB: 247
Buckingham, Lindsey BL: 63; RR: 82–84
Buckingham, Steve CO: 184, 221
Buckle Busters, The FO: 97
Buckner, Clay FO: *165*
Bud and Travis FO: **22**
Budapest String Quartet CL: 200, 201
Buena Vista Social Club BL: 43
Buena Vista Social Club (documentary and recording) JA: 76, 174
Buffalo, New York BL: 8
Buffalo, Norton BL: 185
Buffalo Gals, The FO: **23**
Buffalo Philharmonic Orchestra CL: **39–40**
JoAnne Falletta CL: 75
Lukas Foss CL: 81
Josef Krips CL: 130
Robert Moran CL: 159
William Steinberg CL: 214
Michael Tilson Thomas CL: 223
Buffalo Springfield RR: **34–35,** 44–45, 152, 254
Bull City Red BL: 65
Bulldog RR: 199
Bulleit, Jim CO: 87, 168
Bull Mountain Moonshiners FO: 111
Bullock, Annie Mae. *See* Turner, Tina
Bumble Bee Slim BL: **32**
Bumgarner, Samantha CO: 167; FO: **23**
Bundesen, Jayne CO: 58
Bunn, Teddy BL: 3
Burbridge, Oteil RR: 6
Burch, Curtis FO: 146–147

Burdon, Eric BL: 7, 233; RB: 273; RR: 9, 55
Burke, Clem RR: 26–28
Burke, Joe FO: 2, **23–24**
Burke, Kevin FO: 17, **24**
Burke, Laddie and Alex RB: 239
Burke, Solomon RB: **29–30,** *30,* 239
Burkholder, Peter J. CL: **40**
Burleigh, Henry CL: **40**
Burnett, Chester. *See* Howlin' Wolf
Burnett, Dick CO: 107; FO: 6, 24–25
Burnett, Johnny and Dorsey CO: 176
Burnett, Rev. J. C. BL: 78
Burnett, T-Bone CO: 191; FO: 213; RR: 166
Burnett and Rutherford FO: **24–25**
Burnette, Billy RR: 84
Burnette, Johnny and Dorsey RR: 156, 206
Burns, Jethro BL: 107; CO: 101, 132; FO: 79, 133, 142
Burns, Keith CO: 201
Burns, Robert FO: 166
Burnside, R. L. BL: **32,** 99
Burr, Gary CO: 100
Burrage, Harold RB: 54
Burrell, Kenny JA: 30, 44, 183, 200
Burris, Eddie CO: 154
Burris, J. C. BL: 215
Burroughs, William S. RB: 62, 162; RR: 31, 105
Burrus Mills CO: 218
Bursen, Howie FO: 175
Burton, Cliff RR: 145–147
Burton, Gary JA: **26,** 133, 172, 185, 192
Burton, James RR: 155–156, 166
Burton, Ron JA: 98
Busby, Buzz CO: 38; FO: 60
Busch, Adolf CL: **40,** 204, 205
Busey, Gary RR: 111
Bush, George H. W. JA: 81
Bush, George W. CO: 220
Bush, Roger CO: 75; FO: 115
Bush, Sam
  bluegrass music CO: 16
  J. D. Crowe FO: 47
  Jerry Douglas FO: 55
  mandolin CO: 132; FO: 133
  New Grass Revival FO: 146
  progressive bluegrass FO: 161
Bushwick Bill RB: 279–280
Bushy, Ron RR: 68–69
Butler, Billy RB: **30**
Butler, Burridge D. CO: 148
Butler, Carl and Pearl CO: **27**
Butler, Geezer RR: 106
Butler, Henry BL: 18–19, **32–33,** 252
Butler, Jerry RB: **30–31,** *31*
  Billy Butler RB: 30
  Betty Everett RB: 84
  Impressions, The RB: 130
  Vee-Jay Records RB: 270, 271
Butler, Joe BL: 122
Butram, Hillous CO: 63
Butterfield, Paul BL: **33**
  Elvin Bishop BL: 17
  Michael Bloomfield BL: 20
  blues rock RR: 29
  Bob Dylan FO: 57; RR: 71
  Albert Grossman FO: 84
  Jac Holzman FO: 99
  Sam Lay BL: 111
  Monterey Pop Festival RR: 152
  Geoff Muldaur BL: 142
  Geoff and Maria Muldaur FO: 143
  Mark Naftalin BL: 151
  Newport Folk Festival FO: 149
  David Sanborn JA: 169
  vocal styles BL: 233
  Muddy Waters BL: 239
Butterscotch Fire Department Blues Band BL: 253
Buxton, Glen RR: 43
Buzzington, Ezra CO: 103
"Bye Bye Love" CO: **27,** 70; RR: 78
Byrd, Charlie JA: 74
Byrd, Donald JA: **26;** RB: **31–32**
  Pepper Adams JA: 3
  Paul Chambers JA: 30
  Herbie Hancock JA: 82; RB: 116
  Horace Silver JA: 180
  Timmy Thomas RB: 257
  Stanley Turrentine JA: 200
  Larry Young JA: 219
Byrd, Gary RB: **32**
Byrd, Henry Roelin. *See* Professor Longhair
Byrd, Tracy CO: **27,** 210
Byrds, The FO: **25;** RR: **35–38,** *36*
  Gene Clark FO: 35–36
  country rock CO: 44–45; RR: 43–45
  Bob Dylan RR: 71
  Flying Burrito Brothers CO: 75
  folk-rock FO: 71, RR: 84, 85
  Kentucky Colonels FO: 115
  Monterey Pop Festival RR: 152
  power pop RR: 176
  Pete Seeger FO: 183
  12-string guitar BL: 224

Byrne, David FO: 3; RB: 182; RR: 231, 232
Byrne, Robert CO: 185

C

Cabin in the Sky (movie) BL: 238; JA: 211
Cabrillo Festival of Contemporary Music CL: **41**
Cadence magazine JA: **27**
Cadets/The Jacks, The RB: **33**
Cadillacs, The RB: **33–34**
Cadman, Charles Wakefield CL: **41**
Café Society (New York City) BL: 27, 152; FO: 214; RB: 262
Caffrey, Charlotte CO: 207
Cage, John CL: xii, **41–42**
 Anthony Braxton JA: 21
 Earle Brown CL: 38
 Morton Feldman CL: 77
 4'33" CL: **82**
 Lou Harrison CL: 99
 Ben Johnston CL: 119
 Alvin Lucier CL: 142
 David Tudor CL: 228
 John Zorn JA: 224
Cagle, Chris CO: 99
Cahn, Rolf BL: 234; FO: 49
Cajun music CO: **29–30;** FO: **27**. *See also specific musicians*
Calder, Alexander CL: 38
Caldwell, Gayle FO: 146
Caldwell, Ronnie RB: 10
Cale, J. J. CO: 140
Cale, John RR: 240–242
Calhoun, Cora. *See* Austin, Lovie
Calhoun, Fred CO: 24–25
Calhoun, Roy and Wendell RB: 5
California BL: **35**. *See also* Bakersfield Sound; Los Angeles; Monterey Pop Festival; Oakland; San Francisco; San Francisco Bay Area; surf rock
California, Randy RR: 108–109
California Institute of the Arts CL: 183, 218
Callahan, Homer C. ("Bill") CO: 30
Callahan, Walter T. ("Joe") CO: 30
Callahan Brothers CO: **30;** FO: 138
call-and-response JA: 10, 27, **27**
Callas, Maria CL: **43–44,** *44*
Callier, Terry BL: 249
"Call it Stormy Monday (But Tuesday's Just As Bad)." *See* "Stormy Monday"
Calloway, Blanche RB: 28
Calloway, Cab JA: **27**
 Mario Bauzá JA: 11
 Cozy Cole RB: 46
 Dizzy Gillespie JA: 75
 Sister Rosetta Tharpe BL: 217
 Fats Waller JA: 210
 Ben Webster JA: 213
Calt, Stephen BL: 90, 191
calypso FO: ix, 14, 116
Camel Caravan CO: 117
Cameo RB: **34**
Cameron, Basil CL: 199
Cameron, G. C. RB: 245
Cameron, John RR: 61
Cameron, Matt RR: 167, 168
Camp, Bob FO: 27–28, 76
Camp, Hamilton FO: **27–28,** 76
Campbell, Arthur FO: 166
Campbell, Glen CO: *30,* **30–31**
 Gene Clark FO: 36
 "Gentle on My Mind" CO: 80
 Bobbie Gentry CO: 80
 John Hartford FO: 92
 Alan Jackson CO: 109
 "Rhinestone Cowboy" CO: 172
 Tanya Tucker CO: 204
Campbell, Luther RB: 180
Campbell, Mike RR: 177
Campbell, Milton. *See* Little Milton
Campbell, Orville CO: 93
Campbell, Tom "Harley" FO: 99
Camp Creek Boys FO: 38
Canned Heat (band) BL: **36,** 99, 103, 124, 218; RR: 152
Cannon, Gus/Cannon's Jug Stompers BL: **36**
 banjo BL: 13
 harmonica BL: 72
 jug bands BL: 101
 Noah Lewis BL: 115
 Memphis BL: 131
 Rooftop Singers FO: 175
 "Walk Right In" BL: 236
Cantata Singers CL: **43**
Canticle of the Sun, The (Leo Sowerby) CL: **43**
Canti del Sole (Bernard Rands) CL: **43**
cantometrics BL: 118–119, 229; FO: 127
Cantrell, Jerry RR: 98
Can't You Hear the Wind Howl? (documentary) BL: 140, 141, 249, 251
Caplin, Dalia Ambach JA: 3
capo BL: 43
Cappadonna RB: 284, 285
Captain Beefheart RR: 257
Carabello, Michael RR: 213
Caramoor CL: **43**
Carawan, Candie FO: 28, 33
Carawan, Evan FO: 28

Carawan, Guy FO: **28,** 34, 90
Carey, Mariah RB: 24, **34–35,** *35,* 213
Carlin, Bob FO: **28–29**
Carlisle, Bill CO: 31
Carlisle, Cliff BL: 231; CO: 31; FO: 80
Carlisle Brothers CO: **31–32**
Carlos, Wendy CL: **43,** 218
Carlson, Paulette CO: **32**
Carlton, Carl RB: **35**
Carmen, Eric RR: 177
Carnegie, Andrew CL: 44, 45, 64, 146
Carnegie Hall CL: **44–45;** JA: **27–28**. *See also* From Spirituals to Swing
  Isaac Stern Auditorium CL: **112**
  Weill Recital Hall CL: **237**
  Zankel Hall CL: **245**
Carnes, Kim CO: 44, 178
Carney, Harry JA: 61, 213
Carney, Laurie CL: 8
"Carolina Shout" JA: 107, 116
Carolina Tar Heels FO: 7, **29**
Carpenter, Bob CO: 151
Carpenter, John Alden CL: **45,** 130, 209
Carpenter, Mary Chapin CO: **32**
  Joan Baez FO: 9
  Beausoleil FO: 14
  Cajun music CO: 29
  Joe Diffie CO: 57
  "Down at the Twist and Shout" CO: 61
  Foster and Lloyd CO: 77
Carr, Benjamin CL: **45–46**
Carr, Dora BL: 49
Carr, Eric RR: 130
Carr, James RB: 107
Carr, Leroy BL: xix, **36**
  aliases BL: 5
  Scrapper Blackwell BL: 17
  blues lyrics BL: 25
  "Dust My Broom" BL: 55
  "How Long, How Long Blues" BL: 82–83
  Indianapolis BL: 86
  piano BL: 161
  vocal styles BL: 230
Carr, Sam BL: 94
Carr, Wynona RB: 18
Carroll, Barbara JA: **28**
Carroll, Earl "Speedy" RB: 33, 34
Carroll, Lewis RR: 119
Carroll, Liz FO: **29–30**
Cars, The RR: 158
Carson, Fiddlin' John BL: 158; CO: **33,** 123, 167; FO: 141, 163
Carson, Kit FO: 180
Carson, Kris CO: 118
Carson, Martha CO: **33–34**
Carson, Rosa Lee. *See* Moonshine Kate
Carter, A. P. CO: 34, 115, 219
Carter, Anita CO: 34–35; FO: 144
Carter, Anna CO: 37, 54
Carter, Benny JA: **28–29**
  Cannonball Adderly JA: 3
  Sid Catlett JA: 30
  Ornette Coleman JA: 36
  Roy Eldridge JA: 60
  Art Farmer JA: 69
  Dizzy Gillespie JA: 75
  Coleman Hawkins JA: 87
  Japanese jazz JA: 103
  JATP JA: 106
  jazz firsts JA: 117
  Abbey Lincoln JA: 122
  Carmen McRae JA: 130
  Diane Reeves JA: 163
  George Russell JA: 166
  saxophone JA: 171
  Chick Webb JA: 212
  Ben Webster JA: 213
  Shadow Wilson JA: 218
Carter, Betty JA: **29,** 51, 81
Carter, Bo (Bo Chatmon) BL: **36,** 132, 140
Carter, Calvin RB: 37
Carter, Carlene CO: 35, 36, 187
Carter, Clarence RB: **35–36,** 246
Carter, D. P. "Dad" CO: 37
Carter, Earl RB: 289
Carter, Elliott CL: 6, *46,* **46–47,** 134, 151, 246
Carter, Helen CO: 35
Carter, Janette CO: 35
Carter, Jim CO: 37
Carter, Jimmy CO: 144
Carter, Joe CO: 35
Carter, June CO: 35, 101, 105, 187; FO: 16
Carter, Maybelle FO: *147,* 181
Carter, Mel RB: **36**
Carter, Mother Maybelle CO: 6, *6,* 34, 47, 115
Carter, Ron JA: **29–30**
  Miles Davis JA: 49
  "E.S.P." JA: 63
  Jim Hall JA: 80
  Chico Hamilton JA: 80
  Herbie Hancock JA: 82
  Out There (Dolphy) JA: 150
  Tony Williams JA: 216
Carter, Rose Lola CO: 37
Carter, Sara CO: 34
Carter, Wilf CO: **34**
Carter Family CO: **34–35**
  Chet Atkins CO: 5
  autoharp CO: 6
  Johnny Cash CO: 35
  gospel music CO: 85

"Keep on the Sunnyside" CO: 115
recording FO: 163
record labels CO: 167
Red Clay Ramblers FO: 165
weeper CO: 212
"Will the Circle Be Unbroken?" CO: 219
Carter Sisters CO: *6*
Carthy, Eliza FO: 30
Carthy, Martin FO: **30,** 117, 194
Caruso, Enrique CL: 181; BL: 146
Carver Brothers, The FO: 44
Cary, Annie Louise CL: **47**
Casadesus, Robert CL: 111, 118
Casady, Jack BL: 81; RR: 119–121
Casals, Pablo CL: 93, 112, 148, 200
Casella, Alfred CL: 34
Casey, Harry Wayne RB: 149
Cash, Alvin and the Crawlers RB: 199
Cash, Fred RB: 131, 132
Cash, Johnny CO: **35–36**
"A Boy Named Sue" CO: 21
Rosanne Cash CO: 36
"Cowboy" Jack Clement CO: 38, 39
country rock CO: 45
Glaser Brothers CO: 83
Merle Haggard CO: 91
Buddy Harman CO: 94
Harlan Howard CO: 105
Jan Howard CO: 105
"I Walk the Line" CO: 108
Waylon Jennings CO: 110
Kris Kristofferson CO: 118, 119
Peter La Farge FO: 121
Jerry Lee Lewis CO: 122
Barbara Mandrell CO: 132
Roy Orbison RR: 165, 166
Carl Perkins BL: 158; CO: 162; RR: 169
Sam Phillips RR: 170, 171
Rouse Brothers FO: 177
Statler Brothers CO: 192
Marty Stuart CO: 194
U2 RR: 237
Cash, June Carter. *See* Carter, June
Cash, Rosanne CO: 36, **36,** 48; FO: 36
Cash Money Classics RB: 254
Cassady, Neal RR: 93
Cassone, Cyd BL: 65
Castle, Vernon and Irene JA: 63
Castle Studio CO: 87
Caston, Leonard RB: 63
Castor, Jimmy RB: **36**
Castro, Fidel JA: 174
Casual Gods RR: 232
Catlett, Sid JA: **30,** 157, 169
Cat on a Hot Tin Roof (Tennessee Williams play) BL: 129, 215; FO: 107
"Cattle Call" CO: **36**
Cavaliere, Felix RB: 218; RR: 199
Cavern Club (Liverpool, England) RR: 19
Cavestomp festival RR: 90
CB (citizens band) radio CO: 203
CBGB RR: 188, 198, 231
CBS radio network CO: 123, 179; FO: 107
CBS television network CO: 97; FO: 101
CCC. *See* Civilian Conservation Corps
C+C Music Factory RB: **34**
Cedrone, Danny RR: 104
Cele, Willard JA: 187
Celestin, Papa JA: 10
censorship BL: **36–38**
Centennial Hymn (John Knowles Paine) CL: **47**
Center for Southern Folklore BL: 132
Centers, Roy Lee CO: 191; FO: 193
Cephas, John BL: **38,** 73–74, 223
Cephas and Wiggins FO: **30**
Cerone, David CL: 52
cha-cha JA: 76
Chadbourne, Eugene BL: 243
Chad Mitchell Trio FO: **30–31,** 33, 51, 70, 135
Chadwick, George Whitefield CL: **47**
John Parsons Beach CL: 23
Arthur Farwell CL: 76
Daniel Gregory Mason CL: 149
William Grant Still CL: 215
Chain, Hazel FO: 197
Chain Reaction RR: 1
chamber jazz JA: 24. *See also* Modern Jazz Quartet
Chamberlain, M. F. "Doc" FO: 180
chamber music CL: xvi
Chamber Music Society of Lincoln Center CL: **48,** 123, 133, 203, 228, 235
chamber orchestra/chamber group CL: xvi
Chambers, Paul JA: 19, **30,** 49, 74, 92
Champs, The RR: 115
Chancey, Ron CO: 47
Chandler, Chas BL: 75; RR: 9, 108, 109
Chandler, Dillard CO: 224; FO: 38

Chandler, Gene BL: 180; RB: **36–37,** *37*
Chandler, Len BL: 249; FO: **31**
Chaney, James FO: 34
Chang, Sarah CL: **48**
Channels, The RB: **37–38**
Channing, Chad RR: 159
Chantels, The RB: **38,** 105; RR: 90
Chapel, Jean CO: 33
Chapin, Harry FO: **31**
Chapin, Schuyler CL: **48**
Chapin, Steve FO: 31
Chapin, Tom FO: 31
Chapman, Grady RB: 227
Chapman, Mark David RR: 22
Chapman, Tracy FO: **31–32**
Chapter 8 RB: 7
Chaquico, Craig RR: 120
Charioteers, The RB: 278
Charles, Harry BL: 212
Charles, Ray BL: **38;** CO: viii, **36;** RB: *38,* **38–39**
  Harlan Howard CO: 105
  "I Can't Stop Loving You" CO: 107
  "I'm Moving On" CO: 108
  keyboards RR: 126
  Chaka Khan RB: 152
  Cleo Laine JA: 120
  Brenda Lee CO: 121
  Percy Mayfield BL: 127; RB: 179
  Raeletts, The RB: 217
  rhythm and blues combos BL: 182
  social history and the blues BL: 203
  Stanley Turrentine JA: 200
Charles Ford Band BL: 64
"Charleston" JA: **30–31,** 108
Charlie Daniels Band, The CO: 53
Charlottesville, Virginia RR: 52
Charms, The (Otis Williams & the Charms) RB: **39**
chart, music arrangement JA: **31**
chart, sales JA: **31**
Charters, Ann FO: 32
Charters, Samuel BL: xxi, **38;** FO: **32**
  Lightnin' Hopkins BL: 81
  Furry Lewis BL: 114
  J. B. Long BL: 121
  protest songs BL: 165, 167
  social history BL: 201
  Dave Van Ronk FO: 207
Chase, Gilbert CL: **48–49**
Chatmon, Bo. *See* Carter, Bo
Chatmon, Lonnie BL: 191, 208
Chatmon, Sam BL: 140
Chatterjee, Amit JA: 223
Cheap Suit Serenaders, The FO: 22
Cheap Thrills (Big Brother and the Holding Company) BL: 100; RR: 123
Cheap Trick RR: 177
Checker, Chubby RB: 9, 15, **39–40,** *40,* 237
Chemical Brothers RB: 254
Chenier, C. J. BL: 39; FO: 32
Chenier, Clifton BL: **38–39;** FO: **32**
  accordions FO: 2
  Lonnie Brooks BL: 29
  Cajun music CO: 29; FO: 27
  Sonny Landreth BL: 111
  Lonesome Sundown BL: 120
  Chris Strachwitz FO: 196
  Phillip Walker BL: 236
Cher RR: 6
Cherkassky, Shura CL: **49**
Cherokee Cowboys CO: 163
Cherry, Don JA: *17,* **31–32**
  Gato Barbieri JA: 9
  Ed Blackwell JA: 16–17
  Neneh Cherry RB: 40
  Ornette Coleman JA: 36
  Free Jazz (Ornette Coleman) JA: 71
  Jan Garbarek JA: 73
  Charlie Haden JA: 79
  Abdullah Ibrahim JA: 97
  Steve Lacy JA: 119
  pocket trumpet JA: 156
  Pharoah Sanders JA: 169
  Shape of Jazz to Come, The JA: 174
  Sonny Sharrock JA: 175
  Archie Shepp JA: 177
Cherry, Neneh RB: **40**
Cherry Bombs, The CO: 81, 84
"Cherry Red" BL: 223, 228
Chesapeake FO: 183
Chesnutt, Mark CO: 27, **36–37**
Chess, Leonard BL: **39,** 239; RB: 17; RR: 24
Chess, Marshall BL: 39
Chess, Phil BL: 39
Chessler, Deborah RR: 65
Chess Records BL: **39,** 40, 175, 179
Chess Studios RR: 81, 209, 251
Chester, Pennsylvania RR: 101
Chew, Chris BL: 154
Chic RB: **41**
Chicago, Illinois BL: viii, xix, xx, **39–41,** *40. See also* Chicago blues
  as destination for early New Orleans musicians JA: xxiii
  Dixieland jazz JA: 53
  migration BL: 133, 134
  New Orleans jazz JA: 143
  piano BL: 161
  recordings of early jazz JA: 162

record labels BL: 178
social history BL: 201
talent scouts BL: 212
traditional jazz (classic jazz) JA: 198
Chicago Blues Festival BL: 129, 269
Chicago Civic Opera CL: 85, 119
Chicago Five, The BL: 29
Chicago house RB: 125
Chicago jazz JA: xxiii, **32,** 147, 149, 252*t*
Chicago rhythm and blues RR: ix
Chicago Symphony Orchestra CL: **49–50**
Chicago Underground Trio JA: **32**
Chicago White Sox BL: 247
Chicanos RB: 240
Chicken Shack BL: **41**
Chieftains, The FO: **32–33**
Chiffons, The RB: **41**
Chihara, Paul CL: **50**
Child, Francis FO: viii, 70
Child ballads FO: viii
Children of the Corn RB: 177
children's songs
Cathy Fink FO: 68
Tom Glazer FO: 77, 78
Priscilla Herdman FO: 94
Bessie Jones FO: 112
Si Kahn FO: 113
Frank Luther FO: 129
Tom Paxton FO: 156
Peter, Paul and Mary FO: 157
Sally Rogers FO: 175
Chi-Lites, The RB: **41–42**
Chilton, Alex RR: 177
China CL: 208; FO: 1
Chisholm, George JA: 64
chitlin' circuit BL: 116, 186; RB: 219
Chitwood, Bill FO: 75
Choates, Harry CO: 29
Chopin, Frédéric CL: xxii, 36, 37, 91, 119, 167–168, 194
chops JA: **32**
chord BL: 159–160; JA: **32,** 41, 53, 198
chord progression JA: **32–33**
Chords, The RB: **42;** RR: 65
chorus JA: **33**
Christensen, Jon JA: 208
Christgau, Robert RR: 202
Christian, Charlie JA: **33**
Kenny Clarke JA: 34
Ida Cox BL: 46
electric guitar BL: 58
Jim Hall JA: 79–80
B. B. King BL: 105
Eddie Lang JA: 120
Meade Lux Lewis BL: 114
Wes Montgomery JA: 139
"Tiny" Moore FO: 142
Bud Powell JA: 156
"Stompin' at the Savoy" JA: **188**
T-Bone Walker BL: 236
Christian hip-hop RB: 106
Christianity RR: 200, 236
Christian pop CO: 86
Christian rap RB: 112
Christie, George Washington FO: 72
chromatic harmonica BL: 51, 73, 116
chronology CL: 253–281; BL: 263–267
Chuck Berry—Hail! Hail! Rock 'n' Roll (movie) BL: 94; RR: 25, 209
Chuck D RB: 103, 212–213
Chuck Wagon Gang CO: **37,** 85
Chung, Kyung-Wha CL: **50**
Chung, Myung-Wha CL: **50**
Churchill, Savannah RB: 95
Church of God in Christ BL: 243
Church Street Five, The RB: 22
Cifelli, Jim JA: **33**
Cimarron Boys, The FO: 134
Cincinnati Chamber Orchestra CL: **50–51**
Cincinnati Opera CL: **51**
Cincinnati Symphony Orchestra CL: **51**
Circle (Corea/Holland/Braxton/Altschul) JA: 22, 42, 92
circular breathing JA: **33,** 98, 114
city blues. *See* urban blues
"City of New Orleans, The" FO: 79, 87
Civilian Conservation Corps (CCC) BL: 166, 167, 201
Civil Rights Act of 1964 FO: 34
Civil Rights movement FO: **33–34**
Harry Belafonte FO: 14
James Brown RB: 26
Guy Carawan FO: 28
Len Chandler FO: 31
Barbara Dane FO: 49
Manny Greenhill FO: 82
Si Kahn FO: 113
Curtis Mayfield BL: 127
migration BL: 134–135
Peter, Paul and Mary FO: 157
Nina Simone JA: 181
social history and the blues BL: 203

Civil Rights movement (*continued*)
 Sweet Honey in the Rock FO: 197
 young black country blues artists BL: 249
Civil War CL: xxii
Claborn, Pearl and Logan FO: 191
Clancy, Bobby FO: 35
Clancy, Liam FO: 35, 68
Clancy, Pat FO: 35
Clancy, Tom FO: 35
Clancy, Willie FO: 10, **34–35,** 141
Clancy Brothers, The FO: **35,** 36, 164
Clannad FO: **35**
Clapton, Eric BL: **41;** RR: **39–40**
 Duane Allman BL: 6
 Allman Brothers Band RR: 4
 Cream BL: 46; RR: 45
 Buddy Guy BL: 69
 Robert Johnson BL: 98
 Freddie King BL: 106
 John Mayall BL: 127
 music business BL: 144
 "Nobody Knows You When You're Down and Out" BL: 154
 reggae RR: 199
 roots rock RR: 211
 Yardbirds, The BL: 247, RR: 251
 young black country blues artists BL: 250
clarinet BL: **189;** JA: xxvi, **33–34.** *See also specific clarinettists*
Clark, Cortelia BL: 44
Clark, Dave RB: 17
Clark, Dee RB: **42–43**
Clark, Dick RB: 9, 39, 40, 239; RR: 51, 222. *See also American Bandstand*
Clark, Gene CO: 84; FO: 25, **35–36,** 53, 146; RR: 35–38
Clark, Guy, Jr. CO: 67, 154; FO: **36,** 209
Clark, James "Poppa" RB: 33, 34
Clark, Louis RR: 77
Clark, Roy BL: 30; CO: 22, 27, 38, **38,** 97–98
Clark, Terri CO: **38**
Clark, William Andrews, Jr. CL: 141
Clarke, Kenny JA: **34**
 bebop JA: 12
 Andrew Cyrille JA: 46
 Al Di Meola JA: 52
 Minton's Playhouse JA: 137
 Modern Jazz Quartet JA: 138
 Charlie Parker JA: 151
 "Stompin' at the Savoy" JA: 188
Clarke, Michael CO: 75; FO: 25; RR: 35, 37, 38
Clarke, Stanley JA: 17, 18, **34–35,** 43, 163, 216
Clarke, Vince RR: 158
Clarke, William BL: 194
Clarksdale, Mississippi BL: 26, 47, 72, 75, 80, **137–138,** 255
Clash, The RR: 188, 199
classical music CL: 1–290
classic blues BL: **42.** *See also specific artists, e.g.:* Smith, Bessie
 Louis Armstrong BL: 8
 instruments BL: 87
 jazz and the blues BL: 92
 saxophone, trombone, trumpet, and clarinet BL: 188
 vocal styles BL: 229–230
classic jazz. *See* traditional jazz
classic rock RR: xx, **40–42,** 73, 133
Class of '55 (Roy Orbison, Carl Perkins, Jerry Lee Lewis, Johnny Cash) RR: 165–166, 169
Claunch, Quinton CO: 135; RB: 107
Clavinet RR: 127
Clay, Otis RB: 54
Clayborn, Reverend Edward BL: 192
Claypool, Les RR: 15
Clayton, Adam RR: 235, 236
Clayton, Merry RB: 170–171, 217
Clayton, Paul FO: 11, **36–37,** 37, 155
Clayton, Willie RB: 51
Clear Creek Crossin' FO: 126
Clearwater, Eddie BL: **42**
Clearwater concerts FO: 31
Cleaves, Jessica RB: 97
Clement, Ada CL: 198
Clement, "Cowboy" Jack CO: **38–39,** 41, 170, 215–216; FO: 176
Clements, Vassar FO: 16, **37,** 81, 93, 153, 200
Clemons, Clarence RR: 225
Cleveland, Grover CL: 146
Cleveland, Mississippi BL: **138**
Cleveland Chamber Symphony Orchestra CL: **51–52,** 141
Cleveland Institute of Music CL: 31, **52,** 131, 191, 206
Cleveland Museum of Art CL: 159
Cleveland Orchestra CL: 31–32, **52–53,** 206–207
Cleveland Women's Orchestra CL: **53**
Cliburn, Van CL: xxiv, xxv, *53,* **53–54,** 137

Cliff, Jimmy RB: 133, 222; RR: 201
Clifford, Doug RR: 46, 48
Clifton, Bill FO: **37**
Clinch Mountain Boys, The CO: 190; FO: 193
Cline, Curly Ray CO: 191; FO: 194
Cline, Patsy CO: **39**
 Owen Bradley CO: 21
 Cowboy Copas CO: 43
 "Crazy" CO: 47–48
 Don Gibson CO: 81
 Buddy Harman CO: 94
 Freddie Hart CO: 95
 Hawkshaw Hawkins CO: 96
 Harlan Howard CO: 105
 "I Fall to Pieces" CO: 107
 Jordanaires CO: 112
 k. d. lang CO: 121
 Nashville sound CO: 147
 Willie Nelson CO: 149
 record labels CO: 169
Clinton, Bill CL: 208; CO: 190; JA: 29, 81, 138; RB: 240
Clinton, George RB: 11, *43*, **43–44**
Clinton, Hillary CO: 190
Clivilles, Robert RB: 34
Clooney, Rosemary CO: 93
closed-throat singers BL: 118, 229, 232
Clovers, The RB: **44**
Clovis, New Mexico RR: 112
Club 47 (Cambridge, Massachusetts) BL: 234; FO: 9, 113, 176
Club Nouveau RB: **44–45**
C melody saxophone JA: 199
CMT cable network CO: 16, 113, 150, 151
Coakley, John FO: 18
"Coal Miner's Daughter" CO: **39,** 127
Coasters, The RB: *45*, **45–46**
 Cadets/The Jacks, The RB: 33
 Cadillacs, The RB: 34
 King Curtis RB: 155
 Leiber and Stoller RB: 163–164; RR: 139
 Robins, The RB: 227
"Coat of Many Colors" CO: **39,** 158
Cobain, Kurt RR: 97, 159–161, 203
Cobb, Jimmy JA: 74, 113
Cobb, Kevin CL: 7
Cobham, Billy JA: **35**
 John Abercrombie JA: 1
 Randy Brecker JA: 22
 Jan Hammer JA: 81
 Inner Mounting Flame, The JA: 99
 John McLaughlin JA: 132
 John Scofield JA: 172
Coca-Cola CO: 213
Cochran, Anita CO: 211
Cochran, Eddie RR: **42,** *42*
Cochran, Hank CO: 39, 131, 184; RR: 42
Cockerham, Fred FO: 13, **37–38,** 110
Coconut Grove (Los Angeles) RR: 166
Coe, David Allan CO: **40,** 159, 220; FO: 79
Coerne, Louis CL: **54**
Cohen, Avishai JA: 43
Cohen, Joel CL: 34
Cohen, John FO: **38,** *147*
 Moses Asch FO: 7
 Roscoe Holcomb FO: 98
 New Lost City Ramblers FO: 147–148
 recording FO: 164
 Mike Seeger FO: 181
 Izzy Young FO: 219
Cohen, Larry FO: 188, *188*
Cohen, Leonard CO: 53; FO: 39; RR: 219–220
Cohen, Mike FO: 38
Cohen, Norm FO: 173
Cohen, Paul CO: 169, 212
Cohen, Ronald BL: 118
Cohn, Al JA: 182
Cohn, Mark BL: 132
Coko (Cheryl Gamble) RB: 251
Cold 187 RB: 1, 2
"Cold, Cold Heart" CO: **40,** 217
Cold Chillin' Records RB: **46**
Coldplay RR: 175
cold war CL: ix, xxiv, 53–54
Cole, Bob BL: 137
Cole, Cozy RB: **46**
Cole, Natalie RB: 34, **46–47,** *47*
Cole, Nat "King" JA: **35–36**
 Natalie Cole RB: 46, 47
 jump blues and rhythm and blues BL: 101
 Los Angeles, California BL: 35
 Oscar Peterson JA: 153, 154
 rhythm and blues combos BL: 182
Coleman, Bee FO: 144
Coleman, Deborah BL: **42**
Coleman, Jim FO: 38, 39
Coleman, Michael FO: 23, **38–39,** 66
Coleman, Ornette JA: xxiv, **36–38,** *37*
 Ed Blackwell JA: 16
 Don Cherry JA: 31, 32
 Eric Dolphy JA: 55
 free jazz JA: 71
 Free Jazz JA: **71–72**
 Charlie Haden JA: 79
 Pat Metheny JA: 134
 Shape of Jazz to Come, The JA: **174–175**

Coleman, Ornette (*continued*)
  Cecil Taylor JA: 195
  Attilla Zoller JA: 224
Coleman, Pat FO: 39
Coleman, T. Michael FO: 183
Coley, Doris RR: 217
Colgrass, Michael CL: **54,** *54,* 65–66
collective improvisation JA: 71
Collie, Mark CO: **40–41**
Collins, Aaron RB: 33
Collins, Albert BL: **42–43,** 43, *43,* 49
Collins, Bootsy RB: 276
Collins, Dolly FO: 40
Collins, Judy FO: **39–40,** *40*
  Civil Rights movement FO: 34
  Sandy Denny FO: 51
  Jac Holzman FO: 99
  Joni Mitchell FO: 140
  singer-songwriters RR: 220
  12-string guitar BL: 224
Collins, Lewis RB: 182
Collins, Phil RB: 7; RR: 69, 136, 152, 185
Collins, Shirley FO: **40,** 80, 102
Collins, Tommy CO: 10, **41,** 156
Colomby, Bobby JA: 152
colonial America BL: xv, 195–197
Colorado FO: 121
Color Me Badd RB: **47**
Colter, Jessi CO: **41–42,** 110, 149
Coltrane, Alice JA: **38**
  Ed Blackwell JA: 16
  John Coltrane JA: 40, 41
  Ravi Coltrane JA: 41
  Leroy Jenkins JA: 107
  Pharoah Sanders JA: 170
  Carlos Santana RR: 214
Coltrane, John JA: **38–41,** *39*
  Cannonball Adderly JA: 3
  Birdland JA: 15
  Blue Train JA: 19
  Donald Byrd JA: 26; RB: 31
  Don Cherry JA: 31
  Alice Coltrane JA: 38
  Ravi Coltrane JA: 41
  Miles Davis JA: 49
  Eric Dolphy JA: 54, 55
  Duke Ellington JA: 61
  Giant Steps (John Coltrane) JA: **74**
  Grammy Awards JA: 78
  Johnny Hartman JA: 86
  Coleman Hawkins JA: 88
  "In a Sentimental Mood" JA: **98**
  Elvin Jones JA: 108–109
  Kind of Blue JA: 113
  Love Supreme, A JA: **124**
  Thelonious Monk JA: 139
  Wes Montgomery JA: 139
  multiphonics JA: 142
  "My Favorite Things" JA: **142**
  Courtney Pine JA: 155
  George Russell JA: 167
  Pharoah Sanders JA: 169
  Mongo Santamaria JA: 170
  saxophone JA: 171
  Archie Shepp JA: 177
  Andy Sheppard JA: 177
  Wayne Shorter JA: 178
  McCoy Tyner JA: 200
  Shadow Wilson JA: 218
  Lester Young JA: 220
Coltrane, Ravi JA: **41**
Columbia-Princeton Electronic Music Center CL: **55**
  Milton Babbitt CL: 15
  Mario Davidovsky CL: 65
  Jacob Druckman CL: 70
  Otto Luening CL: 143
  Time's Encomium CL: 225
  Vladimir Ussachevsky CL: 231
Columbus, Georgia BL: 9
Columbus, Ohio RB: 226–227
Colvig, William CL: 99
Colvin, Shawn BL: 223
Colyer, Ken BL: 108
Comacho, Thelma Lou FO: 146
Combelle, Alix JA: 25
combo JA: **41,** 62, 159, 164
combo blues
  acoustic guitar BL: 3
  Big Bill Broonzy BL: 29
  Chicago BL: 40, 41
  electric guitar BL: 57–59
  Lester Melrose BL: 130
Combs, Sean. *See* Puff Daddy
Comeaux, Oscar FO: 5
Comhaltas Ceoltóirí Éireann FO: 23
Commodores, The RB: 223, *224;* RR: 154
communism FO: 174
Communist Party BL: 168; FO: ix, 174, 185–186
Como, Perry FO: 137
competitions CL: xxv, 53
comping JA: **41**
Complete Communion (Don Cherry) JA: 16, 31–32
composer JA: **41**. *See also* arranger; *specific composers*
composition. *See* arrangement; counterpoint
Compton, California RB: 50, 149, 196
Compton, Mike FO: 145
Compton's Most Wanted RB: **47–48**
Concerto for Flute, Strings and Percussion (Linda Wagner) CL: **55**
Concerto for Orchestra (Roger Sessions) CL: **55**

Concerto for Two Pianos and Orchestra (Quincy Porter) CL: **55**
Concerto in F (George Gershwin) CL: **55**
Concord Sonata (Charles Ives) CL: 38, **55,** 88, 114, 126
conductors CL: xvi–xvii. *See also specific conductors*
Cone, Edward T. CL: **55**
Conference of the Birds (Dave Holland) JA: **41,** 92
Con Funk Shun RB: **48**
congas JA: 170; RR: 213
congregational singing CL: xx
Conley, Earl Thomas CO: **42**
Conley, Walt BL: 249
Conlon, James CL: **55–56,** 186
Connecticut JA: 16, 179
Conneff, Kevin FO: 33
Connell, Dudley FO: 111, 183
Connie's Inn JA: 85
Connor, Joanna BL: **43**
Connors, Bill JA: 43
Conried, Heinrich CL: 155
Conroy, Anne FO: 24
Conspiracy of Hope Tour RR: 235
Constanten, Tom RR: 93
Consul, The (Gian Carlo Menotti) CL: **56**
Contemporary Chamber Players (New York) CL: 123
contemporary jazz JA: **42**. *See also specific artists*
Contours, The RB: **48**
contracts BL: 147. *See also* publishing; recording royalties
contra dancing FO: 192
Converse, Frederick CL: **56,** 80, 108, 117, 130
"Convoy" CO: 135, 203
Conway, Bill RB: 11
Cooder, Ry BL: **43**
  acoustic guitar BL: 4
  John Hiatt FO: 95
  Blind Willie Johnson BL: 94
  Taj Mahal BL: 123–124
  Compay Segundo JA: 174
  slide guitar BL: 193
  social history and the blues BL: 204
  Taj Mahal FO: 199
Cook, Don CO: 97
Cook, Greg RB: 266
Cook, Jeffrey Alan CO: 3
Cook, Stu RR: 46, 48
Cooke, Jack CO: 191; FO: 194
Cooke, Sam RB: **48–49,** *49*
  Animals, The BL: 7
  Bumps Blackwell RB: 18
  Clarksdale, Mississippi BL: 137
  holy blues BL: 79
  Little Richard RR: 142
  Ovations, The RB: 201
  Lou Rawls RB: 219
  Bobby Womack RB: 282
Cookery, The BL: 83, 152
Cookies, The RB: **49,** 217
Cooley, Eddie, & the Dimples RB: **49–50**
Cooley, Spade CO: 19, **42–43,** 214; FO: 213
Coolidge, Calvin FO: 97
Coolidge, Rita CO: 119
Coolio RB: **50**
cool jazz JA: xxiv–xxv, 15, **42.** *See also specific artists*
Coon Creek Girls, The FO: 124
Cooney, Michael FO: **41,** 155, 192
coon songs BL: 176
Cooper, Alice RR: **42–43**
Cooper, Carol Lee FO: 41
Cooper, Mike RB: 48
Cooper, Wilma Lee and Stoney CO: 62; FO: **41,** 80
Copas, Cowboy CO: 39, **43,** 117
Copeland, Johnny BL: **43**
Copeland, Miles RR: 158
Copeland, Shemekia BL: 43, *44*
Copeland, Stuart RR: 64
Copenhagen, Denmark JA: 77, 154, 213
Copes, Ronald CL: 121
Copland, Aaron CL: viii–ix, ix, **56–58,** *58*
  Samuel Adler CL: 4
  American Music Center CL: 7
  Appalachian Spring CL: **12**
  Aspen Music Festival and School CL: 13
  Arthur Berger CL: 25
  Leonard Bernstein CL: 26
  Billy the Kid CL: **29–30**
  Fanfare for the Common Man CL: **75**
  Harold Farberman CL: 75
  Irving Fine CL: 78
  Philip Glass CL: 89
  Rubin Goldmark CL: 90
  Roy Harris CL: 99
  Alan Hovhaness CL: 108
  André Kostelanitz CL: 128
  League of Composers CL: **135**
  Lincoln Portrait, A CL: **139**
  Alvin Lucier CL: 142
  William Masselos CL: 150
  Musical Quarterly CL: 160
  recommended listening CL: 250
  William Schuman CL: 202
  Harold Shapero CL: 207
  Lester Trimble CL: 227
  Richard Wernick CL: 238
Copper, James FO: 42

Copper Family, The FO: **42**
copyright BL: 143–146, 158
Copywrite RB: 226, 227
Corea, Chick JA: *42,* **42–43**
Bitches Brew JA: 15, 16
Art Blakey JA: 17
Richard Bona JA: 20
Anthony Braxton JA: 22
Stanley Clarke JA: 34, 35
Miles Davis JA: 49
Al Di Meola JA: 52
Maynard Ferguson JA: 70
Jan Garbarek JA: 73
Dave Holland JA: 92
Bobby McFerrin JA: 131
piano JA: 155
In a Silent Way JA: 98
Tommy Smith JA: 185
Steve Swallow JA: 192
Miroslav Vitous JA: 208
Joe Zawinul JA: 223
Corgan, Billy RR: 98–99
Corigliano, John CL: **59,** *59,* 143, 155
Corman, Roger RR: 198
Corneal, Jon CO: 75
Cornelius, Helen CO: 25, **43–44**
Cornelius Brothers and Sister Rose RB: **50**
Cornell, Chris RR: 98, 167
cornet JA: xxvi, **43**
Cornish, Gene RB: 218; RR: 199
"Cortelia Clark" BL: **44**
Cortez, Dave "Baby" RB: **50**
Cortot, Alfred CL: 136
Coryell, Larry JA: 20, 26, 80
Cosby, Bill JA: 174
Costello, Elvis
Beatles, The RR: 22
Owen Bradley CO: 21
Bill Frisell JA: 72
George Jones CO: 111
Diana Krall JA: 114
Ewan MacColl FO: 131
roots rock RR: 211
Cotton, Elizabeth "Libba" BL: 13, **44,** *45;* FO: **42,** 72–73, 181
Cotton, James BL: **44,** 139, 142, 208, 239
Cotton Club (Harlem) JA: **43–44,** 60, 85, 93; RB: 124
cotton gin BL: 195
Couch, Tommy BL: 124
counterculture. *See* psychedelic; rock festivals
counterpoint JA: 24, **44**
Count Five RR: 14, 89
Country CO: viii
country and western (C&W) CO: vii–viii; RR: xix
country blues BL: 20, 25, **45,** 248–253. *See also* Delta blues; folk blues; Piedmont blues; rural blues
Country Blues, The (Sam Charters) BL: 38; FO: 32
Country Caravan CO: 219
Country Cooking CO: 16; FO: **42–43,** 161, 204
Country Gazette CO: 75; FO: 15, **43,** 115
Country Gentleman (Gretch guitar) CO: 90
Country Gentlemen, The FO: **43–44**
Jerry Douglas FO: 55
Bill Emerson FO: 60, 61
Doyle Lawson FO: 122
Seldom Scene FO: 183
Ricky Skaggs CO: 186
Country Joe and the Fish BL: 7; FO: 32, 135; RR: 151
country music BL: 204, 231, 232; CO: 1–256; FO: viii
Country Music Association (CMA) CO: 175, 195, 245
Country Music Television (CMT) CO: 245
countrypolitan CO: xviii, **44,** 61, 123, 148, 172
country rock CO: **44–45;** RR: xx, **43–45**. *See also specific artists*
Gene Clark FO: 36
psychedelic rock RR: 187
roots rock RR: 210, 211
"Courtesy of the Red, White and Blue" CO: **45**
Courville, Sady CO: 29; FO: 5, 27
Cousin Emmy FO: **44–45,** 148
Cousin Joe. *See* Pleasant Joe
Covay, Don RB: **50–51**
Coverdale, David RR: 136
Covington, Joey RR: 120
Cowan, John FO: 147
Cowboy Ramblers CO: 20
cowboy songs CO: **45–46;** FO: 99, 127, 170. *See also* singing cowboys
Cowell, Henry CL: **59–60,** *60*
John Cage CL: 41
Ruth Crawford Seeger CL: 60
Vivian Fine CL: 78
Percy Goetschius CL: 90
Lou Harrison CL: 99
Charles Ives CL: 114
William Kraft CL: 129
Musical Quarterly CL: 160
Conlon Nancarrow CL: 161
Wallingford Riegger CL: 189
Carl Ruggles CL: 195
Cox, Anthony JA: **44**
Cox, Bill FO: **45**
Cox, Billy RB: 183; RR: 108, 109
Cox, Ida BL: **46,** 89, 242–243
Cox, Jimmie BL: 154
Cox, Sidney FO: 45, 46
Cox, Suzanne FO: 45, 46

Cox, Tony FO: 109, 156
Cox, Willard FO: 45, 46
Cox Family, The FO: **45–46**
Craddock, Billy "Crash" CO: **46–47**
Craddock, Ronald CO: 46
Cramer, Floyd CO: 25, **47,** 55, 147; RB: 210; RR: 181
Crary, Dan FO: **46,** 146
Crary, Hickman, and Berline FO: 15
crash cymbal JA: **44**
Craver, Mike FO: 165, *165*
Crawdaddy Club (Richmond, England) RR: 209, 251
Crawford, Blackie CO: 3
Crawford, Ruth (Seeger) CL: **60–61,** 78
Cray, Robert BL: 26, 43, **46,** 183, 188; RB: 182
Crayton, Pee Wee BL: **46,** 163; JA: 36
"Crazy" CO: 39, **47–48,** 149
"Crazy Arms" CO: **48**
"Crazy Blues" BL: xvii, **46;** JA: 184
Crazy Horse FO: 179; RR: 254
Creach, Papa John BL: 62, 81, 252; RR: 120
Cream BL: **46;** RR: **45–46,** *46*
  blues rock RR: 28–29
  Eric Clapton BL: 41; RR: 40
  "Crossroads Blues" BL: 47
  Skip James BL: 90
Creed, Kyle FO: 38
Creedence Clearwater Revival RR: **46–49,** *47,* 152, 211, 248
Creole Jazz Band (King Oliver) JA: 53, 54, 84, 147–148
Creoles JA: 150
Creston, Paul CL: *61,* **61**
Crew-Cuts, The RR: 65
Crewe, Bob RR: 86
Crickets, The CO: 101; RR: 111, 113, 114. *See also* Holly, Buddy
Crier, Keith RB: 108. *See also* Sweat, Keith
Crispell, Marilyn JA: **44–45,** 46
Criss, Peter RR: 130, 131
Crissman, Maxine FO: 87
Cronquist, Robert L. CL: 53
Crook, General RB: **51**
Crook, Herman FO: 46, 47
Crook, Lewis FO: 46
Crook, Matthew FO: 46
Crook, Max RR: 215
Crook Brothers, The CO: 12; FO: **46–47**
Cropper, Steve
  Booker T. & the MGs RB: 23, *23,* 24
  instrumental rock RR: 116
  Mar-Keys, The RB: 175
  Otis Redding RB: 220
  Stax Records BL: 180
Crosby, Bing CL: 33; CO: 162; JA: 56, 206
Crosby, David FO: 25, 71; RR: 34, 35, 37, 120
Crosby, Stills, and Nash (and Young) RR: 35, 37, 254
Cross, Joe RB: 14
cross harp BL: 72
Crossings (Herbie Hancock) JA: 83, 117
crossover CL: xxvi; JA: **45**
"Cross Road Blues" BL: 31, 47, **47**
crossroads BL: **46–47,** 97, 98
"Crossroads" RR: 40, 46
Croston, John CO: 53
Crouch, Stanley JA: 106
Croudson, Edna's Rhythm Girls JA: 13
Crowe, J. D. CO: 186, 215; FO: 3, **47,** 122, 169
Crowell, Rodney CO: **48**
  Rosanne Cash CO: 36
  Guy Clark FO: 36
  Vince Gill CO: 81
  Emory Gordy, Jr. CO: 84
  Emmylou Harris CO: 95
  Harlan Howard CO: 105
  Nitty Gritty Dirt Band CO: 151
  Lee Ann Womack CO: 220
Crowley, Louisiana BL: 111, 135
Crows, The RB: **51;** RR: 65
Crucible, The (Robert Ward) CL: **61**
Crudup, Arthur "Big Boy" BL: 28, **47,** 217–218; RB: **51–52,** 209; RR: 179
Crum, Simon CO: 106
Crumb, George CL: 8, **61–62,** 73, 193
Crumb, R., and the Cheap Suit Serenaders FO: 22
Crump, E. H. BL: 131; JA: 84
Cruz, Adam JA: 43
"Crying" RR: 165, 166
Crystals, The RB: 21, **52;** RR: 222–223
Cuba. *See also* Latin and Afro-Cuban jazz
  Mario Bauzá JA: 11
  Ruben Gonzalez JA: 76
  Latin and Afro-Cuban jazz JA: 121
  Machito JA: 125
  Chico O'Farrill JA: 147
  Chano Pozo JA: 157
  Gonzalo Rubalcaba JA: 166
  Arturo Sandoval JA: 170
  Mongo Santamaria JA: 170
  Compay Segundo JA: 174
"Cubana Be, Cubana Bop" JA: 157, 166
Cugat, Xavier JA: 125

Culp, Jennifer CL: 131
Culture Club RR: 157
Cumberland Mountains FO: 171–172
Cuney, Waring BL: 170
Cunningham, Agnes "Sis" FO: 19, 57
Cunningham, Carl RB: 10
Cunningham, Johnny FO: 24, 184, 185
Cunningham, Merce CL: 42
Cunningham, Phil FO: 18, 184, 185
Curb, Mike CO: 155
Curless, Dick CO: 202
Curran, Ciarán FO: 4
Curtis, Connie. *See* Crayton, Pee Wee
Curtis, Herman RB: 243, 244
Curtis, Sonny RR: 111, 114
Curtis Institute of Music CL: **62**
 Samuel Barber CL: 17
 Leonard Bernstein CL: 26
 Marc Blitzstein CL: 30
 Jorge Bolet CL: 33
 Shura Cherkassky CL: 49
 Richard Danielpour CL: 65
 Lukas Foss CL: 81
 Sidney Foster CL: 81
 Ivan Galamian CL: 85
 Boris Goldovsky CL: 90
 Richard Goode CL: 91
 Gary Graffman CL: 92
 Hilary Hahn CL: 97
 Josef Hofmann CL: 104
 Lee Hoiby CL: 105
 Mieczyslaw Horszowski CL: 108
 Eugene Istomin CL: 112
 Paarvo Järvi CL: 118
 Young Uck Kim CL: 126
 Anton Kuerti CL: 131
 Jaime Laredo CL: 133
 Ruth Laredo CL: 134
 Jacob Lateiner CL: 134
 Seymour Lipkin CL: 139, 140
 Sergiu Luca CL: 142
 Gian Carlo Menotti CL: 152
 Fritz Reiner CL: 187
 Nadia Reisenberg CL: 188
 George Rochberg CL: 189
 Artur Rodzinski CL: 190
 Ned Rorem CL: 191
 Leonard Rose CL: 191
 Max Rudolph CL: 194
 David Saperton CL: 199
 Thomas Schippers CL: 200
 Peter Serkin CL: 204, 205
 Rudolf Serkin CL: 205
 Oscar Shumsky CL: 208, 209
 Abbey Simon CL: 209
 Felix Slatkin CL: 209
 Robert Spano CL: 212
 Randall Thompson CL: 224
 Hugo Weisgall CL: 237
 Efrem Zimbalist CL: 245
cutting contest JA: **45–46,** 87, 212
cylinder recordings FO: 163
cymbal JA: 44, 91, 164–165
Cymone, Andre RB: **52**
Cypress Hill RB: **52**
Cyrille, Andrew JA: **46**
Cyrus, Billy Ray CO: 1, *48,* **48–49**
Czechoslovakia JA: 80–81, 207–208

D

D-12 RB: 81
Da Basement RB: 258
Daddy-O RB: **53**
Daffan, Ted CO: **51**
Dahl, Ingolf CL: **63**
Daily, Harold "Pappy" CO: **51–52,** 110, 152, 169
Dale, Dick RR: 16, 229
Dalhart, Vernon CO: **52**
 Johnny Bond CO: 19
 Adelyne Hood CO: 103
 Reverend Andrew Jenkins FO: 110
 railroad songs CO: 165
 record labels CO: 167
 Carson J. Robison FO: 175
 Roy Smeck FO: 189
 weeper CO: 211–212
 Henry Whitter FO: 215
 "Wreck of the Old 97, The" CO: 220–221
Dallas, Bobby Lester RB: 186, 187
Dallas, Texas BL: **216;** FO: 123
 Anson Funderburgh BL: 66
 Blind Lemon Jefferson BL: 93
 piano BL: 162
 Sammy Price BL: 165
 Jesse (Babyface) Thomas BL: 219
 Willard (Rambling) Thomas BL: 219
 Jimmy Vaughan BL: 227
 Stevie Ray Vaughan BL: 228
Dallas String Band BL: 208, 236
Dallas Symphony Orchestra CL: **63**
 Antal Dorati CL: 70
 Andrew Litton CL: 140
 Kurt Masur CL: 150
 Yehudi Menuhin CL: 153
 Leonard Pennario CL: 174
 Max Rudolph CL: 194
 Janos Starker CL: 213
Dalton, Lacy J. CO: **53**
Daltrey, Roger RR: 243–246
Daly, Jackie FO: 24, 50
D'Amato, Maria FO: 142. *See also* Muldaur, Maria

D'Ambrosio, Joey RR: 104
Damrosch, Clara CL: 147
Damrosch, Frank CL: 120
Damrosch, Leopold CL: **63–64,** 154–155, 164–165
Damrosch, Walter CL: **64**
  An American in Paris CL: 7
  Concerto in F CL: 55
  Leopold Damrosch CL: 64
  George Gershwin CL: 88
  New York Symphony Society CL: 165
Dana Dane RB: **53**
dance CL: 42, 158; JA: 125, 170–171
dancehall RB: 235–236
dance remixes. *See* remixes
Danderliers, The RB: **53**
Dane, Barbara BL: 35; FO: **49**
Danelli, Dino RB: 218; RR: 68, 199
Danielpour, Richard CL: *64,* **64–65**
Daniels, Charlie CO: **53,** 56, 143, 217
Daniels, Jack CO: 32
Daniels, Jeffrey RB: 184, 237
Daniels, Sam RB: 234
Daniels, Ted RB: 92
Danko, Rick RR: 11, 13
Dankworth, John JA: 120; RB: 178
Darbone, Luderin FO: 89
Darby, Tom BL: 213, 231
Darby and Tarlton FO: **49**
Darin, Bobby RR: *51,* **51–52**
DarkRoom Familia RB: 240
Dark Side of the Moon (Pink Floyd) RR: 172–174, 184
"Dark Was the Night" BL: 79, 94
Darling, Erik BL: 13, 236; FO: 175, 182, 212
Darnell, Rick BL: 220
Dash, Sarah RB: 161
Dashiell, Bud FO: 22
Daughters of the American Revolution CL: 10
Dave Matthews Band, The RR: **52–53,** 118
Davenny, Ward CL: 52
Davenport, Charles "Cow Cow" BL: 26, **49**
Davenport, Danny CO: 201–202
Davenport, Homer FO: 89–90
David, Hal RB: 274
Davidovich, Bella CL: **65**
Davidovsky, Mario CL: 21, 55, **65**
Davidson, Clay CO: 99
Davidson, Eric FO: 210
Davidson, Ken FO: 45, 115
Davies, Cyril BL: 11, 108
Davies, Dave RR: 128
Davies, Debbie BL: **49**
Davies, Dennis Russell CL: 7, 38, **65,** 197
Davies, Gail CO: 32
Davies, Ray RR: 128
Davis, Andrea (Minnie Riperton) RB: 226
Davis, Sir Andrew CL: **65,** 143
Davis, Art (country) CO: 20
Davis, Art (jazz bassist) JA: 41
Davis, Betty Jack CO: 54
Davis, Bill RB: 201
Davis, Billy RB: 8
Davis, Billy, Jr. RB: 88
Davis, Blind John BL: **49**
Davis, Clive RR: 2
Davis, Doc FO: 210
Davis, Eddie "Lockjaw" JA: 174
Davis, Ernestine "Tiny" JA: **47,** 99
Davis, Eva FO: 23
Davis, Rev. Gary BL: **49–50,** *50;* FO: **50**
  banjo BL: 13
  blind musicians and singers BL: 19
  Rory Block BL: 19–20
  Roy Book Binder BL: 28
  Blind Boy Fuller BL: 65
  Manny Greenhill FO: 82
  Stefan Grossman FO: 84
  Ernie Hawkins BL: 74
  holy blues BL: 76, 77
  "If I Had My Way" FO: 106
  Larry Johnson BL: 95
  J. B. Long BL: 120, 121
  New York City BL: 152
  Art Satherly BL: 188
  Terry, Sonny and Brownie McGhee FO: 201
  Dave Van Ronk BL: 227
  vocal styles BL: 230
  Blind Willie Walker BL: 235
Davis, Georgia CO: 55
Davis, Guy BL: 14, **50–51,** 204, 251
Davis, Ivan CL: **65**
Davis, Jesse Ed RR: 4
Davis, Jimmie CO: **53–54**
  Chuck Wagon Gang CO: 37
  Freddy Fender CO: 71–72
  Johnny Gimble CO: 82; FO: 77
  Patsy Montana CO: 141
  "You Are My Sunshine" CO: 224
Davis, Joe RB: 19
Davis, Lynn FO: 126, 152, 153
Davis, Mac CO: **54**
Davis, Marlena RB: 200
Davis, Miles JA: **47–51,** *48, 50*
  Muhal Richard Abrams JA: 1
  acid jazz JA: 2
  Cannonball Adderly JA: 3

Davis, Miles *(continued)*
Birdland JA: 15
Birth of the Cool JA: **15**
Bitches Brew JA: **15–16**
Art Blakey JA: 17
Clifford Brown JA: 23
Benny Carter JA: 29
Ron Carter JA: 30
Paul Chambers JA: 30
Billy Cobham JA: 35
John Coltrane JA: 39, 40
and cool jazz JA: xxiv
Chick Corea JA: 42
Jack DeJohnette JA: 51
Eric Dolphy JA: 55
Duke Ellington JA: 62
"E.S.P." JA: **63**
Bill Evans JA: 65–66
Gil Evans JA: 67–68
fusion JA: 72
and fusion JA: xxv
Kenny Garrett JA: 73
Herbie Hancock JA: 82, 83; RB: 116
Coleman Hawkins JA: 87
Dave Holland JA: 92
Shirley Horn JA: 93
Ahmad Jamal JA: 102
Keith Jarrett JA: 104
jazz firsts JA: 117
Jefferson Airplane RR: 119
Philly Joe Jones JA: 109
Thad Jones JA: 110
Kind of Blue JA: **113**
John McLaughlin JA: 131
Marcus Miller JA: 135
Charles Mingus JA: 136
modal jazz JA: 138
Thelonious Monk JA: 139
Gerry Mulligan JA: 141
Charlie Parker JA: 152
Sonny Rollins JA: 165
Gunther Schuller JA: 172
John Scofield JA: 172
Sonny Sharrock JA: 175
Wayne Shorter JA: 178, 179
In a Silent Way JA: **98**
Horace Silver JA: 180
Clark Terry JA: 196
Eddie "Cleanhead" Vinson BL: 228
Miroslav Vitous JA: 207
wah-wah pedal JA: 209
Weather Report RB: 275
Tony Williams JA: 216
Larry Young JA: 219
Joe Zawinul JA: 223
Davis, Ossie BL: 50, 251
Davis, Peter G. CL: 150
Davis, Raymond RB: 43
Davis, Skeeter CO: 6, 43, **54–55,** 87, 116
Davis, Steve JA: 43, 142
Davis, Tyrone RB: **53–54**
Davis, Walter BL: **51**
Jimmy McCracklin BL: 128
piano BL: 161
"Sweet Home Chicago" BL: 210
talent scouts BL: 211
Henry Townsend BL: 221
vocal styles BL: 230
Davis, William RB: 51
Davis, Willie RB: 33
Davis Sisters, The CO: 54
Davy Jones and the Lower Third RR: 30
Dawkins, Jimmie BL: **51,** 248
Day, Bobby RB: **54**
Day, Morris and the Time RB: 138
Dayton, Ohio BL: 237
Deacon, John RR: 191, 193
Dead, The RR: 96. *See also* the Grateful Dead
Deadheads RR: 92–94, 96
Dean, Ira CO: 201
Dean, Jimmy CO: 13–14, 38, **55**
Dearth, Kathy (Kathy Dee) CO: 213
Deason Sisters CO: 212
death metal RR: 107
Death Row Records RB: **54–55.** *See also* Knight, Suge
DeBarge RB: 55, **55,** 251
DeBarge, El RB: 55, **55,** *55*
de Blasis, James CL: 51
Declaration of Independence CL: 105
de Coteaux, Burt BL: 220
De Danann FO: **50**
"Dedicated to the One I Love" RR: 145, 217
Dee, Joey RB: 218; RR: 199
Dee, Ruby BL: 50, 251
Deele, The RB: 223
Deep Ellum BL: 216
Deep Purple RR: 41
Def Jam Records RB: **55–56**
Def Jam South RB: 171
Def Leppard RR: 106
DeFrancesco, Joey JA: **51**
Deitch, Adam JA: 173
Déjà vu for Percussion Quartet and Orchestra (Michael Colgrass) CL: 54, **65–66**
DeJohnette, Jack JA: **51**
John Abercrombie JA: 1
Bitches Brew JA: 15
Herbie Hancock JA: 83
Dave Holland JA: 92
Charles Lloyd JA: 124
Pat Metheny JA: 134
Michel Petrucciani JA: 154
John Surman JA: 191
Miroslav Vitous JA: 207
Dekker, Desmond RB: 222; RR: 199
Delaney, Clayton CO: 92
Delaney, Mattie BL: 3

De La Soul RB: 192
Delaware Water Gap FO: 28
DeLay, Dorothy CL: 48, **66,** 207
DeLay, Paul BL: **51**
Delfonics, The RB: 15, **56,** 117, 118
Delfs, Andreas CL: **66,** 197
Delgarde, Mario RR: 138
Delicates, The RB: 265
Delicious Vinyl RB: **56**
Dello Joio, Norman CL: **66,** 185
Dells, The RB: **56–57,** *57*
Dell-Vikings, The (Del Vikings) RB: **57–58**
Delmark Records BL: 41, **51–52,** 85, 180. *See also* Koester, Bob
Delmore, Alton CO: 55, 56
Delmore, Lionel CO: 195
Delmore, Rabon CO: 55, 56
Delmore Brothers CO: **55–56,** 97, 112, 200; FO: 189
DeLoach, James RB: 19
Del Rios, The RB: 15
Delta blues BL: xix. *See also* Mississippi Delta; *specific artists*
  acoustic guitar BL: 1, 2
  blues revival BL: 26
  country blues BL: 45
  instruments BL: 87
  slide guitar BL: 191, 192
  vocal styles BL: 230, 232
Delta Blues Museum BL: 137–138
Delta Cultural Center BL: 7
Delta Rhythm Kings RB: 25
Del Tredici, David CL: 2, **66–67,** 111
DeLucia, Paco JA: 52, 132
DeMarcus, Jay CO: 166
de Marky, Paul JA: 153
DeMent, Iris CO: 39; FO: **50–51**
Demon Boyz RB: **58**
DeMore, Anthony RB: 3
Denmark FO: 118
Dennerlein, Barbara JA: **51–52**
Dennis, Willie JA: 19
Denny, Sandy FO: **51,** 64; RR: 135
Densmore, Francis FO: 163
Densmore, John RR: 62, 64
Denson, Ed BL: 90, 241, 242; FO: 84
Denver, Colorado BL: 63, 214, 253
Denver, John CO: viii, **56;** FO: 31, **51–52,** 157
Denver Folklore Center BL: 214, 253
Deodato, Eumir RB: 156
De Palma, Brian FO: 204
De Paur, Leonard BL: 168
Depeche Mode RR: 158
DePreist, James CL: **67**
Depression. *See* Great Depression
Derek and the Dominoes BL: 41; RR: 4, 40
DeReszke Singers FO: 129
Desert Rose Band, The CO: 45; FO: 25
Desmond, Paul JA: 21, 24, 197
Dessau, Paul CL: 82
Destiny's Child RB: **58–59,** *59*
Destri, Jimmy RR: 26–28
Detours, The RR: 244
Detroit, Michigan BL: **52**. *See also* Motown
  migration BL: 133
  piano BL: 161
"Detroit City" CO: 12, **56,** 198
Detroit Symphony Orchestra CL: **67–68**
Dett, Nathaniel BL: 78
Deutsche Grammophone CL: 97
"Devil Went Down to Georgia, The" CO: 53, **56**
Devito, Tommy RR: 86
Devo RR: 158
DeVoe, Ronnie RB: 194
de Waart, Edo CL: 3, **68,** 199
DeWitt, Lew CO: 192
Dexter, Al CO: 162
Dexter, Dave RB: 171
Diabate, Toumani FO: 199
Diamond, David CL: **68,** 224
Diamond, Mike (Mike D) RB: 12
Diamond, Neil CO: 84; RR: 150, 151
Diamond Rio CO: **56–57**
Dibango, Manu JA: 20; RB: 61
Dicaire, David BL: 204
Dickens, Hazel FO: **52,** 76, 83, 181
Dickens, "Little" Jimmy CO: viii, 9, 26, **57,** 161, 176
Dickey, Tom CO: 100
Dickinson, Jim BL: 154, 224; RR: 211
Dickinson, Luther and Cody BL: 154
Dickson, Jim RR: 35
Dicterow, Glenn CL: 156
Diddley, Bo BL: **52,** *52;* RR: **53–56,** *54*
  Fred Below BL: 16
  Bobby Hebb RB: 120
  Rolling Stones, The RR: 209
  Billy Stewart RB: 248
Diddy, P. *See* Puff Daddy
Diffie, Joe CO: 37, **57,** 102–103, 201
DiFranco, Ani FO: 158
Digable Planets RB: **59–60**
Digital Underground RB: **60,** 236
Dillard, Dottie CO: 116

Dillard, Doug
Byron Berline FO: 14, 15
Gene Clark FO: 36
Dillards FO: *52*, 52–53
Steve Frumholz FO: 74
John Hartford FO: 92
Dillard, Rodney FO: 52, 53
Dillard and Clark FO: 15, 36, 115; RR: 37
Dillards, The FO: 14, 18, **52–53,** 125
Dilleshaw, John FO: 53
Dilly and His Dill Pickles FO: **53**
Di Meola, Al JA: 43, **52,** 81, 132
d'Indy, Vincent CL: 159, 182
Dinning, Dolores CO: 58
Dinning, Ella Lucille "Lou" CO: 57, 58
Dinning, Eugenia "Jean" CO: 57–58
Dinning, Marvis CO: 58
Dinning, Virginia "Ginger" CO: 57, 58
Dinning Sisters, The CO: **57–58**
Dion RR: **56–57,** *57*
Dion and the Belmonts RR: 56
"Dipper Mouth Blues" JA: **52–53,** 147
Dirt Nation RB: **60**
"Dirty Dozens, The" BL: **53,** 205
Dirty South RB: 147, 171, 189–190
disco BL: 203; RB: **60–62;** RR: x. *See also specific artists*
disc recording FO: 163
Disposable Heroes of Hiphoprisy, The RB: **62**
dissonance JA: **53,** 139, 194
Distants, The RB: 254
distortion RR: 170
Diva JA: **53**
"Divorce Me C.O.D." CO: **58**
Dixie Chicks CO: **58–59,** *59,* 84
Dixie Cups, The RB: **62**
Dixie Fiddler's Convention FO: 196
Dixie Flyers RB: 16
Dixieland jazz BL: 176; JA: 9, **53,** 91
Dixieliners, The FO: 189
Dixon, Calvin BL: 78
Dixon, Dean CL: **68–69**
Dixon, Dorsey FO: 53, 54
Dixon, George RB: 244, 245
Dixon, George Washington FO: 138
Dixon, Howard FO: 53
Dixon, Luther RB: 105, 238; RR: 217
Dixon, Willie BL: **53;** RB: **62–63**
bass and drums BL: 15
Carey Bell BL: 16
Chicago BL: 40
Fleetwood Mac BL: 63
Howlin' Wolf BL: 82
Led Zeppelin BL: 113; RR: 134
J. B. Lenoir BL: 114
music business BL: 144–145
Rolling Stones, The RR: 209
Sonny Terry BL: 216
Muddy Waters BL: 239, 240
young black country blues artists BL: 250
Dixon Brothers, The FO: **53–54**
DIY (do-it-yourself) RR: 188
DJ (deejay) RB: xvii; RR: 200
DJ Hollywood RB: **63**
DJ Jazzy Jeff RB: 242
DJ Kool Herc RB: 121, 217
DJ Logic JA: 133
DJ Premier RB: 101, 102
DJ Screw RB: **63–64**
DJ Slip RB: 47
DJ Smurf RB: **64,** 180
Dludlu, Jimmy JA: 187
Dobie, J. Frank CO: 174
Dobro CO: **59–61,** 160, 161; FO: **54**
Dobson, Richard FO: 23
Dockery's Plantation BL: 138
Dr. Alban RB: **70**
Dr. Feelgood and the Interns BL: 163
Dr. Jeckyll and Mr. Hyde RB: **72**
Dr. John (Mac Rebennack) BL: **54,** 164; RB: 11–12
Dr Dre RB: **70–71**
Above the Law RB: 1
Coolio RB: 50
Eazy-E RB: 78
Eminem RB: 81
N.W.A. RB: 196
Snoop Doggy Dogg RB: 243
Xzibit RB: 288
Dodd, Coxsone RB: 175
Dodds, Baby JA: 52, **53–54,** 147; RR: 66
Dodds, Johnny BL: 18; JA: 52, **54,** 94, 147
Dodge, Charles CL: **69–70**
Doggett, Bill RB: **64,** 183, 246; RR: 115
Doherty, Denny RR: 145, 146
Dohnányi, Christoph von CL: 53, **70**
Dolenz, Micky RR: 149, 151
Dollywood CO: 18, 158
Dolphy, Eric JA: *54,* **54–55**
Ed Blackwell JA: 16
The Blues and the Abstract Truth JA: 19
John Coltrane JA: 40
Free Jazz (Ornette Coleman) JA: 71
Chico Hamilton JA: 80
Freddie Hubbard JA: 95

Charles Mingus JA: 136
Out There JA: **150**
George Russell JA: 167
saxophone JA: 171
Steve Swallow JA: 191
Tony Williams JA: 216
Lester Young JA: 220
Domingo, Placido CL: 80
Domino, Antoine "Fats" RB: **64–66,** *65;* RR: **57–60,** *58*
James Booker BL: 28
Big Al Downing CO: 61
drums RR: 67
jump blues and rhythm and blues BL: 101
Ricky Nelson RR: 155
New Orleans, Louisiana BL: 121
reggae RR: 200
rhythm and blues combos BL: 182
Big Joe Turner RR: 232
Dominoes, The RB: 181, 281
Domnhaill, Triona Ni FO: 17
Donahue, Jerry FO: 64
Donald, Duck FO: 68
Donaldson, Lou JA: 183, 219
Don and Juan RB: **66**
Donegan, Dorothy JA: **55**
Donegan, Lonnie FO: **54–55**
Donovan FO: 179; RR: **60–62,** *61*
"Don't It Make My Brown Eyes Blue" CO: 44, **61,** 80
"Don't Look Back" RR: 201, 204, 205, 210, 221
"Don't Worry, Be Happy" JA: 131; RB: 180
Doo Bop (Miles Davis) JA: 2, 51, 117
Dooley, Simmie BL: 7
Doors, The FO: 99; RR: **62–64,** *63*
doo-wop RB: vii, xvi, *66,* **66–69,** *68;* RR: x, **64–66.** *See also specific artists*
Dopyera, John CO: 60; FO: 54
Dopyera brothers CO: 160
Doran, Johnny FO: 35
Dorati, Antal CL: **70**
Dallas Symphony Orchestra CL: 63
Detroit Symphony Orchestra CL: 68
Minnesota Orchestra CL: 156
National Symphony Orchestra CL: 162
Dorham, Kenny JA: 180
Dorschug, Doug FO: 96, 97
Dorsey, Jimmy JA: **55–56,** 56, 134, 163, 214
Dorsey, Lee BL: 183, 220, 238; RB: 11, **69–70**
Dorsey, Thomas A. (Georgia Tom) BL: xix, **54**
Atlanta BL: 9
Scrapper Blackwell BL: 17
gospel music CO: 85–86
holy blues BL: 79
instruments BL: 87
protest songs BL: 167
Ma Rainey BL: 177
Tampa Red BL: 212; RB: 253
Sister Rosetta Tharpe BL: 217
Dorsey, Tommy (trombonist and bandleader) JA: **56**
Jimmy Dorsey JA: 55
Fletcher Henderson JA: 89–90
Glenn Miller JA: 134
Ma Rainey JA: 161
Buddy Rich JA: 164
Paul Whiteman JA: 214
Mary Lou Williams JA: 215
double bass JA: xxii, **56,** 164. *See also specific artists*
double time JA: 19, **56**
Double Trouble BL: 228
Doucet, Michael CO: 29; FO: 14, 27, 180
Douglas, Alan RR: 110
Douglas, Jerry FO: **55**
Country Gentlemen FO: 44
J. D. Crowe FO: 47
Dobro CO: 60–61; FO: 54
Alison Krauss CO: 118
Doyle Lawson FO: 122
Mark O'Connor FO: 152
Ricky Skaggs CO: 186
Douglas, K. C. BL: 7, 145
Dowd, Tom RB: 83; RR: 4, 6
"Down at the Twist and Shout" CO: 32, **61;** FO: 14
Down Beat magazine BL: 194; JA: 55, **56–57,** 142
Downes, Olin CL: 56, 152, 163, 245
"Downhearted Blues" BL: **54**
Lovie Austin BL: 9
Alberta Hunter BL: 83; JA: 95
piano BL: 161
Bessie Smith JA: 183
Frank Walker BL: 235
Down Home Music (El Cerrito, California) BL: 7; FO: 196
Down Homers RR: 101
Downing, Big Al CO: **61–62**
downloads RR: 147
Dozier, Lamont RB: 123. *See also* Holland-Dozier-Holland
Drake, Pete CO: 45, **62,** 142
Dramatics RB: **70**
Draper, Rusty CO: **62–63**
Dreadnought guitar CO: 90; FO: 86
Dread Zeppelin RR: 137

Dream House RB: 96
Dregs, The FO: 152
Dreja, Chris RR: 251–253
Drew, Kenny JA: 19
Drew, Ronnie FO: 55
Drifters, The RB: *71,* **71–72,** 181
Drifting Cowboys, The CO: **63,** 163, 216
Driftwood, Jimmy CO: 13, **63–64**
Driggs, Robert BL: 98
"Drinking Wine, Spo-Dee-O-Dee" BL: 129; RB: 180
DRS RB: **72**
Druckman, Jacob CL: 23, **70,** 125, 240
Dru Hill RB: **72–73,** 243
drum and bass RB: **73,** 106–107, 260
drums JA: **57;** RR: **66–69.** *See also* bass and drums; *specific drummers*
  crash cymbal JA: **44**
  hi-hat cymbal JA: **91**
  honky-tonk music CO: 102
  rhythm section JA: 164
  ride cymbal JA: **164–165**
  ride rhythm JA: **165**
  shuffle rhythm JA: 179
Drusky, Roy CO: 62, **64**
Dryden, Spencer RR: 119, 120
dub RB: **73–74,** 222–223; RR: 201
Dubliners, The FO: **55**
DuBois, Tim CO: **64–65,** 98
Dubroven, Issay CL: 199
Dubs, The RB: **74**
Dudek, Les RR: 5
Dudley, Buck CL: **71**
Dudley, Dave CO: **65,** 92, 185, 202
Duffey, John FO: 43, 44, 183
Duffy, Tim BL: 68, 148
Dukays, The RB: 36–37
Duke, George JA: 104, 172; RB: 7
Duke of Paducah, The CO: **65**
Duke Records. *See* Robey, Don
Dukes, Laura BL: 132
Dula, Thomas C. FO: xvi, 160, 203, 210
dulcimer (Appalachian) FO: **55–56,** 131, 150, 172
dulcimer (hammered) FO: 28, **56,** 191
Dunaway, Dennis RR: 43
Duncan, Stuart FO: 145
Duncan, Tommy CO: **65–66,** 183, 214, 218–219; FO: 213
Dunford, Uncle Eck FO: 194, 210
Dunn, Bob CO: 25, 160
Dunn, Donald "Duck" RB: 23, *23,* 24, 175; RR: 15, 116
Dunn, Ronnie CO: 23, 97
Duplicates: A Concerto for Two Pianos and Orchestra (Mel Powell) CL: **71**
Dupree, Champion Jack BL: **54–55;** RR: 57
Dupri, Jermaine RB: **74,** 177, 266, 276
Duran Duran RR: 157
Durham, North Carolina BL: 49, 50, 65, 120
Dust Brothers, The RB: 12
"Dust My Broom" BL: **55,** 90, 98, 130
Dutrey, Honore JA: 52, 147
Dvořák, Antonín CL: vii, viii, xxiii, xxiv, *71,* **71–72**
  Henry Burleigh CL: 40
  Sissieretta Jones CL: 119
  Clara Anna Korn CL: 128
  National Conservatory of Music CL: 161
  From the New World CL: **82–83**
  Carl Ruggles CL: 195
Dwight, John Sullivan CL: **72**
Dyble, Judy FO: 64
Dyer-Bennett, Richard FO: **56–57,** 78
Dylan, Bob BL: **55,** *55;* FO: ix, xvi, **57;** RR: ix, x, **69–71,** *70*
  Animals RR: 9
  Animals, The BL: 7
  "Baby, Please Don't Go" BL: 11
  Joan Baez FO: 9
  Band, The RR: 11
  Beatles RR: 20
  Norman Blake FO: 16
  Michael Bloomfield BL: 20
  Broadside magazine FO: 19
  David Bromberg FO: 19
  Byrds FO: 25; RR: 35, 36
  Johnny Cash CO: 35
  Civil Rights movement FO: 34
  Paul Clayton FO: 36–37
  country rock CO: 44, 45; RR: 43
  Charlie Daniels CO: 53
  Donovan RR: 61
  Electric Light Orchestra RR: 76
  Ramblin' Jack Elliott FO: 60
  Richard and Mimi Fariña FO: 65
  Flatt and Scruggs CO: 74
  folk revival FO: 71
  folk rock RR: 84, 85
  folk-rock FO: 71
  Grateful Dead RR: 96
  Albert Grossman FO: 83–84
  Woody Guthrie FO: 88
  harmonica FO: 92
  Jimi Hendrix RR: 110

Carolyn Hester FO: 95
Highway 61 BL: 75
Peter La Farge FO: 121
Sam Lay BL: 111
Charlie McCoy CO: 136
"Me and Bobby McGee" CO: 139
Newport Folk Festival FO: 149
Roy Orbison RR: 166
Peter, Paul and Mary FO: 157
power pop RR: 178
roots rock RR: 211
singer/songwriter movement FO: 185
singer-songwriters RR: 219
Sing Out! magazine FO: 186
Victoria Spivey BL: 206
Bruce Springsteen RR: 224, 226
Marty Stuart CO: 194
Happy Traum BL: 221
Dave Van Ronk BL: 227; FO: 207
Izzy Young FO: 219
Dyson, Ronnie RB: **75**

E

Eagles, The RR: 45, **73–75,** *74*
Eaglin, Snooks BL: 18, **57**
Eanes, Jim FO: **59**
Earl, Ronnie BL: **57,** 185
Earle, Gene FO: 29
Earle, Steve CO: **67,** 84; FO: 135
Earl Scruggs Revue FO: 81
early jazz. *See* recordings of early jazz; traditional jazz
Early Jazz: Its Roots and Musical Development (Gunther Schuller) JA: **59**
early music CL: 30, 34, 93, 165
Earth, Wind & Fire RB: 7, *77,* **77–78,** 81, 165
"Earth Angel" RB: 205; RR: 64
Earth Opera FO: 83, 177
East, Ernest FO: 38
Eastern Europe FO: 117
Eastman, George CL: 73
Eastman School of Music CL: **73**
Easton, Amos. *See* Bumble Bee Slim
East St. Louis, Illinois BL: 141; JA: 47
East Texas Serenaders FO: **59–60**
Eastwood, Clint BL: xvi; CO: 82, 92; JA: 86
Easy Mo Bee JA: 51, 117
Easy Rider (movie) FO: 25; RR: 12, 228, 229
Eaton, John CL: **73**
Eazy-E RB: 1, 71, **78,** 196, 253
Ebonys RB: **78**
Echart, Wolf FO: 3
Echoes of Joy RB: 283
Echoes of Time and the River (George Crumb) CL: **73**
Eckstine, Billy
Miles Davis JA: 48
Dexter Gordon JA: 77
Johnny Hartman JA: 86
Earl "Fatha" Hines JA: 91
Hank Jones JA: 109
Quincy Jones JA: 110
Charlie Parker JA: 151
Sonny Stitt JA: 187
Sarah Vaughn JA: 205
Ecstasy (drug) RB: 73, 254
Eddy, Duane CO: 41; RR: 115
Edge, The RR: 166, 235, 236
Edison, Thomas BL: 188
Edmonson, Collin FO: 22
Edmonson, Travis FO: 22
Edmonton, Jerry RR: 228
Edmundson, Dave and Suzanne FO: 99
Edsels, The RB: **78–79**
Ed Sullivan Show, The FO: 35; RR: 19, 32, 64, 86
Educated Rapper, The RB: 268
education/educators CL: xv, xix, xxiii, xxv, xxvi; JA: 7, 14. *See also specific educators*
Edwards, Bernard RB: 41; RR: 27
Edwards, Cliff (Ukelele Ike) FO: 138
Edwards, David "Honeyboy" BL: **57**
Edwards, Dennis RB: 48
Edwards, Don CO: **67–68**
Edwards, Jackie RR: 201
Edwards, Stoney CO: **68**
Edwards, Van and Earl FO: 210
effects pedals RR: 111
Egyptian Lover RB: **79**
Ehrling, Sixten CL: **73,** 140
Eichheim, Henry CL: 15, **73**
Einstein, Albert CL: 152, 194
Einstein on the Beach (Philip Glass) CL: **73–74,** 89
Eisenhower, Dwight CL: 10, 124
Eisfeld, Theodore CL: 164, 177
Either/Orchestra JA: **59**
Eklund, Greg RR: 99
Eldridge, Roy JA: 34, 45, **59–60,** 76, 137, 197
electric bass (bass guitar) BL: xxiii; JA: **10–11**. *See also specific electric bass players*
electric blues BL: viii, xvi. *See also* Chicago blues
Electric Flag BL: 20; RB: 183; RR: 152
electric guitar BL: xx, **57–59,** *58.* *See also* guitar

Electric Light Orchestra RR: **75–77**
electric piano JA: 42, 155; RR: 126
electronic keyboards BL: 162–163; JA: 134, 190. *See also* synthesizer
electronic music CL: 158, 218, 233–234; JA: 122
Electronic Wind Instrument (EWI) JA: 22
Elgar, Edward CL: 45, 130
Ellington, Duke JA: xxiii, *5,* **60–62,** *61*
Ivie Anderson JA: 5
Louis Armstrong JA: 6
bebop JA: 12
on bebop JA: xxiv
Tony Bennett JA: 13
"Black and Tan Fantasy" JA: **16**
Jimmy Blanton JA: 18
Buddy Bolden JA: 20
Carnegie Hall JA: 27–28
Benny Carter JA: 28
Cotton Club JA: 44
European jazz JA: 64
Gil Evans JA: 67
And His Mother Called Him Bill (Duke Ellington) JA: **4–5**
Abdullah Ibrahim JA: 97
"In a Sentimental Mood" JA: **98**
"It Don't Mean a Thing (If It Ain't Got That Swing)" JA: **99**
Japanese jazz JA: 103
jazz firsts JA: 116
Lonnie Johnson BL: 95
Cleo Laine JA: 120
Melba Liston JA: 123
Charles Mingus JA: 136
Newport Jazz Festival JA: 144
New York City JA: 144
Oscar Pettiford JA: 154
Django Reinhardt JA: 164
Savoy Ballroom JA: 171
South African jazz JA: 186
Billy Strayhorn JA: 188, 189
"Take the 'A' Train" JA: 193
Clark Terry JA: 196
third stream jazz JA: 197
Ben Webster JA: 213
Ellington, Mercer JA: 61, 73, 130
Elliot, Cass RR: 145, 146
Elliott, Missy "Misdemeanor" RB: **79–80,** 166, 258
Elliott, Ramblin' Jack FO: *60,* **60,** 90
Ellis, Big Chief FO: 30
Ellis, Billy RB: 244
Ellis, Don JA: **62,** 70
Ellis, Herb JA: 153
Ellis, Shirley RB: **80**
Elman, Mischa CL: **74**
El-P RB: 227
"El Paso" CO: **68,** 83, 176
Elton John BL: 11; CO: 174; RR: 175
Ely, Joe FO: 3, 77
Emerson, Bill FO: 43, 44, **60–61**
Emerson, Keith RR: 127, 182, 184
Emerson, Lake, and Palmer RR: 184, 185
Emery, Ralph CO: **68–69**
Eminem RB: **80–81,** 236, 288
Emmet Folk Group FO: 140–141
Emmett, Dan FO: 139
Emmons, Buddy CO: 161
Emotions, The RB: **81–82**
Encyclopedia of Jazz (Leonard Feather) JA: **62,** 70
Enesco, Georges CL: 147
Engberg, Davenport CL: 204
England. *See* Great Britain
Ennis, Seamus FO: 10, **61,** 188
Ennis, Skinnay JA: 67
Eno, Brian RR: 31, 231, 232, 236, 237
Enright, Pat FO: 145
ensemble JA: **62.** *See also* combo
Entwistle, John RR: 15, 243–246
Enuff Z'Nuff RR: 178
En Vogue RB: **82,** 200
Enya FO: 35
"Epistrophy" JA: 34, **62–63,** 218
Epitaph RR: 189
EPMD RB: **82,** 158
Epstein, Brian RR: 19, 21
Epstein, Dena BL: 196–197
Eric B. and Rakim RB: 56, **82**
Erskine, John CL: 121
Ertegun, Ahmet RB: **82–83**
Herb Abramson RB: 2
Atlantic Records BL: 9
Clovers, The RB: 44
R. B. Greaves RB: 111
Clyde McPhatter RB: 181
record labels BL: 179
Ertegun, Nesuhi BL: 9, 179; RB: 2, 82, 83
Ervin, Booker JA: 19
Erwin, Emily CO: 58
Erwin, Martie CO: 58
Escalator Over the Hill (Carla Bley) JA: 18, 127
Eschenbach, Christoph CL: **74,** 108, 176, 186, 207
"E.S.P." JA: **63**
Esquerita RR: 141
Esquires, The RB: **83**
Essex, The RB: **83–84**
Estes, Sleepy John BL: **59–60**
Homesick James BL: 79
Noah Lewis BL: 115

mandolin BL: 125
Charley Patton BL: 157
Yank Rachell BL: 175
talent scouts BL: 212
Sonny Boy Williamson I RB: 279
Etchingham Steam Band FO: 40, 102
Eternals, The RB: **84**
Etheridge, Floyd FO: 46
Ethiopia RR: 200
Ethiopian Serenaders FO: *139*
ethnic humor FO: 139
Ethridge, Chris CO: 75
Eurhythmics RR: 158–159
Eurodisco RB: 61
Europe, James Reese JA: **63,** 116, 162, 207
European jazz JA: **63–65**
Evans, Bill JA: **65–67,** *66*
Tony Bennett JA: 13
Blues and the Abstract Truth, The JA: 19
Jim Hall JA: 80
Herbie Hancock JA: 82
Philly Joe Jones JA: 109
Kind of Blue JA: 113
George Russell JA: 167
David Sanborn JA: 169
Lennie Tristano JA: 199
Waltz for Debby JA: 210
Evans, Dale CO: 94, 179
Evans, David (blues scholar) BL: 18, **60,** 99, 132, 155
Evans, David (the Edge) RR: 235
Evans, Dick RR: 235
Evans, Elgin BL: 15
Evans, Faith RB: 7, 196, 213
Evans, Gil JA: **67–68**
John Abercrombie JA: 1
Miles Davis JA: 49, 51
Steve Lacy JA: 119
Gerry Mulligan JA: 141
progressive jazz JA: 158
Maria Schneider JA: 171
Gunther Schuller JA: 172
Andy Sheppard JA: 177
Tony Williams JA: 216
Evans, Howard FO: 30, 117
Evans, Sara CO: **69,** *69,* 105
Evans, Tom RR: 177
Even Dozen Jug Band BL: 101, 122, 142, 232; FO: 84, 142
Everclear RR: 99
Everett, Betty BL: 180; RB: 31, **84**
Everlast RB: **84–85,** 259
Everly, Don CO: 70; RR: 77, 78
Everly, Ike RR: 77
Everly, Phil CO: 70; RR: 77, 78
Everly Brothers CO: **70;** RR: **77–79,** *78*
Boudleaux and Felice Bryant CO: 26
"Bye Bye Love" CO: 27
country rock CO: 44
Wesley Rose CO: 179
Evers, Medgar JA: 181
EWI (Electronic Wind Instrument) JA: 22
Exciters, The RB: **85**
Exploding Plastic Inevitable RR: 240

F

Fabio RB: 73
Fabulous Thunderbirds BL: 25–26, **61,** 111, 183, 227
Face of the Night, The Heart of the Dark, The (Wayne Peterson) CL: **75**
Fadden, Jimmy CO: 151
Fagen, Donald RR: 226
Fahey, John BL: **61;** FO: *63,* **63**
Skip James BL: 90
Jo Ann Kelly BL: 103
Leo Kottke FO: 118
Charley Patton BL: 157
Bukka White BL: 240
Faier, Billy BL: 13
Fairburn, Bruce RR: 3
Fairburn, Werly RB: 203
Fairfax, Frankie JA: 218
Fairport Convention FO: 51, **64,** 71, 102, 194
Falcons, The RB: **87,** 94, 197, 206
Falletta, JoAnne CL: **75**
Fallon, David FO: 33
falsetto BL: 137, 230
FAME Studio (Muscle Shoals, Alabama)
Duane Allman BL: 6
Atlantic Records BL: 9
Clarence Carter RB: 36
Rick Hall RB: 115
Etta James BL: 90
Malaco Records BL: 124
Muscle Shoals RB: 189
social history and the blues BL: 203
Famous Flames, The RB: 26
Fanfare for the Common Man (Aaron Copland) CL: 57, **75**
fanzines RR: 97, 188
Farberman, Harold CL: **75–76**
Fargo, Donna CO: **71**
Fargo, North Dakota BL: 111
Fariña, Mimi FO: *40, 65,* **65–66**
Fariña, Richard FO: *65,* **65–66,** 95
Farish Street BL: 138–139
Farish Street Blues Museum BL: 139
Farmer, Addison JA: 69
Farmer, Art JA: **69**
Jim Hall JA: 80

Farmer, Art (*continued*)
- Lionel Hampton JA: 81
- Chico O'Farrill JA: 147
- Horace Silver JA: 180
- Billy Strayhorn JA: 189
- Steve Swallow JA: 192
- Miroslav Vitous JA: 207
- Nancy Wilson JA: 218

farming. *See* sharecropping
Farr brothers CO: 189
Farrell, Joe JA: 43
Farwell, Arthur CL: **76,** 99, 237
Fascinations, The RB: **87**
Fastball RR: 178
Fat Boys, The RB: **87–88**
Father MC RB: 213
Faurot, Charlie FO: 38
Favors, Malachi JA: 6, **69**
Fay, Amy CL: **76–77**
Fay, Charles Norman CL: 223
Fay, Martin FO: 33
Feather, Leonard BL: 238; JA: 62, **69–70,** 172
Feathers, Charlie RR: 205
Featherstonhaugh, Buddy JA: 64
Federici, Danny RR: 225
feedback composers CL: 142
Felder, Don RR: 74
Feldman, Morton CL: **77**
Feliciano, José RB: 274; RR: 64
Fell, Terry CO: 202
Feltsman, Vladimir CL: **77**
feminism BL: 187, 242–243; CO: 127; FO: 79; RR: 91
Fender, Freddy CO: **71–72;** RB: 182
Fender, Leo BL: 58; CO: 90, 200; JA: 10; RR: 14
Fender bass. *See* electric bass
Fender Guitars BL: 15, 58
Fender Precision Bass RR: 14
Fender Rhodes electric piano RR: 126
Fender Stratocaster RR: 111
Fender Telecaster CO: 10
Fenning's All Star Band FO: 191
Ferguson, Bob CO: 44, 187
Ferguson, Buster FO: 96
Ferguson, Jimmy FO: 106, 107
Ferguson, Maynard JA: **70**
- Pepper Adams JA: 3
- Stan Kenton JA: 112
- Oscar Peterson JA: 153
- Wayne Shorter JA: 178
- Dinah Washington JA: 211
- Joe Zawinul JA: 223

Festival of American Folklife (Smithsonian Institution) FO: 30, 170–171
Festival of Two Worlds CL: **77,** 152, 200, 235. *See also* Spoleto Festival
festivals. *See specific festivals*
fiddle BL: 14, 30, **61–62,** 86, 95; CO: **72–73;** FO: **66–67**
fiddle contests/fiddler's conventions FO: 14, 67, 115, 203
Fiddle Fever FO: 43
Fiedler, Arthur CL: 34, **77–78**
Fiedler, Max CL: 35
field hollers BL: xvii, **62,** 77
field recording BL: 119, 188; FO: 36, 127
Fields, Ernie RB: 184
fife and drum music BL: 75, 139, 223–224; FO: 69
Fifer, Julian CL: 171
5th Dimension, The RB: *88,* **88**
Fifty-four Studies for Player Piano (Conlon Nancarrow) CL: **78**
52nd Street, New York City JA: 184, 213
file-sharing RR: 147
file trading FO: 164
fill JA: **70**
Fillmore East (New York City) BL: 106; RR: 4–5
Fillmore West (San Francisco) BL: 104, 105; JA: 124; RR: 46, 122
Finckel, David CL: 48
Fine, Irving CL: 25, **78,** 142, 207, 238
Fine, Vivian CL: **78**
Fingerett, Sally FO: 121
finger-picking BL: xxii, 6–7, 11, 115, 232, 250
fingerpicks BL: 4, 13
Fink, Cathy FO: *67,* **67–68,** 113, 125
Finland BL: 29; RR: ix
Finn, Alec FO: 50
Finney, Ross Lee CL: 21, **78–79**
Firkusny, Rudolf CL: **79**
Firm, The RB: 26; RR: 136
First Choice RB: **88–89**
First Edition CO: 178; FO: 146
First Generation Band FO: 37
First National Band FO: 145
Fisher, Archie FO: **68**
Fisher, Ray FO: 68
Fishman, Jonathan RR: 118
Fitzgerald, Ella JA: **70–71;** RB: **89**
- "A-Tisket A-Tasket" JA: **7**
- Ray Brown JA: 24
- Duke Ellington JA: 61
- Dizzy Gillespie JA: 75
- Norman Granz RB: 110
- Jim Hall JA: 80
- Chico Hamilton JA: 80
- Japanese jazz JA: 103
- JATP JA: 106
- Hank Jones JA: 109
- Louis Jordan BL: 100
- Oscar Peterson JA: 153
- Savoy Ballroom JA: 171
- scat singing JA: 171
- Clark Terry JA: 196
- Dinah Washington JA: 211

Chick Webb JA: 212
Shadow Wilson JA: 218
Fitzgerald-Hartley CO: 64
Fitzhugh, McKie RB: 92
Five Breezes RB: 63
Five Discs RB: **89**
Five Echoes RB: 254
Five Hand Reel FO: 75
Five Keys RB: **89–90**
"5" Royales RB: **90**
Five Satins RB: **90–91;** RR: 64
Five Sharps RB: **91–92**
Five Spot (New York City) JA: 36
Five Thrills RB: **92**
Flack, Roberta FO: 131; JA: 135; RB: **92–93,** 118
Flagler, H. H. CL: 165
Flamingos, The RB: *93,* **93–94**
Flamin' Groovies RR: 177, 198
Flanagan, Tommy JA: 74, 185
Flares, The RB: 33, **94**
Flash Cadillac RR: 208
Flatlanders, The FO: 76–77
flat pick BL: xxii, 59
flatpicking FO: 115
Flatt, Lester CO: 15, 73–75, 141, 194; FO: 81, 217
Flatt and Scruggs CO: **73–75,** *74*
bluegrass music CO: 15, 16
Dobro CO: 60; FO: 54
"Foggy Mountain Breakdown" CO: 75–76
Buck (Uncle Josh) Graves FO: 80–81
Lilly Brothers FO: 126
Del McCoury FO: 134
Benny Martin FO: 133
Bill Monroe CO: 141
rube/hillbilly humor CO: 180
Chubby Wise FO: 216
Mac Wiseman FO: 216
Flavor Flav RB: 212
Flea RR: 15
Fleck, Béla CO: 12; FO: 55, *68,* **68–69,** 147, 205; RR: 118
Flecktones, The FO: 68–69
Fleetwood, Mick BL: 62, 63, 127; RR: 81, 83, 84
Fleetwood Mac BL: **62–63,** *63,* 205; RR: 28, **81–84,** *83*
Fleisher, Leon CL: **79,** 236
Fleming, Renée CL: *79,* **79–80**
Flight into Egypt, The (John Harbison) CL: **80**
Flint, Michigan BL: 185
Flivver Ten Million (Frederick Converse) CL: 56, **80**
Florence, Alabama BL: 71
Flores, Rosie FO: **69**
Florida BL: 6, 197; JA: 3, 152, 170; RR: 4
Flower, Mary BL: **63,** *64*
Floyd, Carlisle CL: **80**
Floyd, Eddie RB: 87, **94**
Floyd, Harmonica Frank BL: 103
flugelhorn JA: **71**
flutes FO: **69–70;** JA: **71**
Flying Burrito Brothers CO: **75**
Byron Berline FO: 15
Byrds CO: 45; FO: 25; RR: 37
Country Gazette FO: 43
country rock RR: 45
Kentucky Colonels FO: 115
Barry and Holly Tashian FO: 199
"Flying Home" JA: 81, 101
Flying Machine, The FO: 200
Flynn, Pat FO: 147
FM radio RR: 8, 40
Focus RR: 183
Foerster, Therese CL: 102
Fogerty, John BL: 138; RR: 46, 48
Fogerty, Tom RR: 46, 48–49
Foggy Mountain Boys CO: 73
"Foggy Mountain Breakdown" CO: 73, **75–76**
Foley, Ged FO: 13, 24
Foley, Red CO: **76**
Debby Boone CO: 19
Callahan Brothers CO: 30
Grand Ole Opry CO: 87
Grandpa Jones CO: 112
Jordanaires CO: 112
Lulu Belle and Scotty FO: 127
"Peace in the Valley" CO: 159
Porter Wagoner CO: 209
Kitty Wells CO: 213
Foley, Sue BL: **63–64**
folk ballad (real and imitation) CO: 13–14, 68, 78, 104, 187
folk blues BL: xviii–xix, xxii, 230, 248–253. *See also* country blues; Delta blues
folk-blues revival BL: xx, 35, 101, 231, 232, 248–249. *See also* blues revival
folk festivals. *See* Newport Folk Festival
Folklore Associates FO: 78
Folklore Center, The FO: 219
Folklore Productions FO: 82
folk music FO: 1–260
folk process FO: xv
folk revival FO: xv–xvi, **70–71**
folk-rock FO: **71;** RR: x, xx, **84–85,** 176, 219. *See also specific artists*
Folksmiths, The FO: 96
Folksong Society FO: 82
Folk Songs of the Hills (Merle Travis) CO: 185, 200
Folkways Records BL: **64,** 180; FO: 163–164, 189–190. *See also* Asch, Moses

Folsom Prison CO: 35
Fontana, D. J. RB: 210; RR: 67, 180, 205
Fontenot, Adam FO: 5
Fontenot, Canray FO: 5
Fontenot, Hadley FO: 12
Foote, Arthur CL: **80–81**
Force MD's, The RB: **94,** 259
Ford, Henry FO: 192, 196
Ford, Pennye RB: 244
Ford, Robben BL: **64–65,** 148, 245
Ford, Tennessee Ernie CO: **76–77,** 185, 191
Foreign Objects, The RB: 230
Forest City Joe BL: **65**
Forester, Christy CO: 77
Forester, June CO: 77
Forester, Kathy CO: 77
Forester, Kim CO: 77
Forester Sisters CO: 13, **77**
Forest Hills, Queens RR: 198, 217
form. *See* song form
Forster, Nick FO: 100
Fortune, Jimmy CO: 192
Fortune, Sonny JA: 108
Fort Worth, Texas BL: 106; FO: 96; JA: 36
45 (45 RPM record) BL: 179; RR: 90
Foss, Lukas CL: **81**
  Brooklyn Philharmonic Orchestra CL: 38
  Buffalo Philharmonic Orchestra CL: 40
  Michael Colgrass CL: 54
  Alvin Lucier CL: 142
Foster, David RB: 47
Foster, Fred CO: 170
Foster, Garley FO: 7, 29
Foster, Gwen FO: 7, 29
Foster, Lawrence CL: **81**
Foster, Radney CO: 77
Foster, Ruthie BL: **65**
Foster, Sidney CL: **81**
Foster, Stephen FO: **71–72,** 139
Foster and Lloyd CO: **77**
Fotheringay FO: 51
Fotomaker RR: 199
Four Aces of Western Swing RR: 101
Four Bitchin' Babes FO: 121–122
4'33" (John Cage) CL: 41, **82**
Fournier, Vernel RB: 270
Four Rebels CO: 46
Four Seasons, The RB: 271; RR: **85–87,** *86*
Four Tops, The RB: **94–95,** *95*
Four Tunes, The RB: **95**
Fowler, Wally CO: 39, 153
Fowlkes, Eddie "Flashin'" RB: **95–96**
Fox, Carol CL: 143
Fox, Norman & the Rob Roys. *See* Rob Roys
Foxxx, Freddie RB: **96**
Foxy RB: **96**
frailing FO: 12
Fraley, Danielle FO: 72
Fraley, J. P. and Annadeene FO: **72**
Frame, Pete RR: xi
Frank, Claude CL: **82**
Frank, Leo FO: 141
Frank, Michael BL: 51
Franklin, Aretha RB: **96–97,** *97*
  Duane Allman BL: 6
  Rick Hall RB: 115
  holy blues BL: 79
  Quincy Jones JA: 110
  keyboards RR: 126
  King Curtis BL: 106; RB: 155
  Marcus Miller JA: 135
  Muscle Shoals RB: 189
  Otis Redding RB: 220
  social history and the blues BL: 203
  Spinners, The RB: 245
Franklin, C. L. RB: 96
Franklin, John Hope BL: 195
Franklin, Melvin RB: 254, 255
Franks, Tillman CO: 104, 105, 162
Frantz, Chris RR: 231, 232
Franz, Dennis CO: 84
Frazier, Dallas CO: 106
Freed, Alan RB: 105, 154, 187; RR: 24, 207
Freedman, Max RR: 102
Freedom Riders FO: 34
Freedom Singers, The BL: 249
free jazz/free improvisation JA: xxiv, **71–72,** 97, 142, 252*t. See also* avant-garde; *specific artists*
Free Jazz (Ornette Coleman Double Quartet) JA: 55, 71, **71–72**
Freeland, Charles R. CO: 170
Freeman, Bud JA: 25
Freeman, Dave CO: 170; FO: 164
Freeman, Lawrence CL: **82**
Freeman, Paul CL: **82**
Freeman, Von RB: 270
free reed instruments FO: 1
A Free Song (William Schuman) CL: **82**
Frehley, Ace RR: 130, 131
"Freight Train" BL: 44; FO: 42, **72–73**
French, Robert RB: 10
French horn CL: 201; JA: 67, **72,** 111, 171, 176
Fresh Prince. *See* Smith, Will
Freund, John C. CL: 160
Frey, Glenn RR: 73, 75
Friars Point, Mississippi BL: **138**

Fricke, Janie CO: 10, 47, **77–78**
Frieberg, David RR: 120
Friedman, David JA: 44
Friedman, Don JA: 224
Friend, Cliff CO: 125
Friendly Gospel Singers FO: 12
"Friends in Low Places" CO: **78**
Friends of Distinction RB: **97**
Friends of Old Time Music FO: 219
Friesen, Gordon FO: 19, 57
Fripp, Robert RR: 185
Frisell, Bill JA: **72,** 80, 124
Fritts, Donnie RB: 115
Frizzell, David CO: 78, 214
Frizzell, Lefty CO: **78**
  "Always Late (With Your Kisses)" CO: 3
  Moe Bandy CO: 10
  Callahan Brothers CO: 30
  Freddie Hart CO: 95
  "If You Got the Money, Honey, I've Got the Time" CO: 107
  Jimmie Rodgers BL: 184
From Spirituals to Swing (Carnegie Hall concert)
  boogie-woogie BL: 27
  Big Bill Broonzy BL: 29; FO: 21
  Ida Cox BL: 46
  John Hammond, Sr. BL: 71
  Pete Johnson BL: 96
  Robert Johnson BL: 98
  New York City BL: 152
  Sonny Terry BL: 215
  Terry, Sonny and Brownie McGhee FO: 201
  Big Joe Turner BL: 223; RB: 262; RR: 232
From the Diary of Virginia Woolf (Dominick Argento) CL: **82**
From the New World (Antonín Dvořák) CL: xxiii, 72, **82–83,** 161
Frost, Frank BL: 7, 94
Fruit Jar Drinkers CO: 129; FO: **73,** 136
Frumholz, Steve FO: **73–74**
Fry, William Henry CL: xxii, **83,** 135
Fuchs, Joseph CL: **83**
Fugees, The RB: **97–98**
"Fugitive, The" CO: **78,** 91
Fugs, The FO: 98
Fuleihan, Anis CL: **83**
Fuller, Blind Boy BL: **65**
  Rev. Gary Davis BL: 49; FO: 50
  holy blues BL: 77
  Homesick James BL: 79
  Larry Johnson BL: 95
  J. B. Long BL: 120, 121
  Brownie McGhee BL: 129
  Art Satherly BL: 188
  Baby Tate BL: 213
  Sonny Terry BL: 215
  Terry, Sonny and Brownie McGhee FO: 201
  Ralph Willis BL: 245
Fuller, Blind Boy #2 (Brownie McGhee) BL: 5, 65, 77
Fuller, Bobby RR: 114
Fuller, Curtis JA: 19
Fuller, Jesse BL: 35, **65–66,** 188, 224
Full Force RB: 219, 267
Full-Tilt Boogie Band RR: 124
Fulson, Lowell BL: **66,** 181
Funderburgh, Anson BL: **66**
funk JA: 3, 26, 85, 88, 143; RB: **98**. *See also specific artists*
Funkadelic RB: 43–44
Funk Brothers, The RR: 153
Funkdoobiest RB: **98**
funk punk RB: 98, **98–99**
Fuqua, Harvey RB: 103, 139, 186, 187, 245
Furay, Richie RR: 34, 35
Furious Five, The RB: 108
Furnier, Vincent RR: 43
Furtwängler, Wilhelm CL: 18, 19
fusion (jazz-rock fusion) JA: xxv, **72,** 117, 207, 252*t. See also specific artists*
Future Shock (Herbie Hancock) JA: 81, 83, 165; RB: 117
Future Tones, The RB: 246

G

G., Kenny JA: 45; RB: 243
G. Schirmer CL: **95**
  Harold Bauer CL: 21
  Robert Russell Bennett CL: 25
  Ernest Bloch CL: 31
  Arthur Farwell CL: 76
  Lukas Foss CL: 81
  Percy Grainger CL: 93
  Minnie Hauk CL: 100
  Victor Herbert CL: 102
  Scott Joplin CL: 120
  William Schuman CL: 202
  Oscar Sonneck CL: 211
  Wa-Wan Press CL: 237
Gabler, Milt BL: 76; RR: 102
Gabriel, Debby FO: 23
Gabriel, Peter JA: 74; RR: 184, 185
Gabrilovich, Ossip CL: 67, **85**
Gadd, Steve RR: 69
Gaelic FO: 35
Gaines, Charley BL: 100
Gaines, Chris (Garth Brooks) CO: 23
Gaither, Bill BL: 5, 36

Gaither, Tommy RB: 200
Galamian, Ivan CL: 50, **85,** 133
Galax, Virginia FO: 67, 110, 115
Galax, Virginia, fiddlers' convention FO: 7–8, 38
Gales, Weston CL: 67
Gallagher, Liam RR: 163
Gallagher, Noel RR: 163
Gallagher, Rory BL: **67**
Galland, Stephane JA: 223
Gallimore, Byron CO: 139
Galveston, Texas BL: 30
Gambetta, Beppe FO: 46
Gamble, Kenny RB: 15, 237
Gamble, Kenny, and Leon Huff
  Archie Bell and the Drells RB: 14
  Jerry Butler RB: 31
  disco RB: 61
  Ebonys RB: 78
  Intruders, The RB: 132
  O'Jays, The RB: 199
  Teddy Pendergrass RB: 204
  Lou Rawls RB: 219
  the Soul Survivors RB: 244
gamelan CL: 73
Gangsta Pat RB: **101**
gangsta rap. *See specific artists*
Gang Starr RB: **101–102**
Gap Band, The RB: **102**
Garage, Inc. (Metallica) RR: 146, 147
garage rock RR: xx, **89–90**
Garbarek, Jan JA: **73,** 167, 208
Garbousova, Raya CL: **85**
Garcia, Jerry CO: 45; FO: 83, 153; RR: 44, 93, 95, 120
Garcia, Simon CO: 100
García Lorca, Federico CL: 8
Garden, Mary CL: **85–86**
Gardner, Ava JA: 176
Gardner, Carl RB: 45, 227
Garfunkel, Art RR: 217, 218
Garland, Hank BL: 107; CO: 76; RB: 210
Garland, Jim FO: 109
Garland, Mary Magdalene. *See* Jackson, Aunt Molly
Garland, Red JA: 26, 49, 109
Garner, Erroll JA: 15, **73,** 86, 109, 218
Garrett, Amos BL: 33
Garrett, Kenny JA: **73–74**
Garrison, Jimmy JA: 40, 41, 124
Gary, Indiana BL: 104, 107
Gary G-Wiz RB: **102–103**
Gaslight, The (Greenwich Village) FO: 156
Gaston, Pat RB: 243
Gate of Horn (Chicago) BL: 8; FO: 76, 83, 90
Gates, Rev. J. M. BL: 78
Gateway (Abercrombie/Holland/DeJohnette) JA: 1
Gateway Singers, The BL: 249; FO: 49
Gatlin, Larry CO: 79
Gatlin, Rudy CO: 79
Gatlin, Steve CO: 79
Gatlin Brothers CO: **79**
Gatti-Casazza, Giulio CL: **86,** 155, 225
Gatton, Danny RR: 116
Gaudio, Bob RR: 86, 87
Gaudreau, Jimmy FO: 47
Gaughan, Dick FO: 18, **75**
Gavin, Frankie FO: 50
gay culture, disco and RB: 60–61
Gaye, Marvin RB: *103,* **103,** 187, 188, 277; RR: 154
Gayle, Crystal CO: 44, 61, **80,** 144
Gaylord Entertainment Group CO: 65, 88
Gaynor, Gloria RB: **103–104,** 182
gay rights movement RR: x
Gayten, Paul RB: 36, **104**
Gebhard, Heinrich CL: **86**
Geddins, Bob BL: **67**
  Lowell Fulson BL: 66
  Jimmy McCracklin BL: 128
  record labels BL: 181
  San Francisco Bay Area BL: 35
  Chris Strachwitz BL: 207
  Jesse (Babyface) Thomas BL: 219
Gee, Grant RR: 196
Gee, Jack BL: 194
Geer, Will FO: 100
Geils, J. BL: 94
Gellen, Annie RB: 263
Gellert, Lawrence BL: **67–68**
  censorship BL: 37–38
  protest songs BL: 165, 166, 168, 170–171
  social history and the blues BL: 202
Gems, The RB: 226
Gene Autry's Melody Ranch CO: 7, 19
Generation X RR: 160
Genesis RR: 184, 185
Genies, The RB: 231
Genius/GZA RB: 283, 284
Gentele, Goeran CL: 48
"Gentle on My Mind" CO: 31, **80;** FO: 92
Gentry, Bobbie CO: **80,** 154
Gentry, Teddy Wayne CO: 3
Gentry, Troy Lee CO: 142
Genus, James JA: 185
geographical history of early jazz JA: 251*m*
George, Franklin FO: 66, 115
Georgia Cotton Pickers BL: 240

"Georgia on My Mind" CO: 36; RR: 204
Georgia Sea Islands FO: 112
Georgia Sea Island Singers FO: 112
Georgia Wildcats CO: 200; FO: 187
Georgia Yellow Hammers FO: **75–76**
Georgio RB: **104–105**
Gerde's Folk City BL: 153
Geremia, Paul BL: **68,** 234
Gerlach, Fred BL: 50, **68**
Gerrard, Alice FO: 52, **76,** 83, 148, 181
Gershon, Russ JA: 59
Gershwin, George CL: xxiv, **86–88,** *87*
- *An American in Paris* CL: **7**
- Concerto in F CL: **55**
- Rubin Goldmark CL: 90
- Herbie Hancock JA: 83
- Oscar Levant CL: 136
- *Porgy and Bess* CL: **181–182**
- *Rhapsody in Blue* CL: **188**
- Paul Whiteman JA: 214
- Earl Wild CL: 239

Gershwin, Ira CL: 86
Geto Boys RB: 279, 280
Getz, David RR: 122
Getz, Stan JA: **74**
- Birdland JA: 15
- Joanne Brackeen JA: 21
- Gary Burton JA: 26
- Anthony Cox JA: 44
- *Getz/Gilberto* JA: **74**
- Astrud Gilberto JA: 75
- Woody Herman JA: 90
- Dave Holland JA: 92
- Antonio Carlos Jobim JA: 107
- Charles Mingus JA: 136
- Oscar Pettiford JA: 154
- Diane Schuur JA: 172
- Horace Silver JA: 179
- Steve Swallow JA: 192

Getz/Gilberto (Stan Getz, João Gilberto) JA: **74**
Ghione, Franco CL: 67
ghost bands RR: 104
Ghostface Killah RB: 284, 285
Giants in the Earth (Douglas S. Moore) CL: **88**
Giant Steps (John Coltrane) JA: 40, **74**
Gibb, Barry RB: 13, 14
Gibb, Maurice RB: 13, 14
Gibb, Robin RB: 13, 14
Gibbons, Billy BL: 255
Gibson, Bob FO: 9, 28, **76,** 83, 156
Gibson, Clifford BL: 184
Gibson, Don CO: 41, **80–81,** 107; FO: 11
Gibson, Orville CO: 131; FO: 132–133
Gibson, William RR: 237
Gibson Flying V BL: 104, 123
Gibson F-5 mandolin CO: 132; FO: 133
Gibson Jumbo guitar FO: 86
Gibson Les Paul guitar RR: 100, 137
Gibson Mastertone banjo CO: 12; FO: 12
Gibson Musical Instruments BL: 58, 105, 125; CO: 90, 161
Gielen, Michael CL: 51
gig JA: **75**
Gilbert, Henry F. B. CL: **88**
Gilbert, Ronnie FO: 182, 212
Gilberto, Astrud JA: 74, **75,** 224
Gilberto, João JA: 74, 75, 107, 117, 191
Gilbmer, Jimmy FO: 95
Gilchrist, William W. CL: **88**
Gilels, Emil CL: 53
Gilkinson, Jeff FO: 53
Gill, Johnny RB: 194
Gill, Vince CO: *81,* **81–82**
- bluegrass music CO: 16
- Tim DuBois CO: 64
- Emory Gordy, Jr. CO: 84
- Emmylou Harris CO: 95
- Ricky Skaggs CO: 186

Gillespie, Dizzy JA: xxiii, xxiv, **75**
- Mario Bauzá JA: 11
- bebop JA: 11
- Birdland JA: 15
- Dee Dee Bridgewater JA: 23
- Clifford Brown JA: 24
- Ray Brown JA: 24
- Cab Calloway JA: 27
- Benny Carter JA: 29
- Kenny Clarke JA: 34
- John Coltrane JA: 38
- cutting contest JA: 45
- Miles Davis JA: 48
- Roy Eldridge JA: 60
- Malachi Favors JA: 69
- Dexter Gordon JA: 77
- Johnny Hartman JA: 86
- Coleman Hawkins JA: 87
- Woody Herman JA: 90
- Earl "Fatha" Hines JA: 91
- JATP JA: 106
- jazz firsts JA: 117
- Antonio Carlos Jobim JA: 107
- Latin and Afro-Cuban jazz JA: 121
- Mel Lewis JA: 122
- Melba Liston JA: 123
- Minton's Playhouse JA: 137
- Modern Jazz Quartet JA: 138
- Lee Morgan JA: 140
- Red Norvo JA: 145
- Chico O'Farrill JA: 147

Gillespie, Dizzy (*continued*)
Charlie Parker JA: 151
Oscar Peterson JA: 153
Oscar Pettiford JA: 154
Bud Powell JA: 156, 157
Chano Pozo JA: 157
Max Roach JA: 165
George Russell JA: 166, 167
"Salt Peanuts" JA: **169**
Arturo Sandoval JA: 170
Mongo Santamaria JA: 170
Diane Schuur JA: 172
Stuff Smith JA: 184
Sonny Stitt JA: 188
Sarah Vaughn JA: 205
Mary Lou Williams JA: 216
Gillett, Charlie RB: xvi, xvii; RR: ix
Gilley, Mickey CO: **82,** 122, 178
Gilley's (nightclub) CO: 82
Gilliand, Henry FO: 173
Gillum, Jazz BL: **68,** 238
Gilman, Lawrence CL: **88**
Gilmore, Jimmie Dale FO: **76–77**
Gilmore, John JA: 190
Gilmour, David RR: 172–174
Gimble, Johnny CO: **82–83;** FO: 60, **77**
Gimme Shelter (documentary) RR: 206, 210
Gin Blossoms RR: 178
Gingold, Joseph CL: 24, **88–89**
Girl Can't Help It, The (movie) JA: 122; RR: 141
"Girl from Ipanema, The" JA: 74, 75
girl groups RB: **105–106;** RR: **90–91,** 216–217. *See also specific artists*
Girls of the Golden West CO: 46, **83**
Gitler, Ira JA: 40, 62
Giuffre, Jimmy BL: 93
Giulini, Carlo Maria CL: **89,** 142
Givens, David and Candy BL: 255
Glackin, Paddy FO: 17, 24
Gladden, Texas FO: 190
glam rock RR: x, **91–92,** 106
Glaser, Chuck CO: 83
Glaser, Jim CO: 83, 84
Glaser, Matt FO: 43
Glaser, Tompall CO: 83, 84, 105, 110, 149
Glaser Brothers CO: **83–84**
Glasgow International Jazz Festival JA: 185
Glass, Philip CL: 73–74, **89,** 129, 177
Glazer, Tom FO: **77–78**
Gleason, Frederick G. CL: **90**
Gleason, Patrick JA: 83, 117
Gleason, Ralph J. RR: 121, 241
Glen, Alan RR: 253
Glenside Céili Band FO: 24
glitter rock. *See* glam rock
Glosson, Lonnie BL: 72
Glover, Henry BL: 107, 121
Glover, Tony "Little Sun" BL: 108, 233; FO: 118
Gluck, Alma CL: 245
Goad, Millie and Dolly CO: 83
"God Bless the Child" BL: 76; JA: **76,** 92
Godchaux, Donna RR: 93
Godchaux, Keith RR: 93
Goden, Sam RB: 131, 132
Godfrey, Arthur RB: 191
Godowsky, Leopold CL: 88, **90,** 199
God's Original Gangstaz RB: **106**
Goetschius, Percy CL: **90**
Goffin, Gerry RR: 91, 150, 217, 221
Goins, Melvin FO: 78
Goins, Ray FO: 78
Goins Brothers FO: **78**
Gold, Dave RB: 107
Gold, Julie FO: 82
Goldberg, Barry BL: 20
Golden, Bill CO: 153–154
Golden Gate Quartet FO: 123
Golden Ring FO: 156
Golden Tones, The RB: 240
Golden West Cowboys CO: 43, 117, 197
Goldflies, Dave RR: 6
Goldie RB: 73, **106–107**
Goldkette, Jean JA: 206
Goldmark, Rubin CL: 56, **90**
Goldner, George RB: 5, 51, 93
Goldovsky, Boris CL: **90**
Goldsboro, Bobby RB: 188
Goldstar Studio RB: **107**
Goldstein, Jerry RB: 274
Goldstein, Kenneth S. FO: **78**
Mick Moloney FO: 141
New York City BL: 153
Sandy Paton FO: 155
U. Utah Phillips FO: 158
recording FO: 164
Izzy Young FO: 219
Goldwax Records RB: **107–108**
Golschmann, Vladimir CL: **90–91**
Golson, Benny JA: 137, 138
Go Mach RB: 1
Gomelsky, Giorgio RR: 251
Goners, The FO: 95
"Gonna Move to Kansas City" BL: **103**
Gonzalez, Ruben JA: **76,** 174
Good, Rick FO: 99
"Goodbye, Earl" CO: **84**
Goode, Richard CL: **91,** 148
Goodman, Al RB: 185
Goodman, Andrew FO: 34

Goodman, Benny JA: **76,** *77*
- Pepper Adams JA: 3
- Carnegie Hall JA: 27–28
- Barbara Carroll JA: 28
- Benny Carter JA: 28
- Charlie Christian JA: 33
- clarinet JA: 33
- Roy Eldridge JA: 60
- Lionel Hampton JA: 81
- Fletcher Henderson JA: 90
- Harry James JA: 102
- Japanese jazz JA: 103
- jazz firsts JA: 116, 117
- Hank Jones JA: 109
- Gene Krupa JA: 114–115
- Peggy Lee JA: 121
- Mel Lewis JA: 122
- Marian McPartland JA: 133
- Glenn Miller JA: 134
- Red Norvo JA: 145
- Savoy Ballroom JA: 171
- Zoot Sims JA: 182
- Steve Swallow JA: 191
- Jack Teagarden JA: 195
- Sister Rosetta Tharpe BL: 217
- Mary Lou Williams JA: 215
- Attilla Zoller JA: 224

Goodman, Jerry JA: 99, 132
Goodman, Shirley RB: 244
Goodman, Steve CO: 101; FO: **79,** 160
"Goodnight Irene" FO: **79**
- folk revival FO: 70
- Lead Belly BL: 112; FO: 124
- John Lomax BL: 120
- Pete Seeger FO: 182
- Weavers FO: 212

Good Ol' Persons FO: **79,** 125
"Good Rockin' Tonight" BL: 74; RB: 27, 118; RR: 170, 180
Goossens, Eugene CL: 51
Gordon, Dexter JA: **76–77**
- Dee Dee Bridgewater JA: 23
- Donald Byrd RB: 32
- Don Cherry JA: 31
- Lionel Hampton JA: 81
- Herbie Hancock JA: 82
- Barry Harris JA: 86
- Melba Liston JA: 123
- Bud Powell JA: 157
- "Watermelon Man" JA: 211
- Lester Young JA: 220

Gordon, Jimmie BL: 167
Gordon, Mike FO: 118; RR: 118
Gordon, Robert (folklorist) FO: 4, 163
Gordy, Anna RB: 103
Gordy, Berry RB: xvi
- girl groups RB: 106
- Holland-Dozier-Holland RB: 122
- Marv Johnson RB: 144
- Motown RB: 188; RR: 153, 154
- Motown Records BL: 180–181
- Diana Ross RB: 231
- Mary Wells RB: 276

Gordy, Emory, Jr. CO: 42, **84,** 125
Gordy-Lupper, Gwen RB: 121
Gorodnitzky, Sascha CL: 65, **91,** 168
Gosdin, Vern CO: **84–85**
Gosdin Brothers FO: 36
Gosfield, Reuben (Lucky Oceans) CO: 5
gospel music CL: vii; CO: **85–86;** RB: vii, xvi. *See also* holy blues; *specific artists*
Gossard, Stone RR: 167, 168
Gottehrer, Richard RR: 27
Gottlieb, Danny JA: 52
Gottschalk, Louis Moreau CL: xxii, **91–92**
Gould, Darby RR: 121
Gould, Glenn CL: 236
Gould, Morton CL: **92,** 217
Gouldman, Graham RR: 251
Gourdine, Anthony RB: 167–168
Governar, Alan BL: 30
G.Q. RB: **108**
Graceland (mansion) RR: 179, 182
Graffman, Gary CL: 62, **92**
Grafton, Wisconsin BL: 178
Graham, Bill
- Allman Brothers Band RR: 4
- Band, The RR: 12
- Grateful Dead RR: 92
- B. B. King BL: 105
- Led Zeppelin RR: 136
- rock festivals RR: 207

Graham, Billy BL: 238; CO: 93
Graham, Davey FO: **79–80**
Graham, Larry JA: 34; RB: 242; RR: 15
Graham, Martha CL: 12, 189
Grainger, Percy CL: **92–93;** FO: 163
Gramercy Five JA: 176
Grammer, Billy BL: 107
Grammy Awards JA: **77–78, 259–272**
Grand Canyon Suite (Ferde Grofé) CL: **93**
Grande, Johnny RR: 104
Grandmaster Flash RB: **108,** *109*
- Kurtis Blow RB: 21
- hip-hop RB: 121–122
- Positive-K RB: 209
- Sylvia Robinson RB: 229
- social history and the blues BL: 203
- Sugar Hill RB: 249

Grandmaster Slice RB: **109**

Grandmixer DST JA: 165; RB: **109–110**
Grand Ole Opry CO: vii, viii, **86–88;** FO: viii
- Roy Acuff CO: 1, 2
- "Whispering" Bill Anderson CO: 4
- Chet Atkins CO: 5
- Bailes Brothers CO: 9; FO: 10
- DeFord Bailey CO: 9–10
- Dr. Humphrey Bate and The Possum Hunters CO: 12
- Binkley Brothers Dixie Clodhoppers FO: 15–16
- bluegrass music CO: 15
- Boxcar Willie CO: 20
- Browns, The CO: 25
- Carlisle Brothers CO: 31
- Martha Carson CO: 33
- Carter Family CO: 35
- Wilma Lee and Stoney Cooper FO: 41
- Cowboy Copas CO: 43
- Crook Brothers FO: 46–47
- Skeeter Davis CO: 55
- Delmore Brothers CO: 55
- "Little" Jimmy Dickens CO: 57
- Drifting Cowboys CO: 63
- Roy Drusky CO: 64
- Duke of Paducah, The CO: 65
- Ralph Emery CO: 69
- Everly Brothers, The RR: 77
- Flatt and Scruggs CO: 73, 74
- Red Foley CO: 76
- Fruit Jar Drinkers FO: 73
- Don Gibson CO: 81
- Vince Gill CO: 81
- Glaser Brothers CO: 84
- gospel music CO: 85
- Buck (Uncle Josh) Graves FO: 80
- Jack Greene CO: 88
- Gully Jumpers FO: 86
- Theron Hale and Daughters FO: 89
- George Hamilton, IV CO: 93
- Buddy Harman CO: 94
- harmonica BL: 72; FO: 92
- Hawkshaw Hawkins CO: 96
- Hay, George D. CO: 96, 97
- David Holt FO: 98
- David Houston CO: 104–105
- Jim and Jesse FO: 111
- Grandpa Jones CO: 112
- Bradley Kincaid FO: 116
- Pee Wee King CO: 117
- Alison Krauss CO: 118
- *Louisiana Hayride* CO: 123
- Louvin Brothers CO: 124
- Robert Lunn FO: 128
- Charlie McCoy CO: 136
- Mel McDaniel CO: 136
- Sam McGee FO: 136, 137
- Uncle Dave Macon CO: 129
- Benny Martin FO: 133
- Grady Martin CO: 134
- Jimmy Martin FO: 134
- Bill Monroe CO: 141
- George Morgan CO: 143
- *National Barn Dance* CO: 148
- Jimmy "C" Newman CO: 150; FO: 148
- Osborne Brothers FO: 154
- Brad Paisley CO: 157
- Minnie Pearl CO: 160
- Pickard Family FO: 158
- Webb Pierce CO: 162
- Elvis Presley RR: 180
- railroad songs CO: 166
- Jim Reeves CO: 171
- Riders in the Sky FO: 170
- Marty Robbins CO: 176
- Tommy Scott FO: 180
- Jeannie Seely CO: 184
- Connie Smith CO: 187
- Hank Snow CO: 188
- Stanley Brothers, The CO: 191
- Ernest "Pop" Stoneman FO: 195
- Stringbean CO: 194
- Marty Stuart CO: 194
- Uncle Jimmy Thompson FO: 203
- Pam Tillis CO: 199
- Travis Tritt CO: 202
- Ernest Tubb CO: 203
- Porter Wagoner CO: 209
- Steve Wariner CO: 211
- Kitty Wells CO: 213
- Dottie West CO: 213
- Whites FO: 215
- Hank Williams CO: 217
- Faron Young CO: 225

Grand Puba RB: **110,** 209
Grant, Amy CO: 86
Grant, Bill and Delia Bell FO: **80**
Grant, Peter RR: 133, 136
Grant Street FO: 125
Granz, Norman RB: **110**
- Toshiko Akiyoshi JA: 3
- Japanese jazz JA: 103
- JATP JA: 106
- Hank Jones JA: 109
- Gene Krupa JA: 115
- Machito JA: 125
- Oscar Peterson JA: 153

Grappelli, Stephane
- European jazz JA: 64
- David Grisman FO: 83
- Coleman Hawkins JA: 87
- Hot Club de France JA: 94
- Yehudi Menuhin CL: 153
- Oscar Peterson JA: 153
- Django Reinhardt JA: 164

Stuff Smith JA: 184
violin JA: 207
Grateful Dead, The RR: **92–97**
country rock CO: 45
Rev. Gary Davis BL: 50
jam bands RR: 117
Jefferson Starship RR: 120
keyboards RR: 127
Mamas and the Papas RR: 145
Monterey Pop Festival RR: 151
psychedelic rock RR: 187
rock festivals RR: 206, 207
roots rock RR: 211
Grau, Maurice CL: 155
Gravediggaz RB: **110,** 284
Gravenites, Nick BL: 20
Graves, Buck (Uncle Josh) CO: 60, 75, 180; FO: 11, 54, **80–81**
Graves, Milford JA: 46
Gray, Arvella BL: *40*
Gray, Mark CO: 221
Gray, Otto CO: 65
Gray, Tom FO: 44, 183
Grayson, G. B. CO: 221; FO: 215
Grayson and Whitter FO: 215
"Grazing in the Grass" JA: 129, 187; RB: 178
Great American Country (GACTV) CO: 245
Great American Music Band FO: 82, 83
Great Awakening BL: 196
Great Britain BL: viii, xvi, xx; RR: x. *See also* United Kingdom
Frankie Armstrong FO: 5–6
bagpipes FO: 9–10
Bruce Bastin BL: 16
Beatles RR: **18–22**
Ivy Benson JA: 13–14
Eric Clapton RR: 39–40
Bill Clifton FO: 37
Michael Coleman FO: 39
Shirley Collins FO: 40
Copper Family FO: 42
Demon Boyz RB: 58
Sandy Denny FO: 51
Lonnie Donegan FO: 54–55
drum and bass RB: 73
Ramblin' Jack Elliott FO: 60
Fairport Convention FO: 64
Leonard Feather JA: 69–70
folk-rock FO: 71
glam rock RR: 92
Goldie RB: 106–107
Davey Graham FO: 79–80
Groove Corporation, The RB: 112–113
guitar RR: 100
Bill Haley and His Comets RR: 102
heavy metal RR: 105
Dave Holland JA: 92
Buddy Holly RR: 113–114
Hot Chocolate RB: 124–125
house RB: 125
Ashley Hutchings FO: 102
Incredible String Band FO: 106
Andy Irvine FO: 107
Jamiroquai RB: 140
Junior RB: 147
Cleo Laine JA: 119–120
Led Zeppelin RR: 133
A. L. Lloyd FO: **126–127**
Alan Lomax BL: 118
Ewan MacColl FO: 131
John McLaughlin JA: 131–133
Marian McPartland JA: 133
music business BL: 144–145
new wave RR: 156, 157
Oasis RR: **163–164**
Pentangle FO: 156
Carl Perkins RR: 169
Courtney Pine JA: 155–156
Pink Floyd RR: **172–175**
power pop RR: 177
progressive rock RR: 183
psychedelic rock RR: 186
punk rock RR: 187, 188
reggae RR: 200
John Renbourn FO: 167
Jean Ritchie FO: 172
rockabilly RR: 206
rock festivals RR: 206–207
Del Shannon RR: 216
Andy Sheppard JA: 177
Simon and Garfunkel RR: 217
ska/bluebeat revival RB: 241
Percy Sledge RB: 241
Steeleye Span FO: 194
John Surman JA: 191
vocal styles BL: 231, 233
Muddy Waters BL: 239
Who, The RR: 243–246
Steve Williamson JA: 216–217
Wire, The (magazine) JA: 218
Jimmy Witherspoon BL: 245
young black country blues artists BL: 250
Great Depression BL: xv; FO: viii
Allen Brothers FO: 4
Emry Arthur FO: 6
blues lyrics BL: 22
boogie-woogie BL: 27
Bill Boyd CO: 20–21
Burnett and Rutherford FO: 25
Carolina Tar Heels FO: 29
classic blues BL: 42
Vernon Dalhart CO: 52
Darby and Tarlton FO: 49

Great Depression (*continued*)
Dilly and His Dill Pickles FO: 53
Georgia Yellow Hammers FO: 75
Woody Guthrie FO: 87
Kelly Harrell FO: 92
Haywire Mac FO: 94
Hill Billies FO: 97
holy blues BL: 78
Homesick James BL: 79
honky-tonk music CO: 102
Frank Hutchison FO: 103
Lonnie Johnson BL: 96
Kansas City BL: 140
Buell Kazee FO: 114
Clark Kessinger FO: 115
Robert Lunn FO: 128
migration BL: 134
Linda Parker FO: 155
Harry Partch CL: 174
protest songs BL: 166, 167
Yank Rachell BL: 175
Ravinia Festival CL: 186
record labels BL: 178
George Reneau FO: 168
social history BL: 201–202
Ernest "Pop" Stoneman FO: 194
Stripling Brothers FO: 196
"This Land Is Your Land" FO: 202
Peetie Wheatstraw BL: 241
Henry Whitter FO: 215
young black country blues artists BL: 248
Great Migration. *See* migration
Great Society, The RR: 119, 120
Great Speckled Bird (band) FO: 106
Greaves, R. B. RB: **110–111**
Grech, Rick BL: 41; RR: 40
Green, Al (singer) BL: 79; RB: **111–112,** *112,* 185
Green, Archie FO: 29, 173
Green, Charlie BL: 92, 189, 194
Green, Doug CO: 46, 182; FO: 170, *171*
Green, Jerome BL: 52; RR: 55, 56
Green, Juanita BL: 194
Green, Peter BL: 62, 63, *63,* 127; RR: 81–82, 213
Greenberg, Florence RB: 238; RR: 216, 217
Greenbriar Boys, The FO: **81,** 170
Greenburg, Noah CL: **93,** 165
Greene, Gene JA: 115
Greene, Jack CO: **88,** 184
Greene, Richard FO: **81–82**
David Grisman FO: 83
Bill Keith FO: 114
Kentucky Colonels FO: 115
Jim Kweskin FO: 119
Muleskinner FO: 143, 144
Jim Rooney FO: 176
Peter Rowan FO: 177
Greenfield, Howard RR: 175
Green Fields of America FO: 29
Green Grass Gringos FO: 177
Greenhill, Manny FO: **82**
Greenhill, Mitch FO: 82
Greenhouse, Bernard CL: 23, **93**
Green Mansions (Louis Gruenberg) CL: **93**
Green River (band) RR: 167
Greenville, Mississippi BL: **138**
Greenville, South Carolina BL: 213, 242
Greenwich, Ellie RB: 62, 142; RR: 34, 91, 223
Greenwich Village
Eric Anderson FO: 4
Rory Block BL: 19
Len Chandler FO: 31
Harry Chapin FO: 31
Clancy Brothers FO: 35
Judy Collins FO: 39
Dion RR: 56–57
Bob Dylan FO: 57; RR: 70–71
Richard and Mimi Fariña FO: 65
Stefan Grossman FO: 84
John Hammond, Jr. BL: 71
Tim Hardin FO: 90
Richie Havens FO: 93
Jimi Hendrix BL: 75
Carolyn Hester FO: 95
Jac Holzman FO: 99
Janis Joplin RR: 122
Peter La Farge FO: 121
Christine Lavin FO: 121
Mamas and the Papas RR: 145
Geoff and Maria Muldaur FO: 142
New Lost City Ramblers FO: 148
New York City BL: 153
Phil Ochs FO: 151
Tom Paxton FO: 156
Peter, Paul and Mary FO: 156, 157
protest songs BL: 168
Rooftop Singers FO: 175
Patrick Sky FO: 187
Mark Spoelstra FO: 192
Happy and Artie Traum FO: 204
Dave Van Ronk BL: 227
Weavers FO: 212
Greenwood, Colin RR: 195
Greenwood, Jonny RR: 195
Greenwood, Lee CO: **88–89**
Greenwood, Mississippi BL: 68, 97, **138**
Greenwood Blues Heritage Museum and Gallery BL: 138

Greer, Sonny JA: 60
Gretsch Guitars CO: 90
Grier, Lamar FO: 76
Griesar, Peter RR: 52
Griffes, Charles T. CL: **93–94**
Griffin, Rex CO: **89,** 125
Griffith, Nanci CO: 18, 67, 135; FO: 2, **82,** 164
Griffiths, Marcia RB: 134
Grimes, Tiny JA: 194
grindcore RR: 107
Grisman, David FO: **83**
Red Allen FO: 3
bluegrass music CO: 16
Bob Brozman BL: 32
Alice Gerrard FO: 76
Grateful Dead, The RR: 96
Richard Greene FO: 82
Bill Keith FO: 114
Kentucky Colonels FO: 115
Del McCoury FO: 135
mandolin BL: 125; CO: 132; FO: 133
Muleskinner FO: 144
New York City BL: 153
Mark O'Connor FO: 152
Old and in the Way FO: 153
progressive bluegrass FO: 161
Tony Rice FO: 169
Peter Rowan FO: 177
Grits RB: **112**
Grofé, Ferde CL: 93, **94**
Grohl, Dave RR: 159–161
groove RR: 117
Groove Corporation, The RB: **112–113**
Grooverider RB: 73
Gross, Clifford FO: 96
Grossman, Albert FO: **83–84**
Bob Dylan FO: 57
Bob Gibson FO: 76
Frank Hamilton FO: 90
Ian and Sylvia FO: 105–106
Janis Joplin BL: 100; RR: 123
Gordon Lightfoot FO: 125
Newport Folk Festival FO: 149
Peter, Paul and Mary FO: 156
Jim Rooney FO: 176
Grossman, Stefan BL: *152;* FO: **84**
Rory Block BL: 19, 20
Rev. Gary Davis BL: 50; FO: 50
Davey Graham FO: 80
Son House BL: 82
New York City BL: 153
John Renbourn FO: 167
Groucutt, Kelly RR: 77
Gruenberg, Louis CL: 93, **94–95**
grunge RR: xx, 6, **97–99,** 178, 189. *See also* Nirvana; Pearl Jam
Guard, Dave FO: 116–117
Guess, Don RR: 111
Guggenheim fellowship JA: 38, 167
Guibeau, Gib CO: 75
Guida, Frank RB: 22, 23
Guilet, Daniel CL: 23
guitar. *See also specific guitarists*
acoustic guitar BL: **1–4**
bass guitar JA: **10–11**
country music CO: **89–90**
electric (blues) BL: **57–59**
folk music FO: **84–86,** *85*
pedal steel CO: **160–161**
rock and roll RR: **99–100**
slide BL: **191–193**
synthesizer JA: **78**
tunings BL: **222–223**
12-string BL: **224–225**
"Guitar Boogie" BL: 26; RR: 115
Guitar Gabriel BL: **68,** 148
Guitar Junior. *See* Brooks, Lonnie
Guitar Slim (Eddie Jones) BL: **68,** 194
guitar synthesizer JA: **78**
Guitar Town (Steve Earle) CO: 67, 84
guitar tunings. *See* tunings, guitar
Guit-Steel guitar CO: 24
Gulah FO: 112
Gulda, Friedrich JA: 223
Gully Jumpers FO: **86**
Gunning, Sarah Ogan CO: 107; FO: 6, 109
Gunther, Cornell RB: 34, 46
Guralnick, Peter BL: **69;** RB: 83; RR: 182
Gurewitz, Brett RR: 189
Gurley, James RR: 122
Guru Keith E RB: 101–102
Gussow, Adam BL: 188, **188**
Guthrie, Arlo FO: 24, 79, **86–87,** 124, 183
Guthrie, Woody FO: ix, **87–88**
Archive of American Folk Song FO: 4
Moses Asch BL: 8; FO: 7
Hoyt Axton FO: 8
Bob Dylan FO: 57; RR: 70
Ramblin' Jack Elliott FO: 60
folk revival FO: 70, 71
guitar FO: 86
Arlo Guthrie FO: 86
harmonica FO: 92
Cisco Houston FO: 100
Lead Belly BL: 112; FO: 123
Harold Leventhal FO: 124
Alan Lomax BL: 118
Robert Lunn FO: 128
mandolin FO: 133
protest songs BL: 167, 168
"Reuben James" FO: 168

Guthrie, Woody (*continued*)
- Pete Seeger FO: 182
- Alec Seward BL: 189
- "So Long, It's Been Good to Know You" FO: 190
- Sonny Terry and Brownie McGhee FO: 201
- Bruce Springsteen RR: 224, 226
- "This Land Is Your Land" FO: 202
- U2 RR: 237
- Weavers FO: 212

Gutiérrez, Horacio CL: **95,** 148
Guy, Audrey Sheppard. *See* Williams, Audrey
Guy, Billy RB: 45
Guy, Buddy BL: **69**
- Elvin Bishop BL: 17
- Chicago BL: 40
- electric guitar BL: 59
- Jimi Hendrix BL: 75
- Kenny Neal BL: 151
- Derek Trucks BL: 222
- Junior Wells BL: 241

Guy, Joe JA: 188
Gyrlz RB: 266

H

Hackberry Ramblers, The FO: **89**
Hackett, Bobby JA: 13, 48
Hackford, Taylor RR: 25
Hadden, Martin FO: 185
Haden, Charlie JA: **79**
- Don Cherry JA: 31
- Ornette Coleman JA: 36
- *Free Jazz* (Ornette Coleman) JA: 71
- Bill Frisell JA: 72
- Keith Jarrett JA: 104
- Joe Lovano JA: 124
- Pat Metheny JA: 134
- Michel Petrucciani JA: 154
- Gonzalo Rubalcaba JA: 166
- *The Shape of Jazz to Come* JA: 174

Hadley, Henry CL: 199
Hadley, Elder J. J. BL: 5, 77
Hagerty, Lee FO: 155
Haggard, Merle CO: viii, **91–92**
- Bakersfield Sound CO: 10
- Janie Fricke CO: 78
- "The Fugitive" CO: 78
- Johnny Gimble CO: 82, 83; FO: 77
- "Tiny" Moore FO: 142
- "Okie from Muskogee" CO: 154
- Bonnie Owens CO: 155
- Johnny Paycheck CO: 159
- Jimmie Rodgers BL: 184
- Marty Stuart CO: 195
- Townes Van Zandt FO: 208
- Western Swing FO: 213
- western swing CO: 214
- Bob Wills CO: 219

Hahn, Hilary CL: **97**
Haig, Al JA: 169
Haight-Ashbury RR: 92, 121, 152
Hail, Abigail FO: 172
Haile Selassie RR: 200
Hair (Broadway musical) RB: 75, 188
hair metal RR: 106
Hale, Elizabeth FO: 89, 90
Hale, Mamie Ruth FO: 89, 90
Hale, Theron and Daughters FO: **89–90**
Haley, Bill, and His Comets BL: 223; RR: **101–105,** *103,* 170, 208
Haley, Ed FO: 66, 72, 115
Hall, Adelaide JA: 193
Hall, Edmond BL: 114
Hall, Jim JA: 72, **79–80,** 224
Hall, Rene RB: 34
Hall, Rick RB: **115,** 189
Hall, Roy FO: 59
Hall, Tom T. CO: *48,* 65, **92**
Hall, Willie RB: 24, 101
Hall and Oates RR: 159
Halsey, Jim CO: 61
Ham, Pete RR: 177
Hamblen, Stuart CO: **92–93**
hambone rhythm RR: 55
Hamburg, Germany RR: 18–19
Hamelin, Marc-André CL: 229
Hamfat BL: 163
Hamilton, Chico JA: **80**
- John Abercrombie JA: 1
- Ron Carter JA: 30
- Eric Dolphy JA: 55
- Jim Hall JA: 80
- Gerry Mulligan JA: 142
- Steve Swallow JA: 191–192

Hamilton, Frank FO: 76, 83, **90,** 212
Hamilton, George, IV CO: 55, 62, **93–94**
Hamilton, Harlye CL: 141
Hamilton, Roy RB: **115–116**
Hamilton, Tom RR: 1
Hamilton Camp. *See* Camp, Hamilton
Hammer, Jan JA: 65, **80–81,** 99, 132, 192, 207
Hammer, MC. *See* MC Hammer
Hammerstein, Arthur CL: 88
Hammett, Kirk RR: 146
Hammond, John, Jr. (singer and guitarist) BL: **71**
- acoustic guitar BL: 4
- Jimi Hendrix RR: 109
- Robert Johnson BL: 98
- New York City BL: 153
- Duke Robillard BL: 183
- vocal styles BL: 233

Hammond, John, Sr. (record producer) BL: **71**
boogie-woogie BL: 27
Big Bill Broonzy BL: 29; FO: 21
Bob Dylan FO: 57
John Hammond, Jr. BL: 71
Carolyn Hester FO: 95
Helen Humes BL: 83
Robert Johnson BL: 98
New York City BL: 152
Bessie Smith BL: 194
social history BL: 201
Stevie Ray Vaughan BL: 228
Hammonds, Burl FO: 115
Hammonds Family, The FO: 66
Hammons, Will and Cloet FO: 59
Hampton, Lionel JA: **81**
Betty Carter JA: 29
Mel Carter RB: 36
Art Farmer JA: 69
Benny Goodman JA: 76
Dexter Gordon JA: 76
Illinois Jacquet JA: 101
Quincy Jones JA: 109
King Curtis RB: 154
Kwamé RB: 159
Charles Mingus JA: 136
Wes Montgomery JA: 139; RB: 186
Oscar Peterson JA: 153
Jimmy Scott JA: 173
Sir Charles Thompson JA: 197
Dinah Washington BL: 238; JA: 211; RB: 275
Joe Williams BL: 244
Shadow Wilson JA: 218
Han, Wu CL: 48
Hancock, Butch FO: 3, 77
Hancock, Herbie JA: *50,* **81–83,** *82;* RB: **116–117**
Richard Bona JA: 20
Michael Brecker JA: 22
Ron Carter JA: 30
Miles Davis JA: 49
"E.S.P." JA: 63
Grandmixer DST RB: 109
Headhunters JA: **88**
Joe Henderson JA: 90
Dave Holland JA: 92
jazz firsts JA: 117
Bill Laswell RB: 162
Bobby McFerrin JA: 131
Jaco Pastorius JA: 152
piano JA: 155
Diane Reeves JA: 163
"Rockit" JA: **165**
In a Silent Way JA: 98
synthesizer JA: 192
Miroslav Vitous JA: 207
"Watermelon Man" JA: 211
Tony Williams JA: 216
Attilla Zoller JA: 224
Handel and Haydn Society CL: xxii, **97**
Handy, John JA: 19
Handy, W. C. BL: vii, xvi, xvii, **71–72;** JA: **84**
acoustic guitar BL: 1
Cleveland, Mississippi BL: 138
field hollers BL: 62
Memphis BL: 131
New York City BL: 152
record labels BL: 178
"St. Louis Blues" BL: 187–188; JA: 187
slide guitar BL: 192
Tutwiler, Mississippi BL: 140
Handy Awards BL: 214
"(Hang Down Your Head) Tom Dooley" FO: xvi, 116, 160, **203–204,** 210–211
Hanna, Jeff CO: 151
Hanson, Howard CL: 90, **97–98,** 151, 236
"Happy Trails" CO: **94,** 179
Harbison, John CL: 80, *98,* **98**
hard bop JA: xxiv, xxxii, **84,** 252*t. See also specific musicians*
Harder They Come, The (movie) RB: 133, 222; RR: 201
Hardesty, Herbert RR: 58
Hardin, Lil JA: **84**
"Dipper Mouth Blues" JA: 52
Baby Dodds JA: 53
Hot Five and Hot Seven JA: 94
Alberta Hunter JA: 95
King Oliver JA: 147
women in jazz JA: xxx
Hardin, Tim FO: **90**
Hardison, Roy FO: 86
hard rock RR: 41, 91
Hardwicke, Otto JA: 60
Hardy, Lynn FO: 38
Hargrove, Roy JA: **84–85**
Harkreader, Sid CO: 129
Harlan County, Kentucky FO: 213
Harlem JA: **85**
Cotton Club JA: **43–44**
Rev. Gary Davis FO: 50
Billie Holiday JA: 91
Brownie McGhee BL: 129
Minton's Playhouse JA: **137**
New York City BL: 152
Bobby Robinson BL: 183
Satan & Adam BL: 188
Savoy Ballroom JA: **170–171**
Mamie Smith JA: 184
social history and the blues BL: 201
"Stompin' at the Savoy" JA: 188
Chick Webb JA: 212
Harlem Hamfats, The BL: 128, 215

Harlem Hellfighters JA: 63
Harlem Playgirls JA: 47
Harlem Renaissance BL: 201; JA: **85**
Harley, Rufus JA: **85–86**
Harman, Buddy CO: **94,** 147, 187
harmonica BL: **72–74;** FO: **90–92,** *91*
  instruments BL: 86
  jazz and the blues BL: 92
harmony CL: xix; BL: 85–86; FO: 184; JA: 12, 53. *See also* chord; chord progression
Harmony Four, The RB: 278
Harper, Ben BL: 233, 251–252
"Harper Valley P.T.A." CO: 92, 173
Harpo, Slim BL: **74;** RB: **117**
harpsichordists CL: 105, 127
harp-zither FO: 131
Harrell, Andre RB: 20, 72, 266
Harrell, Bill FO: 43, 168
Harrell, Kelly FO: **92**
Harrell, Lynn CL: **98,** 191
Harrington, David CL: 131
Harris, Addie "Micki" RB: 238; RR: 217
Harris, Barry JA: **86**
Harris, Corey BL: 33, **74,** 251, 252
Harris, Craig JA: 44
Harris, Cyril M. CL: 2
Harris, David FO: 9
Harris, Don "Sugarcane" BL: 125
Harris, Eddie JA: 1
Harris, Emmylou CO: **94–95,** *95*
  Guy Clark FO: 36
  Earl Thomas Conley CO: 42
  country rock CO: 45; RR: 45
  Rodney Crowell CO: 48
  Emory Gordy, Jr. CO: 84
  Vern Gosdin CO: 85
  Bill Grant and Delia Bell FO: 80
  Buddy and Julie Miller FO: 137, 138
  Dolly Parton CO: 158
  Ricky Skaggs CO: 186
  Barry and Holly Tashian FO: 199
  Townes Van Zandt FO: 208
  Gillian Welch FO: 213
  Whites FO: 214
  Don Williams CO: 216
Harris, Joe RB: 265, 266
Harris, Major RB: 56, **117–118**
Harris, Marian BL: xvii
Harris, Michael W. BL: 54
Harris, Phil CO: 188
Harris, Roy CL: **98–99,** 199, 213
Harris, Sue FO: 117
Harris, Thurston RB: 174
Harris, Wynonie BL: **74;** RB: **118,** 183; RR: 170
Harrison, George
  Beatles RR: 18, 20–22
  Eric Clapton RR: 40
  Cream RR: 46
  Donovan RR: 60
  Electric Light Orchestra RR: 76, 77
  guitar RR: 100
  Buddy Holly RR: 114
  Roy Orbison RR: 165, 166
  Carl Perkins BL: 158; CO: 162; RR: 169
  power pop RR: 177
  Phil Spector RR: 221, 223
Harrison, Jerry RR: 231, 232
Harrison, Jimmy JA: 195
Harrison, Lou CL: **99–100,** 115
Harrison, Nigel RR: 27, 28
Harrison, Wilbert BL: 89, 103, 183; RR: 138
Harrison, William Henry CL: 119–120
Harry, Debbie RR: 26, 28
Hart, Alvin Youngblood BL: **74,** 251, 252
Hart, Billy JA: 83
Hart, Bobby RR: 150, 151
Hart, Clarence RB: 171
Hart, Freddie CO: **95–96**
Hart, Mickey RR: 93, 96
Hart, Tim FO: 194
Hartford, John FO: **92–93,** *93*
  Norman Blake FO: 16
  Albert E. Brumley FO: 22
  Byrds FO: 25
  Glen Campbell CO: 31
  Bob Carlin FO: 28
  "Cowboy" Jack Clement CO: 39
  Vassar Clements FO: 37
  Dillards FO: 52, 53
  "Gentle on My Mind" CO: 80
  Benny Martin FO: 134
  recording FO: 164
  Tut Taylor FO: 200
Hartford Music Company CO: 26; FO: 22
Hartman, Johnny JA: **86**
Harvey, Roy FO: 159
Harvey, Ted BL: 213
Hastings Street (Detroit) BL: 52, 161, 204
Hatcher, Lib CO: 201
Hatfield, Bobby RB: 225, 226; RR: 204, 205
Hathaway, Donnie RB: 92, **118**
Hauk, Minnie CL: **100**
Hauptmann, Gerhart FO: 212
Hauser, Tim JA: 126
Havana, Cuba JA: 76, 174

Havens, Richie BL: 250; FO: **93;** RR: 247
Hawaii FO: 116
Hawaiian music
- Bob Brozman BL: 32; FO: 21–22
- Carlisle Brothers CO: 31
- "Cowboy" Jack Clement CO: 38
- Ted Daffan CO: 51
- Dobro CO: 60; FO: 54
- Adolph Hofner CO: 100
- pedal steel guitar CO: 160
- slide guitar BL: 191–192

Hawes, Bess Lomax FO: 112
Hawkins, Barbara Ann and Rosa Lee RB: 62
Hawkins, Coleman JA: *87,* **87–88**
- "Body and Soul" JA: **19**
- Benny Carter JA: 28
- cutting contest JA: 45
- Andrew Cyrille JA: 46
- Miles Davis JA: 48
- Roy Eldridge JA: 60
- Duke Ellington JA: 61
- European jazz JA: 64
- Dizzy Gillespie JA: 75
- Barry Harris JA: 86
- Fletcher Henderson JA: 89
- Hank Jones JA: 109
- Oscar Pettiford JA: 154
- Max Roach JA: 165
- Sonny Rollins JA: 165
- saxophone JA: 171
- Horace Silver JA: 179
- Mamie Smith JA: 184
- Jack Teagarden JA: 195
- Sir Charles Thompson JA: 197
- Ben Webster JA: 212
- Lester Young JA: 219, 220

Hawkins, Ernie BL: **74**
Hawkins, Erskine RB: 221
Hawkins, Hawkshaw CO: 39, 43, **96**
Hawkins, Roger RB: 115, 189
Hawkins, Ronnie BL: 32; RR: 11
Hawkins, Roy BL: 220
Hawkins, Screamin' Jay RB: **118–119**
Hawkins, Ted (blues, R&B) BL: **74–75**
Hawkins, Ted (country) BL: 125
Hawks, The RR: 11
Hay, George D. CO: vii, *96,* **96–97**
- DeFord Bailey CO: 9, 10
- Crook Brothers FO: 46
- *Grand Ole Opry* CO: 86, 87
- Theron Hale and Daughters FO: 89
- Bill Monroe CO: 141
- *National Barn Dance* CO: 148
- Uncle Jimmy Thompson FO: 203

Hayes, Alfred FO: 174
Hayes, Edgar JA: 34
Hayes, Isaac RB: *119,* **119–120,** 234, 244, 247
Hayes, Jimmy "Bro" RB: 205
Hayes, Wade CO: **97**
Hayes and Prater BL: 62
Haynes, Henry D. CO: 101
Haynes, Roy JA: 19, 40
Haynes, Warren RR: 6
Hays, Lee BL: 168; FO: 87, 157, 182, 183, 212
Hays, Will S. CO: 123
Hayton, Lennie JA: 80
Haywire Mac FO: **93–94**
Hazard, Tony CO: 92
Hazel, Eddie RB: 43
Hazelwood, Lee CO: 41; RR: 222
head JA: **88**
head arrangement JA: **88**
Head Hunters (Herbie Hancock) JA: 81, 83, **88;** RB: 117
headliner JA: **88**
H.E.A.L. (Human Education Against Lies) RB: 157
Healer, The (John Lee Hooker) BL: 80, 185
Hearts, The RB: 274
Heath, Percy JA: 138
Heavy D RB: 213, 266
heavy metal RR: 29, 41, 97, **105–107,** 185
Hebb, Bobby RB: **120**
Hebb, Hal RB: 120
Heckle, Bob CO: 175
"Heebie Jeebies" JA: 6, **88–89,** 116, 162
Hee Haw CO: **97–98**
- Boxcar Willie CO: 20
- Roy Clark CO: 38
- Grandpa Jones CO: 112
- Charlie McCoy CO: 136
- Buck Owens CO: 156
- rube/hillbilly humor CO: 181–182
- Stringbean CO: 194

Hefti, Neal JA: 90
Hegamin, Lucille BL: 206
Heifetz, Benar CL: 4
Heifetz, Jascha CL: **100,** 134, 178
Heinrich, Anthony Philip CL: xxii, **101**
Heinz Hall CL: *101,* **101,** 179
Helena, Arkansas
- Arkansas BL: 7
- Elmore James BL: 90
- Little Walter BL: 116
- Robert Lockwood, Jr. BL: 117
- Robert Nighthawk BL: 154

Helena, Arkansas (*continued*)
  Houston Stackhouse BL: 206
  Joe Willie Wilkins BL: 243
Helfand, Marshall "Buzzy" RB: 229
Hell Divers JA: 47
Hellerman, Fred FO: 182, 212
Hellman, Lillian CL: 31
"Hello Darlin'" CO: **98,** 206
"Hello Walls" CO: **98,** 149
Hells Angels RR: 206
Helm, Levon RR: 11, 13, 68
Helms, Chet RR: 122
Helms, Don CO: 63
"Help Me Make It through the Night" CO: **98,** 118, 119
Hembree, Mark FO: 145
Hemphill, Jessie Mae BL: **75**
Hemphill, Sid BL: 101, 139
Henahan, Donal CL: 99, 205
Henderson, Fletcher JA: *89,* **89–90**
  Benny Carter JA: 28
  Sid Catlett JA: 30
  Roy Eldridge JA: 59
  Dexter Gordon JA: 77
  Coleman Hawkins JA: 87
  jazz firsts JA: 116
  piano BL: 162
  Ma Rainey JA: 161
  recordings of early jazz JA: 162
  Don Redman JA: 163
  Savoy Ballroom JA: 171
  Bessie Smith JA: 183
  Sun Ra JA: 189
  Jack Teagarden JA: 195
  Sir Charles Thompson JA: 197
  Fats Waller JA: 209
  Ethel Waters JA: 211
  Ben Webster JA: 213
Henderson, Joe JA: 16, **90,** 140, 154, 180
Henderson, Rosa BL: 245
Hendricks, Jon JA: 120; RB: 180
Hendricks, Scott CO: 2, 23, **98–99**
Hendrix, Al RR: 110
Hendrix, Jimi BL: **75;** RR: **107–111,** *109*
  Animals RR: 9
  "Junior" Brown CO: 24
  electric guitar BL: 59
  Gil Evans JA: 68
  guitar RR: 100
  heavy metal RR: 106
  Little Richard RR: 140, 142–143
  Buddy Miles RB: 183
  Monkees RR: 151
  Monterey Pop Festival RR: 151, 152
  New York City BL: 153
  psychedelic rock RR: 186
  wah-wah pedal JA: 209
  Woodstock RR: 247, 248
  Larry Young JA: 219
  young black country blues artists BL: 250
Hendrix, Margie RB: 49, 217
Hendryx, Nona RB: 161, 162
Henhouse FO: 69
Henley, Don CO: 223; RR: 73, 75
Hennacy, Ammon FO: 158
Henry, Clarence "Frogman" RB: 104
Henry, Ernie JA: 23
Henry, Sonny RR: 213
Henschel, George CL: 35
Hentoff, Nat JA: 114, 213
Herald, John FO: 81
Herbert, Victor CL: **101–102,** 179
Herbig, Gunther CL: 68
Herdman, Priscilla FO: **94**
"Here's a Quarter (Call Someone Who Cares)" CO: **99,** 202
Herman, Woody JA: **90–91**
  Tony Bennett JA: 13
  Stan Getz JA: 74
  Joe Lovano JA: 124
  Oscar Pettiford JA: 154
  Tito Puente JA: 158
  Zoot Sims JA: 182
  Shadow Wilson JA: 218
Herndon, Mark Joel CO: 3
Herndon, Ty CO: **99**
Heron, Mike FO: 106
Herrick, Jack FO: *165*
Hertz, Alfred CL: 199
Herz, Djane Lavoie CL: 60
Herzhaft, Gerard BL: 82
Herzog, Arthur, Jr. JA: 76
Hess, Myra CL: 129
Hester, Carolyn FO: 65, 83, **95**
Hetfield, James RR: 145, 147
Hewson, Paul. *See* Bono
"Hey Joe" CO: **99;** RR: 90, 110
Heyward, DuBose CL: 181
Heywood, Eddie JA: 76
Hiatt, John BL: 111; CO: 77; FO: **95**
Hickerson, Joe FO: **95–96**
Hickman, John FO: 46
Hicks, Bessie FO: 160
Hicks, Bill FO: 164
Hicks, Bobby FO: 11, 47, 122
Hicks, Charley BL: 15
Hicks, Laney CO: 136
Hicks, Michael RR: 186
Hicks, Robert. *See* Barbecue Bob
Hidalgo, David CO: 72
Hi Flyers, The FO: **96**
Higgins, Billy JA: 31, 36, 71, 174, 211
Higgins, Monk RB: 199

Higginson, Henry Lee CL: 35, 218
High Inergy RB: **121**
Highlander Research and Education Center FO: 28, 33
Highlanders, The FO: 159
Highley, Brewster M. FO: 99
High Numbers, The RR: 244
Hightower, Rosetta RB: 200
Highway 49 BL: 47
Highway 61 BL: 47, **75**
Highway 101 (band) CO: 32, 105
Highwaymen, The CO: 35, 110, 119, 149; FO: 114
Highway QC's RB: 48, 254, 283
Highwoods Stringband, The FO: **96–97,** 187
hi-hat cymbal JA: **91**
Hilgado, Elvira de CL: 43
Hill, Bertha "Chippie" BL: 17, **76,** 214, 222
Hill, Dusty BL: 255
Hill, Edward Burlingame CL: **102–103**
  Leonard Bernstein CL: 26
  Elliott Carter CL: 46
  Irving Fine CL: 78
  Ross Lee Finney CL: 78
  Walter Piston CL: 178
  Randall Thompson CL: 224
  Virgil Thomson CL: 224
Hill, Faith CO: 99, **100,** 138, *138,* 139
Hill, Goldie CO: 187
Hill, Joe FO: ix
Hill, Lauryn RB: 97, 98, 231
Hill, Raymond RB: 25
Hill, Teddy JA: 59, 137
Hill, Thomas Lee RB: 205
Hill, Tommy CO: 186
Hill, Ureli Corelli CL: **103,** 164, 177
Hill, Z. Z. BL: **76**
Hill Billies (Al Hopkins and the Hill Billies) FO: **97**
hillbilly CO: vii
Hilliard Ensemble JA: 73
Hillis, Margaret CL: **103**
Hillman, Chris
  Byrds FO: 25; RR: 35, 37
  Gene Clark FO: 36
  country rock CO: 45
  Flying Burrito Brothers CO: 75
  Vern Gosdin CO: 84
  Tony Rice FO: 169
Hillmen, The CO: 84
Hill & Range Publishers BL: 47, 218
Hills, Anne FO: 94
Hillyer, Robert CL: 121
Hilton, Joe RB: **121**
Hindemith, Paul CL: **103–104**
  Samuel Adler CL: 4
  Norman Dello Joio CL: 66
  Lukas Foss CL: 81
  Ulysses Kay CL: 124
  Daniel Pinkham CL: 178
  Mel Powell CL: 183
  Harold Shapero CL: 207
  Francis Thorne CL: 224
Hines, Earl "Fatha" BL: 186; JA: 86, **91,** 94, 218
Hinojosa, Tish FO: **97**
Hinton, Joe RB: **121**
hip-hop JA: 2–3; RB: vii–viii, xvii, **121–122**. *See also specific artists*
Hispanic Americans CO: 71–72; RB: 250
Hitchcock, H. Wiley CL: 111
Hite, Bob BL: 36
Hite, Les BL: 236
Hitler, Adolf BL: 202
Hitmen, The RB: 177
Hit Squad RB: 158
Hitsville USA RR: 153
"Hit the Road, Jack" BL: 127; RB: 179
Hobbs, Cliff FO: 45
Hobson, Wilder JA: 4
Hodes, Art BL: 247
Hodges, Johnny JA: 39, 61, 212
Hoener, Clayton CL: 34
Hoffman, Ernst CL: 108
Hoffman, Richard CL: **104**
Hofmann, Josef CL: 29, 49, **104–105,** 204
Hofner, Adolph CO: **100–101**
Hofner, Emil CO: 100
Hogan, Ernest BL: 136
Hog Farm RR: 249
Hogg, Smokey BL: **76**
Hogwood, Christopher CL: 97, 197
Hohner RR: 126, 127
Hoiby, Lee CL: **105**
hokum BL: xix, 54, 208; FO: 3
Holcomb, Roscoe BL: 232; FO: 7, 38, **97–98,** 149
Holder, Terrence JA: 215
Holiday, Billie BL: **76;** JA: **91–92**
  Barbara Carroll JA: 28
  Miles Davis JA: 48
  "God Bless the Child" JA: **76**
  Pleasant Joe BL: 163
  Savoy Ballroom JA: 171
  Artie Shaw JA: 176
  Lester Young JA: 220
Holiday Inn RR: 171
Holidays, The RB: 11
Holiness Church FO: 110
Holland, Brian RB: 123. *See also* Holland-Dozier-Holland
Holland, Dave JA: **92**
  John Abercrombie JA: 1
  Bitches Brew JA: 15
  Anthony Braxton JA: 22

Holland, Dave (*continued*)
- *Conference of the Birds* JA: **41**
- Chick Corea JA: 42
- Anthony Cox JA: 44
- Miles Davis JA: 49
- Charles Lloyd JA: 124
- John McLaughlin JA: 131
- *In a Silent Way* JA: 98

Holland, Eddie RB: 122–123, 277. *See also* Holland-Dozier-Holland

Holland, W. S. "Fluke" CO: 161, 162

Holland-Dozier-Holland RB: **122–123,** 123, 177; RR: 153

Holloway, Red RB: 270

Holly, Buddy CO: **101;** RR: **111–114,** *112*
- Boudleaux and Felice Bryant CO: 27
- Bob Dylan RR: 69–70
- guitar CO: 90
- Carolyn Hester FO: 95
- Waylon Jennings CO: 110
- keyboards RR: 125
- Roy Orbison RR: 165
- rockabilly RR: 205
- Rolling Stones RR: 209
- Ritchie Valens RR: 239

Holly Ridge, Mississippi BL: **138**

Hollywood, California CL: 128; BL: 143; FO: 174

Hollywood String Quartet CL: 5, **105,** 210

Holmes, Richard "Groove" JA: **92,** 129, 148

Holmes, Salty CO: 33

Holst, Gustav CL: 46

Holt, David FO: **98**

holy blues BL: 18, 49–50, **76–79,** 94, 217. *See also* gospel music

Holyfield, Wayland CO: 216

Holy Modal Rounders FO: 67, **98**

Holzman, Jac FO: **99,** 135, 164

"Home on the Range" FO: **99,** 127

Homer and Jethro CO: **101–102,** 108, 181

Home Service FO: 102

Homesick James BL: **79–80,** 123, 148, 171

Homespun Tapes BL: 54, 221; FO: 204

homosexuality BL: 24; RR: 141, 191. *See also* gay culture, disco and

Honegger, Arthur CL: 21

Honey Cone, The RB: **123**

Honeydrippers, The RR: 136, 180

Honeysuckle Rose (movie) CO: 149, 154

honky-tonk music CO: viii, xvii, 87, **102–103**. *See also specific artists*

"Honky Tonk Train Blues" BL: 27, 114

Hood, Adelyne CO: **103**

Hood, David RB: 115, 189

Hooker, Earl BL: **80**
- Louis Myers BL: 148
- Robert Nighthawk BL: 152
- Pinetop Perkins BL: 157
- Son Seals BL: 187
- slide guitar BL: 191
- Muddy Waters BL: 237

Hooker, John Lee BL: **80,** *80;* RB: **123–124**
- aliases BL: 5
- Animals, The BL: 7
- R. L. Burnside BL: 32
- Detroit BL: 52
- Eddie Kirkland BL: 107
- music business BL: 147
- Roy Rogers BL: 185
- San Francisco Bay Area BL: 35
- social history BL: 203
- Baby Boy Warren BL: 237
- young black country blues artists BL: 252

Hoopii, Sol CO: 60; FO: 189

Hoose, David CL: 43

Hoosier Hot Shots CO: **103**

Hoover, Herbert CL: 239; BL: 166, 201

Hoover, Sylvester BL: 138

Hope, Daniel CL: 23

Hopkins, Al CO: 180; FO: 97

Hopkins, Lightnin' BL: **81**
- acoustic guitar BL: 4
- Albert Collins BL: 42
- Guitar Gabriel BL: 68
- Houston, Texas BL: 217
- Chris Strachwitz BL: 207; FO: 195

Hopkins, Mary RR: 60

Hopkinson, Francis CL: viii, xx–xxi, **105,** 160

Hoppers, The FO: 119

Hoppers, Lonnie FO: 46

Hopps, Jimmy JA: 98

Hora Novissima (Horatio Parker) CL: **106**

H.O.R.D.E. festival RR: 53

Horn, Jim CO: 216

Horn, Paul JA: 80

Horn, Shirley JA: *93,* **93**

Horne, Lena JA: 80, **93–94,** 117, 176, 211; RB: **124**

Horne, Marilyn CL: **106**

Hornsby, Bruce JA: 127; RB: 176; RR: 93

Hornsby, Dan BL: 212

Horowitz, Adam (Ad-Rock) RB: 12

Horowitz, Vladimir CL: xxiii, *106,* **106–108**
Ivan Davis CL: 65
Gary Graffman CL: 92
Byron Janis CL: 117
Nathan Milstein CL: 156
Arthur Rubinstein CL: 193
horse operas CO: 46
Horszowski, Mieczyslaw CL: **108,** 139, 148, 204
Horton, Big Walter BL: 16, 73, **81,** 116, 132
Horton, Johnny CO: 13, 63, **103–104,** 112; FO: 6
Horvitz, Wayne JA: 72
Hoskins, Tom BL: 83; FO: 102
hot JA: **94**
Hot Chocolate RB: **124–125**
Hot Chocolates (revue) JA: 27, 210
Hot Club de France JA: **94**
Hot Five and Hot Seven JA: xxiii, **94**
Louis Armstrong JA: 6
Baby Dodds JA: 53
Johnny Dodds JA: 54
Lil Hardin JA: 84
"Heebie Jeebies" JA: **88–89**
Earl "Fatha" Hines JA: 91
Lonnie Johnson BL: 95
recordings of early jazz JA: 162
Hot Harlem Revue RB: 258
hot jazz JA: xxiii, xxxii, 47, 94, **94–95,** 144, 163
Hot Mud Family FO: **99–100**
Hot Rize FO: 43, **100,** 151
Hot Tuna BL: **81;** RR: 120
"Hound Dog" BL: 219; RB: 163, 258; RR: 138
Hour Glass RR: 4
house RB: xvii, 112–113, **125,** 254, 260
House, Son BL: **81–82**
acoustic guitar BL: 3
Willie Brown BL: 31
Canned Heat BL: 36
Cleveland, Mississippi BL: 138
Robert Johnson BL: 97, 98
John Mooney BL: 141
Charley Patton BL: 157
slide guitar BL: 192
vocal styles BL: 229, 230, 232
house band JA: **95,** 212
House of Blues BL: xvi, 143
House of Pain RB: 85
"House of the Rising Sun" BL: 7; CO: 30; RR: 8–9, 84
House Un-American Activities Committee (HUAC) BL: 170, 242; FO: 78, 107, 214
Houston, Cisco FO: 88, **100–101,** 121
Houston, Cissy RB: **125,** 126, 274
Houston, David CO: **104–105**
Houston, Texas BL: **216–217**
Lightnin' Hopkins BL: 81
Robert Earl Keen FO: 114
Lead Belly FO: 123
Amos Milburn BL: 135
Peacock Records BL: 155–156
Big Mama Thornton BL: 217
Eddie "Cleanhead" Vinson BL: 226
Houston, Whitney CO: 158; RB: 25, 125, *126,* **126–127,** 162
Houston Symphony Orchestra CL: **108**
Hovhaness, Alan CL: **108–109**
Howard, Camille RB: 184
Howard, Clint FO: 8
Howard, Frank BL: 136
Howard, Harlan CO: **105**
Patsy Cline CO: 39
Sara Evans CO: 69
Jan Howard CO: 105
Melba Montgomery CO: 142
Ricky Van Shelton CO: 184
Mel Tillis CO: 199
Howard, Jan CO: 4, 105, **105–106**
Howard Theater (Washington, D.C.) JA: 99
Howe, Elias FO: 66
Howe, Steve RR: 184
Howell, Peg Leg BL: 9, 61, **82**
Howlin' Wolf BL: **82**
James Cotton BL: 44
Tommy Johnson BL: 99
Led Zeppelin RR: 134
Little Junior Parker RB: 203
Bonnie Raitt BL: 177
Jimmy Rogers BL: 184
Otis Spann BL: 205
Hubert Sumlin BL: 208
Walls, Mississippi BL: 140
Baby Boy Warren BL: 237
West Point, Mississippi BL: 140
Sonny Boy Williamson II BL: 244
Mighty Joe Young BL: 248
"How Long, How Long Blues" BL: 36, **82–83**
How to Play the 5-String Banjo (Pete Seeger) FO: 13, 170, 182
HUAC. *See* House Un-American Activities Committee
Hubbard, Freddie JA: **95**
Art Blakey JA: 17
Blues and the Abstract Truth, The JA: 19
John Coltrane JA: 40
Malachi Favors JA: 69
Free Jazz (Ornette Coleman) JA: 71
Kenny Garrett JA: 73

Hubbard, Freddie (*continued*)
- Joe Henderson JA: 90
- Michel Petrucciani JA: 154
- Diane Reeves JA: 163
- Miroslav Vitous JA: 207
- "Watermelon Man" JA: 211

Hubbard, Greg "Hobie" CO: 183
Hudson, Garth RR: 11, 13
Hues Corporation RB: **127**
Huff, Dann CO: 166
Huff, Leon RB: 15. *See also* Gamble, Kenny, and Leon Huff
Huggar, R. L. RB: 195
Hughes, Allen CL: 181
Hughes, Jimmy RB: 189
Hughes, Langston FO: 199
Hugo, Chad RB: 193–194
Hugo and Luigi (record producing team) FO: 216
Human Be-In RR: 94
Human League, The RR: 158
Humes, Helen BL: **83**
Humphrey, Bobbi JA: 135
Humphrey, Mark BL: 78
Huneker, James CL: 171
Hungary CL: 198, 213; JA: 224
Hunt, Bill FO: 103
Hunt, Charley BL: 125
Hunter, Alberta BL: **83;** JA: **95**
- Lovie Austin BL: 9; JA: 7
- "Downhearted Blues" BL: 54
- New York City BL: 152, 153
- piano BL: 161
- record labels BL: 178
- Fats Waller JA: 209

Hunter, Ivory Joe RB: **127**
Hunter, Robert RR: 93
Huntington's chorea FO: 87, 88
Hurok, Sol CL: 10, 214; FO: 56
Hurricane RB: 4
Hurston, Zora Neale FO: 199
Hurt, Mississippi John BL: **83–84;** FO: **101–102**
- Avalon, Mississippi BL: 137
- Newport Folk Festival FO: 149
- Harry Smith FO: 190
- "Spike Driver Blues" BL: 205
- vocal styles BL: 229, 232

Hurt, Zack FO: 96
Husky, Ferlin CO: 41, 101, **106,** 177
Hussain, Zakir JA: 132
Hutchence, Michael RR: 237
Hutcherson, Bert FO: 86
Hutcheson, Ernest CL: **109,** 121
Hutchings, Ashley FO: 40, 64, **102,** 117, 194
Hutchinson, Gregory JA: 185
Hutchison, Frank BL: **84,** 231; FO: **103**
Hutto, J. B. BL: 40
Hutton, Danny RR: 149
Huxley, Aldous RR: 62
Hylton, Jack JA: 25, 87
hymns FO: 183–184
Hynde, Chrissie RR: 128, 157

I

"I Am a Man of Constant Sorrow" CO: **107;** FO: 6
Ian, Janis FO: **105**
Ian and Sylvia FO: *105,* **105–106,** 125
Ibbotson, Jimmy CO: 151; FO: 136
"I Believe I'll Dust My Broom." *See* "Dust My Broom"
Ibrahim, Abdullah JA: **97,** 186, 187; RB: 178
"I Can't Stop Loving You" CO: 81, **107**
Ice Cube RB: *129,* **129–130**
- Color Me Badd RB: 47
- Dr Dre RB: 71
- Kam RB: 149
- N.W.A. RB: 196
- Westside Connection RB: 277

Ice Field (Henry Brant) CL: 37, **111**
Ice–T RB: 84, **130**
Ichiban Records BL: **85**
Ickes, Harold L. BL: 201
Idan, John RR: 253
"I Didn't Hear Nobody Pray." *See* "Wreck on the Highway"
"I Fall to Pieces" CO: 39, 105, **107**
"I Feel Like I'm Fixin' to Die Rag" FO: 135, 196
"If I Had My Way (Samson and Delilah)" BL: 50, 78; FO: **106**
"If You Could Read My Mind" FO: 126; RR: 221
"If You Got the Money, Honey, I've Got the Time" CO: 78, **107**
Iglauer, Bruce BL: 5, 51, **85,** 189, 213
"I'll Fly Away" CO: 26, 37, 86; FO: 22
Illinois BL: 74, 140, 221. *See also* Chicago
Illusion RR: 253
"I'm a Lonesome Fugitive." *See* "The Fugitive"
Imbrie, Andrew CL: **111**
immigrants/immigration CL: xix, xxi, xxiv; BL: 125, 133, 137; FO: 66. *See also* migration
"I'm Moving On" CO: 36, **107–108,** 188
Impressions, The RB: 30–31, **130–132**
improvisation BL: **85–86;** JA: xxviii, **97,** 185, 192; RR: 94, 96–97
"I'm Walkin'" RR: 58–59, 155

"In a Sentimental Mood" JA: **98**
In a Silent Way (Miles Davis) JA: **98**
  Chick Corea JA: 42
  Miles Davis JA: 49
  Dave Holland JA: 92
  jazz firsts JA: 116
  John McLaughlin JA: 131
  Joe Zawinul JA: 223
Incognito JA: 2
Incredible Jazz Guitar of Wes Montgomery, The JA: **98**
Incredible String Band, The FO: **106**
indentured servitude BL: 195
independent record distributors BL: 106–107
independent record labels BL: 178, 179; FO: ix. *See also* record labels
India FO: 100
Indiana BL: **86**
Indianapolis, Indiana BL: **86**
Indian music CL: 89
Indianola, Mississippi BL: 104, **138,** 190
indie rock RR: 97. *See also* alternative rock
Industrial Workers of the World (IWW) FO: ix, 94, 158
"I Never Promised You a Rose Garden." *See* "Rose Garden"
Infante, Frank RR: 27, 28
Inflated Tear, The (Rahsaan Roland Kirk) JA: **98,** 114
inflection JA: **98**
Ingersoll, Charles RB: 289
Ingram, Luther RB: 247
Ingram, Philip RB: 251
the Ink Spots RR: 65
In Memory of a Summer Day (David Del Tredici) CL: 66, **111**
Inner City RB: **132**
Inner Mounting Flame, The (John McLaughlin and the Mahavishnu Orchestra) JA: **99**
Instant Funk RB: **132**
Institute for Studies in American Music CL: **111**
Institute of Musical Art CL: 66, 83, 120, 170, 188. *See also* Juilliard School of Music
Instrumental Music of the Southern Appalachians BL: 11; FO: 11
instrumental rock RR: xix, **115–116**
instruments (blues) BL: **86–87**
integration BL: 202; JA: 196
Intelligent Hoodlum RB: **132**
International Association of Jazz Educators JA: 196
International Society for Contemporary Music. *See* League of Composers/International Society for Contemporary Music
International Sweethearts of Rhythm JA: xxx–xxxi, 47, **99,** 130
Internet CL: 251; BL: 148; FO: 164; RR: 53, 196
"In the Jailhouse Now" CO: **108,** 162, 177
Intruders, The RB: **132**
Invictus/Hot Wax RB: 122, 123
Iommi, Tony RR: 106
Iovine, Jimmy RB: 81; RR: 236
Irakere JA: 170
Iraq War (2003) CO: 45
Ireland/Irish music FO: 10, 66, 69, 70. *See also specific musicians*
Irie, Clement RB: 10
Irish Rovers, The FO: **106–107**
Iron Butterfly RR: 41
Iron Maiden RR: 106
Irons, Jack RR: 168
Irvine, Andy FO: 19, 24, **107,** 158
Irwin, Bill FO: 165
Irwin, Ken BL: 186
Isaacs, Bud CO: 161, 186
Isaac Stern Auditorium CL: 45, **112,** 215
"I Saw the Light" CO: 37, 216
Isbin, Sharon CL: *112,* **112**
"I Shot the Sheriff" RR: 40, 199, 201
Islam RB: 132, 149, 256
Island Records RB: **133**. *See also* Blackwell, Chris
Isle of Wight Festival RR: 206–207
Isles, Bill RB: 199
Isley, Ernie RB: 134
Isley, Ronald RB: 134
the Isley Brothers RB: *133,* **133–134,** 184, 281
Istomin, Eugene CL: **112–113,** 191, 214
Italian-Americans RB: 67–68
"It Don't Mean a Thing (If It Ain't Got That Swing)" JA: 5, **99,** 116
Ithaca, New York FO: 42–43, 96
I-Threes RB: **134**
"It Wasn't God Who Made Honky Tonk Angels" CO: 102, 212–213, 215
Iverson, Ethan JA: 9
Ives, Burl FO: 94, **107,** 118
Ives, Charles CL: **113–115**
  John J. Becker CL: 24
  Peter J. Burkholder CL: 40
  Elliott Carter CL: 46
  Concord Sonata CL: **55**
  Lawrence Gilman CL: 88

Ives, Charles (*continued*)
  Lou Harrison CL: 99
  John Kirkpatrick CL: 126
  William Masselos CL: 150
  114 Songs CL: **168**
  recommended listening CL: 250
  Wallingford Riegger CL: 189
  Carl Ruggles CL: 195
Ives, George CL: 113
Ivey, Michael RB: 11
Iveys, The RR: 177
"I Walk the Line" CO: 35, **108**
"I Want to Be a Cowboy's Sweetheart" CO: 46, **108,** 141
Izquierdo, Tony RB: 261

J

Jackie & Gayle FO: 146
Jack Johnson (Miles Davis) JA: 131, 175
Jackson, Al, Jr. BL: 104; RB: 10, 23, *23,* 24
Jackson, Al, Sr. RB: 185
Jackson, Alan BL: 7, 145; CO: 64, **109,** *109,* 193
Jackson, Aunt Molly FO: 70, **109,** 214
Jackson, Brian RB: 235
Jackson, Bruce RR: 71
Jackson, Bull Moose RB: **135,** 183
Jackson, Chuck RB: 58
Jackson, D. D. JA: **101**
Jackson, Fruteland BL: 251, 252
Jackson, Jack FO: 16
Jackson, Jackie RB: 1
Jackson, Janet RB: **135–136,** 138
Jackson, Jermaine RB: 251
Jackson, Jim BL: **89,** 103, 114, 205
Jackson, John BL: 13, **89**
Jackson, Mahalia BL: 79
Jackson, Michael RB: *136,* **136–138,** *137*
  Beatles, The RR: 22
  Quincy Jones JA: 109, 110
  Lionel Richie RB: 224–225
  Jimmy Smith JA: 183
Jackson, Millie RB: **138**
Jackson, Milt JA: 62, 90–91, 123, 138, 188
Jackson, Mississippi BL: **138–139**
  Lillian McMurry BL: 129
  record labels BL: 181
  H. C. Speir BL: 206
  Houston Stackhouse BL: 206
  Johnny Temple BL: 215
  Cassandra Wilson JA: 217
Jackson, Papa Charlie BL: xviii, 14, 18, 45, **89**
Jackson, Paul JA: 88
Jackson, Stonewall CO: 136
Jackson, Tommy BL: 107; CO: 72
Jackson, Wanda CO: 38, 61, 198; FO: 69
Jackson, Wayne RB: 175, 182
Jackson 5, The RB: 135, *136,* 137; RR: 154
Jacksonville, Florida BL: 18
Jacobs, Paul CL: 229
Jacobs, Walter. *See* Little Walter
Jacquet, Illinois JA: 81, 86, **101,** 197; RB: 92
Jagger, Mick
  David Bowie RR: 32
  Chieftains FO: 33
  Jan Hammer JA: 81
  Motown RR: 153
  reggae RR: 201
  Rolling Stones, The BL: 185; RR: 208, 210
jail. *See also* Angola Penitentiary; Parchman Penitentiary
  Texas Alexander BL: 4
  Chuck Berry BL: 16
  blues lyrics BL: 22
  Freddy Fender CO: 71–72
  Merle Haggard CO: 91
  Ted Hawkins BL: 74–75
  Lead Belly BL: 112; FO: 123
JALC. *See* Jazz at Lincoln Center
jam JA: **102**
Jam, The RR: 188
Jam, Jimmy and Terry Lewis RB: 94, 135, **138,** 195, 235
Jamaica RB: 18, 73–74, 133, 221–223; RR: 199–201
Jamal, Ahmad JA: **102**
"Jambalaya" CO: 29, 217
jam bands JA: 133, 173; RR: xx, **117–118**. *See also specific bands*
  psychedelic rock RR: 187
Jamboree U.S.A. (WWVA radio show) CO: 143, 157
Jamerson, James RR: 15, 153
James, Elmore BL: xx, **90**
  acoustic guitar BL: 3
  Chicago BL: 40
  "Dust My Broom" BL: 55
  Homesick James BL: 79
  Robert Johnson BL: 98
  Lillian McMurry BL: 130
  slide guitar BL: 193
  Big Joe Turner RR: 232
  vocal styles BL: 231
James, Etta BL: 39, **90,** *91;* RB: **138–139**
James, Fanita RB: 21
James, Harry JA: 48, **102,** 198
James, Homesick BL: 28, 90; RB: 279
James, J. L. FO: 169
James, Jimmy, and the Blue Flames RR: 108–109
James, Rick RB: 98, 99, **139–140,** *140,* 189; RR: 154
James, Skip BL: **90**
  Bentonia, Mississippi BL: 137

John Fahey BL: 61
holy blues BL: 77
Jack Owens BL: 155
Johnny Temple BL: 215
tunings BL: 223
vocal styles BL: 230, 232
young black country blues artists BL: 250
James, Sonny CO: 27, 155
James, Steve BL: **91**
Jamestown, Virginia BL: 195
Jamiroquai RB: **140**
Jamison, Roosevelt RB: 283
Jam Master Jay RB: 219, 232
jam session JA: 45–46, **102,** 106, 137
jangle pop RR: 176
Janis, Byron CL: **117,** 148
Jans, Tom FO: 66
Jansch, Bert FO: 79, **109,** 156, 167
Jansons, Mariss CL: **117,** 179
Janssen, Werner CL: **117–118**
Japan JA: 3–4, 116, 126, 197; RR: ix
Japanese jazz JA: **102–103**
Jardine, Al RR: 15
Jarman, Joseph JA: 6
Jarobi RB: 260
Jarreau, Al JA: **103–104**
Jarrell, B. F. FO: 67, 110
Jarrell, Ben FO: 37, 110
Jarrell, Tommy FO: 29, 37, 67, 76, **110**
Jarrett, Keith JA: *104,* **104–105**
Art Blakey JA: 17
Jack DeJohnette JA: 51
Jan Garbarek JA: 73
Charlie Haden JA: 79
Charles Lloyd JA: 124
Ja Rule RB: **140**
Järvi, Neeme CL: 68, **118,** 163
Järvi, Paarvo CL: 51, *118,* **118**
Jarvis, Felton BL: 44
JATP. *See* Jazz at the Philharmonic
Jay and the Americans RR: 226
Jayhawks, The RB: **140–141**
Jayne, Mitch FO: 52
Jaynetts, The RB: **141**
Jay-Z RB: 140, **141–142,** 185, 191
jazz JA: xxi. *See also specific artists*
Jazz Age, The JA: xxiii, **105–106,** 144, 188–189, 206
jazz and the blues BL: **91–93**
Jazz at Lincoln Center (JALC) CL: 148; JA: x–xi, **106,** 128
Jazz at Lincoln Center Hall of Fame JA: **273**
Jazz at the Philharmonic (JATP) JA: **106**
Ray Brown JA: 24
cutting contest JA: 45–46
Roy Eldridge JA: 60
Dizzy Gillespie JA: 75
Coleman Hawkins JA: 87–88
Illinois Jacquet JA: 101
Japanese jazz JA: 103
Hank Jones JA: 109
Gene Krupa JA: 115
Oscar Peterson JA: 153
Ben Webster JA: 213
Lester Young JA: 220
jazz clubs JA: 14–15
Jazz Composer's Orchestra JA: 9, 18, 79, 127, 170
Jazz Epistles JA: 117, 186; RB: 178
jazz festivals BL: 245; JA: 129, 139, 143, 144
jazz firsts JA: 116–117
Jazz Hall of Fame (Jazz History Museum) JA: x–xi
Jazz: Hot and Hybrid (Winthrop Sargeant) JA: **106,** 116, 117
Jazz in Africa (Jazz Epistles) JA: 97, 117
Jazz Institute of Chicago JA: **106**
jazz instruments JA: xxv–xxvii. *See also specific musical instruments*
Jazz Maniacs JA: 186
Jazz Messengers CL: 148; JA: 17, 21, 137–138, 180
Jazz Passengers RR: 28
Jazz Profiles (NPR program) JA: 218
Jazz Record Mart (Chicago) BL: 41, 108
Jazz Revellers JA: 186
jazz-rock fusion. *See* fusion
jazz styles, evolution of JA: 252*t. See also specific styles, e.g.:* bebop
Jazztet (Art Farmer, Benny Golson) JA: 69
Jazz Times JA: **106**
Jazz Warriors JA: 217
Jean, Wyclef RB: 97–98; RR: 214
Jefferson, Blind Lemon BL: xviii, **93–94**
acoustic guitar BL: 1
blind musicians and singers BL: 18, 19
blues lyrics BL: 20
Ishmon Bracey BL: 29
Chicago BL: 41
country blues BL: 45
Dallas, Texas BL: 216
holy blues BL: 77
Lightnin' Hopkins BL: 81
Lead Belly BL: 112; FO: 123
music business BL: 144
Carl Perkins BL: 158
protest songs BL: 167
"See That My Grave Is Kept Clean" BL: 189

Jefferson, Blind Lemon (*continued*)
Victoria Spivey BL: 206
vocal styles BL: 231
T-Bone Walker BL: 236
Jefferson Airplane (Jefferson Starship) BL: 62, 81; RR: 61, **118–121,** 151, 248
Jefferson Starship—The Next Generation RR: 121
Jelly Beans, The RB: **142**
Jenkins, Bobo BL: 237
Jenkins, DeWitt "Snuffy" CO: 73; FO: 59, 110, 111
Jenkins, Gordon FO: 212
Jenkins, Johnny RB: 220
Jenkins, Leroy JA: 7, **106–107**
Jenkins, Reverend Andrew FO: **110**
Jenkins, Verl FO: 110
Jenkins and Sherrill FO: **110–111**
Jenkins String Band FO: 110
Jennings, Greg CO: 98
Jennings, John CO: 32
Jennings, Mary FO: 87
Jennings, Waylon CO: **110,** *110*
Bobby Bare CO: 12
Johnny Cash CO: 35
Guy Clark FO: 36
"Cowboy" Jack Clement CO: 39
Jessi Colter CO: 41, 42
cowboy songs CO: 46
Buddy Holly CO: 101; RR: 113
Kris Kristofferson CO: 119
"Mamas Don't Let Your Babies Grow up to Be Cowboys" CO: 131
Willie Nelson CO: 149
Hank Williams, Jr. CO: 217
Jensen, Ingrid JA: **107**
Jericho CO: 13
Jerk, The RB: 162
Jerrigan, Doug FO: 37
Jessop, Craig CL: 159
Jethro Tull RR: 184–185
J. Geils Band BL: **94**
Jim and Jesse (McReynolds) BL: 125; CO: 202; FO: 37, **111**
"Jim Crow" BL: 166, 168
Jimenez, Flaco CO: 72; FO: 177, 202
Jimi Hendrix Experience RR: 109
Jim Kweskin's Jug Band. *See* Kweskin, Jim
Jive Bombers, The RB: **142**
Jobim, Antonio Carlos JA: 74, 75, **107**
Jodeci RB: 79, 258
Joel, Billy RR: 205
Joe's King Biscuit Boys BL: 243
Johannesen, Grant CL: 52, **118**
Johansen, Gunnar CL: **118–119**
Johanson, Jai Johanny BL: 6; RR: 4, 6
John, Little Willie RB: **142–143**
John, Mabel RB: 217
Johnnie and Jack CO: 123, 212; FO: 133
Johnnie and Joe RB: 141
"Johnny B. Goode" RR: ix, 23
Johnny Moore's Three Blazers BL: 30; RB: 25, **143**
Johns, Glyn RR: 74
Johns, Paul Emile CL: **119**
Johnson, Al RB: 266
Johnson, Beverly CL: 80
Johnson, Big Jack BL: **94**
Johnson, Bill JA: 52, 112, 147
Johnson, Blind Willie BL: 76–79, **94,** 192, 230, 242
Johnson, Budd JA: 212
Johnson, Corinthian "Kripp" RB: 57, 58
Johnson, Courtney FO: 146, 147
Johnson, Doug CO: 99
Johnson, Edward CL: **119**
Johnson, Gene CO: 56
Johnson, George and Louis RB: 25
Johnson, George W. JA: 183
Johnson, J. J. JA: 15, 23, 29
Johnson, J. Rosamund BL: 136, 137
Johnson, Jack (boxer) JA: 44
Johnson, James P. JA: xxiii, **107–108**
Count Basie JA: 10
"Charleston" JA: **30–31**
jazz firsts JA: 116
New York City JA: 144
piano JA: 155
ragtime and the blues BL: 176
Bessie Smith JA: 183
social history and the blues BL: 201
stride piano JA: 189
Fats Waller JA: 209, 210
Johnson, James "Steady Roll" BL: 62
Johnson, James Weldon BL: 136
Johnson, Jimmy (Chicago blues singer/guitarist) RB: **143**
Johnson, Jimmy (Muscle Shoals studio guitarist) RB: 115, 189
Johnson, Johnnie BL: **94–95;** RB: **143;** RR: 24
Johnson, Larry BL: 28, **95,** 233, 250
Johnson, Le Dell BL: 99
Johnson, Leslie. *See* Lazy Lester
Johnson, Lonnie BL: *95,* **95–96;** RB: **144**
acoustic guitar BL: 1, 3
Texas Alexander BL: 4
Scrapper Blackwell BL: 17
Chicago BL: 41

country blues BL: 45
fiddle BL: 62
Helen Humes BL: 83
B. B. King BL: 105
New Orleans BL: 121
St. Louis BL: 140
Jesse (Babyface) Thomas BL: 219
Johnson, Lulu Grace. *See* Howard, Jan
Johnson, Luther "Georgia Boy" BL: 126
Johnson, Lyndon B. FO: 209
Johnson, Marv RB: **144,** 188
Johnson, Pete BL: 27, **96,** 114, 223; RB: 262
Johnson, Plas BL: 182
Johnson, Robert BL: xvi, xix, xxi, **96–99**
acoustic guitar BL: 3
Kokomo Arnold BL: 8
boogie-woogie BL: 28
Big Bill Broonzy BL: 29
Willie Brown BL: 31
Eric Clapton BL: 41–42
crossroads BL: 46–47
"Crossroads Blues" BL: 47
"Dust My Broom" BL: 55
David "Honeyboy" Edwards BL: 57
Friars Point, Mississippi BL: 138
Greenwood, Mississippi BL: 138
Peter Guralnick BL: 69
John Hammond, Sr. BL: 71
improvisation BL: 86
Elmore James BL: 90
Led Zeppelin RR: 134
Robert Lockwood, Jr. BL: 116
Morgan City, Mississippi BL: 139
music business BL: 143, 145
Johnny Shines BL: 191
slide guitar BL: 192
H. C. Speir BL: 205
"Sweet Home Chicago" BL: 210
Henry Townsend BL: 221
vocal styles BL: 230
Elijah Wald BL: 235
Sonny Boy Williamson II BL: 244
young black country blues artists BL: 251
Johnson, Syl RB: 51
Johnson, Thor CL: 51, **119;** BL: 128
Johnson, Tommy (Delta blues guitarist) BL: **99**
Ishmon Bracey BL: 29
Canned Heat BL: 36
Robert Johnson BL: 97
mandolin BL: 125
Houston Stackhouse BL: 206
Walter Vinson BL: 228
vocal styles BL: 230
Johnson, Tommy (funk musician) RB: 25
Johnson, Willie BL: 19
Johnson Mountain Boys CO: 16; FO: **111**
Johnston, Ben CL: **119,** 174
Johnston, Bob FO: 194
Johnston, Bruce RR: 16, 18
Johnstons, The FO: 19, **111–112,** 141
Jolson, Al CL: 86
Jones, Bessie FO: **112**
Jones, Booker T. BL: 132, 180; RB: *23,* 23–24, 282; RR: 125. *See also* Booker T. & the MGs
Jones, Brian BL: 185; RR: 208
Jones, Chuck CO: 154
Jones, Coley BL: 125
Jones, Creadel "Red" RB: 41, 42
Jones, Curtis BL: **99,** 162
Jones, Davy RR: 149, 151
Jones, Elvin JA: *108,* **108–109**
John Coltrane JA: 40, 41
Ravi Coltrane JA: 41
Anthony Cox JA: 44
Joey DeFrancesco JA: 51
Abdullah Ibrahim JA: 97
"In a Sentimental Mood" JA: 98
Japanese jazz JA: 103
A Love Supreme JA: 124
"My Favorite Things" JA: 142
Courtney Pine JA: 155
Sonny Rollins JA: 166
Sonny Sharrock JA: 175
Cecil Taylor JA: 195
Larry Young JA: 219
Jones, Eva Thompson FO: 203
Jones, George CO: ix, **110–111,** *111*
Harold "Pappy" Daily CO: 52
Emory Gordy, Jr. CO: 84
Freddie Hart CO: 95
Alan Jackson CO: 109
Brenda Lee CO: 121
Melba Montgomery CO: 142
George Morgan CO: 143
Eddie Noack CO: 152
Johnny Paycheck CO: 159
record labels CO: 169
"She Thinks I Still Care" CO: 185
Tammy Wynette CO: 221
yodeling CO: 224
Jones, Glenn RB: **144–145**
Jones, Gordon FO: 185
Jones, Grandpa CO: 56, **111–112,** 180, 200
Jones, Hank JA: **109,** 218
Jones, Isham JA: 90
Jones, James Earl III RB: 244

Jones, Jimmy RB: **145**
Jones, Joe (singer and manager) RB: 11, 62
Jones, John Paul BL: 113; RR: 60, 133, 134, 136
Jones, Kenny RR: 246
Jones, Norah CO: 40
Jones, Ollie RB: 19, 218
Jones, Paul RR: 34
Jones, Philly Joe JA: 19, 30, 46, 49, **109,** 169
Jones, Quincy JA: 81, **109–110,** 123, 196; RB: 137
Jones, Richard M. BL: 162, 211, 222
Jones, Robert FO: 149
Jones, Robert Lewis. *See* Guitar Gabriel
Jones, Sissieretta CL: **119–120;** BL: xv
Jones, Sonny BL: 68
Jones, Thad JA: 3, **110,** 122, 136, 187, 191
Jones, Thad—Mel Lewis Orchestra JA: 3, 23, 109, 110, 122
Jones, Tom BL: 233
Jones, Will "Dub" RB: 33, 46
Jon Spencer Blues Explosion BL: 32, **99**
Joplin, Janis BL: **99–100**
  Austin, Texas BL: 216
  Albert Grossman FO: 84
  "Kansas City Blues" BL: 103
  Kris Kristofferson CO: 118–119
  "Me and Bobby McGee" CO: 139
  Monterey Pop Festival RR: 151
  Port Arthur, Texas BL: 217
  Bessie Smith BL: 194
  Big Mama Thornton BL: 219
Joplin, Laura BL: 100
Joplin, Scott CL: **120;** JA: **110**
  "Maple Leaf Rag" JA: 127
  New York City BL: 152
  ragtime JA: 161
  ragtime and the blues BL: 176
  St. Louis, Missouri BL: 140
  Gunther Schuller JA: 172
Jorda, Enrique CL: **120,** 199
Jordan, Charley BL: 241
Jordan, Louis BL: **100;** RB: *145,* **145–146**
  Annisteen Allen RB: 5
  jump blues BL: 101
  Lambert, Hendricks, and Ross JA: 120
  rhythm and blues combos BL: 182
  social history and the blues BL: 202
  Eddie "Cleanhead" Vinson BL: 228
Jordanaires CO: 86, **112–113,** 147; RB: 210; RR: 156, 181
Joseph, Papa John JA: 10
Josephson, Barney BL: 83; FO: 21
Josephson, Nancy FO: 23
Joshua Tree, The (U2) RR: 235, 236
Joyce, Teddy, and the Girlfriends JA: 13
Judaism FO: 117–118
Judas Priest RR: 106
Judd, Cledus T. CO: **113**
Judd, Naomi CO: 113
Judd, Wynonna CO: 113
Judds, The CO: **113,** 131
Judson, Arthur CL: 169, 190
jug bands BL: **100–101**
Juice Crew, The RB: 176
"Juke" BL: 73, 116
jukebox CO: 102
Julian, Don RB: 162
Juilliard, August D. CL: 120
Juilliard School of Music CL: xxiv, xxv, **120–121**
Juilliard String Quartet CL: 2, **121**
jump blues BL: 74, 100, **101**
jungle RB: xvii, 73, **146**
Jungle Brothers RB: **146–147,** 192
Junior RB: **147**
junking BL: viii
Just-Ice RB: **147**
Justis, Bill CO: 173; RR: 171
Justman, Seth BL: 94
Juvenile RB: **147**
JXL RR: 182

K

Kaapana, Led FO: 22
Kabongo, Sabine JA: 223
Kahane, Jeffrey CL: 141
Kahn, Eric Itor CL: **123**
Kahn, Si FO: **113,** *113*
Kalb, Danny BL: 25
Kalem, Rachel FO: 188
Kalichstein, Joseph CL: **123**
Kalish, Gilbert CL: **123**
Kallick, Kathy FO: 79, 125
Kam RB: **149**
Kamen, Michael RR: 147
Kaminski, Mik RR: 77
Kaminsky, Max JA: 15
Kanawha River Valley FO: 66, 115
Kane, Barry FO: 146
Kane, Big Daddy RB: 209
Kangol Kid RB: 268
Kansas BL: 133; FO: 129, 174–175
"Kansas City" BL: 183; RR: 138

Kansas City, Missouri See also Kansas City jazz BL: **140**
Jay McShann BL: 130
migration BL: 133
Jimmy Rushing BL: 188
Big Joe Turner BL: 223; RB: 261–262; RR: 232
"Kansas City Blues" BL: 89, **103**
Kansas City jazz JA: xxiii, **111**
American Jazz Museum JA: 4
Count Basie JA: 10
Coleman Hawkins JA: 87
Bennie Moten JA: **141**
Charlie Parker JA: 151
time line JA: 252*t*
Mary Lou Williams JA: 215
Kantner, Paul RR: 119–121
Kapell, William CL: **123**
Kaplan, Fats BL: 28
Kapp, Richard CL: 177
Karl and Harty FO: 155
Katchen, Julius CL: **123**
Katz, Gary RR: 226
Katz, Mickey CO: 185
Katz, Mike FO: 13
Katz, Steve BL: 25, 153
Kaukonen, Jorma BL: 81; RR: 119, 120
Kavafian, Ani CL: **123,** 221
Kay, Connie JA: 138
Kay, Jason "Jay" RB: 140
Kay, John RR: 228, 229
Kay, Stanley JA: 53
Kay, Ulysses CL: **124**
Kay–Dots CO: 213
Kaye, Carol RR: 14
Kay Gee RB: 192, 195
Kaylan, Howard RR: 258
Kazan, Elia FO: 78
Kazee, Buell FO: **113–114**
KC & the Sunshine Band RB: **149**
K-Doe, Ernie BL: 220; RB: **149–150**
Keane, Bob RR: 239
Keane, Dolores FO: 50
Keane, Jimmy FO: 29
Keane, Sean FO: 33
Keb Mo'. *See* Mo', Keb
Keen, Robert Earl FO: **114**
Keenan, Paddy FO: 17
Keene, Christopher CL: **124**
Keepnews, Orrin JA: 158
"Keep on Pushing" BL: 25, 203
"Keep on the Sunnyside" CO: **115**
Kegrize, Michael CL: 204
Keil, Charles BL: 104
Keilholz, Heinrich CL: 5
Keillor, Garrison CO: 180–181
Keita, Salif JA: 223
Keith, Bill FO: **114**
Kenny Baker FO: 11
bluegrass music CO: 15–16
Richard Greene FO: 81
David Grisman FO: 83
Jim Kweskin FO: 119
Del McCoury FO: 134
Muleskinner FO: 143, 144
Jim Rooney FO: 176
Happy and Artie Traum FO: 204
Tony Trischka FO: 205
vocal styles BL: 231
Keith, Toby CO: 45, **115–116,** 150, 197
Keith vaudeville circuit CO: 31
Kekuku, Joseph BL: 191–192; CO: 60
Kelley, Edgar Stillman CL: **124**
Kelley, Kevin RR: 37
Kellogg, Clara Louise CL: **124**
Kellogg, Paul CL: 164
Kellogg's Corn Flakes CO: 101
Kelly, Jo Ann BL: **103,** 133
Kelly, Luke FO: 55
Kelly, Mark FO: 4
Kelly, R. RB: **150**
Kelly, Wynton JA: 74, 113, 211
Kelso, Beverly RB: 175
Keltner, Jim FO: 95
Kemp, Rick FO: 194
Kendrick, Nat RB: 276
Kendricks, Eddie RB: **151,** 254, 255
Kennedy, Frankie FO: 4
Kennedy, Jerry CO: 169
Kennedy, John F. CL: 10, 125, 205; RR: 32
Kennedy, Peter FO: 42
Kennedy Center for the Performing Arts CL: **124–125**
Leonard Bernstein CL: 27
Lionel Hampton JA: 81
Yo-Yo Ma CL: 145
Mary Lou Williams Women in Jazz Festival JA: 129
Mass (Bernstein) CL: **149–150**
National Symphony Orchestra CL: 162
Kenny, Bill RR: 65
Kenny G. *See* G., Kenny
Kenton, Stan JA: **111–112**
Pepper Adams JA: 3
Maynard Ferguson JA: 70
Mel Lewis JA: 122
progressive jazz JA: 158
Zoot Sims JA: 182
third stream jazz JA: 197
Kentucky Club (New York) JA: 60
Kentucky Colonels, The FO: **114–115**
Kentucky Thunder CO: 16, 186
Keppard, Freddie JA: *112,* **112–113**
Baby Dodds JA: 53
jazz firsts JA: 115
Original Dixieland Jazz Band JA: 149, 150

Keppard, Freddie (*continued*)
    recordings of early jazz JA: 162
Kernis, Aaron Jay CL: **125,** 134
Kerouac, Jack RR: 93
Kerr, Anita CO: **116**. *See also* Anita Kerr Singers
Kerr, Janet FO: 148
Kerrick, Jack FO: 165
Kerrville Folk Festival FO: 184
Kershaw, Doug CO: 29, **116**
Kershaw, Nelson "Pee Wee" CO: 116
Kershaw, Rusty CO: 29, 116
Kershaw, Sammy CO: 143
Kesey, Ken RR: 93
Kessinger, Clark W. FO: 66, **115**
Kessinger, Luke FO: 115
Kessinger Brothers FO: 115
Kettering, Frank CO: 103
keyboards BL: 162–163; RR: **125–128,** 182, 184, 185. *See also specific keyboard instrument, e.g.:* synthesizer
Keyes, Johnny RB: 174
Keys, Alicia RB: *151,* **151–152**
"Key to the Highway" BL: 29, **103–104**
KFDM (Beaumont, Texas) RB: 127
KFFA (Helena, Arkansas) BL: 73, 90, 117, 175; RB: 279. *See also* King Biscuit Radio Show
Khan, Chaka RB: **152**
Khan, Erich Itor CL: 4
Khan, Taka Boom RB: 266
Kid 'N Play RB: **152**
Kid Rock CO: 40, 217
Kid Stormy Weather BL: 165
Kiker, Harry FO: 53
Kikoski, Dave JA: 185
Kilbride, Pat FO: 13
Killebrew, Willie "Sonny" RB: 244
Killen, Buddy CO: 136
Killen, Edgar Ray FO: 34
Kilmer, Val RR: 64
Kim, Earl CL: 98, **126**
Kim, Young Uck CL: **126**
Kimbrough, Junior BL: **104**
Kimmel Center for the Performing Arts CL: **126,** 160, 170, 176, 199
Kincaid, Bradley CO: 112; FO: **116,** 173
Kincaid, Jesse BL: 68
Kindler, Hands CL: 162
Kind of Blue (Miles Davis) JA: 3, 49, 65–66, **113,** 117, 138
King, Albert BL: **104;** RB: **152–153**
    Michael Bloomfield BL: 20
    Rory Gallagher BL: 67
    Indianola, Mississippi BL: 138
    Memphis BL: 132
    Son Seals BL: 189
    Mighty Joe Young BL: 248
    young black country blues artists BL: 250
King, B. B. BL: xvi, xx, **104–106,** *105;* RB: *153,* **153–154**
    Johnny Ace RB: 2
    Bobby "Blue" Bland BL: 18; RB: 19
    Eric Clapton BL: 42
    electric guitar BL: 59
    improvisation BL: 85
    Indianola, Mississippi BL: 138
    Magic Sam BL: 123
    Memphis BL: 131, 132
    Pinetop Perkins BL: 159
    radio BL: 175
    social history BL: 203
    "The Thrill Is Gone" BL: 220
    T-Bone Walker BL: 236
    Joe Willie Wilkins BL: 243
    young black country blues artists BL: 248, 250
King, Ben E. RB: 72
King, Bnois BL: 109
King, Carole
    girl groups RR: 91
    Monkees RR: 150, 151
    pop rock RR: 175
    Shirelles RR: 217
    singer-songwriters RR: 221
King, David JA: 9
King, Don BL: 165
King, Don (vocalist) CO: 183
King, Freddie BL: **106;** RB: **154**
    Tyrone Davis RB: 54
    Smokin' Joe Kubek BL: 109
    Lonnie Mack BL: 123
    T-Bone Walker BL: 236
    young black country blues artists BL: 250
King, Pee Wee CO: 5, 43, 87, **116–117,** 191, 197
King, Rodney RB: 20, 130, 280
King Bees RR: 30
King Biscuit Boys BL: 206
King Biscuit Radio Show
    Arkansas BL: 7
    harmonica BL: 73
    Elmore James BL: 90
    Robert Lockwood, Jr. BL: 117
    Robert Nighthawk BL: 154
    Pinetop Perkins BL: 158
    radio BL: 175
    Joe Willie Wilkins BL: 243
    Sonny Boy Williamson II BL: 244
King Crimson RR: 183–185
King Curtis BL: **106;** RB: **154–155**
    Annisteen Allen RB: 5
    Duane Allman BL: 6

the Coasters RB: 46
Guitar Gabriel BL: 68
Freddie King BL: 106
rhythm and blues combos BL: 182
King David Jug Band BL: 125
"King of the Road" CO: **117,** 140
King Records BL: **106–107**. *See also* Nathan, Syd
record labels CO: 169
King Sisters CO: 58
Kings of Rhythm (Ike Turner band) RB: 262; RR: 170
Kingston, Jamaica RR: 200
Kingston, North Carolina BL: 120
Kingston Trio FO: ix, xv–xvi, **116–117**
folk revival FO: 70
Frank Proffitt FO: 160
"Tom Dooley" FO: 203, 204
"Wimoweh" FO: 215–216
Kinks, The RR: **128**
Kinsey, Lester "Big Daddy" BL: **107**
Kinsey Report, The BL: 107
Kinsmen, The FO: 22
Kiokee, George Leile BL: 196
Kirby, Fred CO: 31
Kirby, Marion FO: 150
Kirby, Pete. *See* Oswald, Bashful Brother
Kirchner, Leon CL: 2, 34, **126**
Kirk, Andy JA: 109, 213, 215
Kirk, Rahsaan Roland JA: *113,* **113–114;** RB: **155**
circular breathing JA: 33
Andrew Cyrille JA: 46
Inflated Tear, The JA: **98**
Keith Jarrett JA: 104
Leroy Jenkins JA: 107
Charles Mingus JA: 136
George Russell JA: 167
Kirkland, Eddie BL: 52, **107,** 237
Kirkpatrick, Darrell FO: 96
Kirkpatrick, John CL: 55, 114, **126**
Kirkpatrick, John (folk artist) FO: 30, **117,** 194
Kirkpatrick, Ralph CL: **127**
Kirkwood, Cris and Curt RR: 161
Kirshner, Don RB: 106
Kirwan, Danny BL: 63; RR: 81, 82
KISS RR: *129,* **129–131**
Kittredge, George Lyman FO: 127
Klein, Larry FO: 140
Klein, Mondi FO: 183
Klein, Oscar BL: 251
Kleinow, "Sneaky Pete" CO: 75, 161
Klemperer, Otto CL: **127,** 141, 179, 239
klezmer music FO: **117–118**
KLF (band) CO: 221
Kline, Lofton CO: 215
KMBC (Kansas City, Missouri) CO: 134
K.M.G. the Illustrator RB: 1
KMOX (St. Louis) CO: 83
KMPC (Los Angeles) CO: 22
Knebworth Festival RR: 207
Kneisel, Franz CL: 54, 83, **127,** 130
Kneisel Hall Chamber Music Festival CL: 16, 127, **127,** 140
Knepper, Jimmy JA: 19
Knight, Gladys CO: 119; RB: **155–156,** *156*
Knight, Madame Marie BL: 217
Knight, Peter FO: 194
Knight, Richard BL: 75
Knight, Suge RB: 7, 54, 55, 70, 71, 236
Knights of Pythias, The (band) BL: 72
Knopfler, Mark BL: 69; CO: 6
Knowles, Beyoncé RB: 58, 59, *59*
Knowles, Mathew RB: 58, 59
Knowling, Ransom BL: 15
Knox, Buddy CO: 19, 20
Knuckles, Frankie RB: 125
Kobluk, Mike FO: 30
Koda, Cub BL: **107**
Kodály, Zoltán CL: 70
Koehler, Esther "Violet" FO: 124
Koerner, Ray, and Glover BL: **108,** 233; FO: 118
Koerner, Spider John BL: 108, *108,* 233; FO: **118**
Koester, Bob BL: 5, 51–52, 59–60, 85, **108,** 213
Koff, Robert CL: 121
Koken, Walt FO: 96, 97
Kolisch, Rudolf CL: **127**
Koller, Hans JA: 223
Konitz, Lee JA: 15, 80, 112, 154, 199
Kool and the Gang RB: **156–157,** *157*
Kool Mo Dee RB: 243
Kooper, Al BL: 25; RR: 127, 152
Koot Tee RB: 4
Koppelman, Charles FO: 32
Kopple, Barbara FO: 52
Korean War BL: 83, 170, 202; FO: 22, 121, 158
Korn, Clara Anna CL: **128**
Korner, Alexis BL: 11, **108–109;** FO: 79; RR: 209
Kornfeld, Artie RR: 248
Korngold, Erich CL: 5, **128**
Kortchmar, Danny FO: 200
Kosek, Kenny FO: 42, 43

Kostelanitz, André CL: **128,** 139
Kotick, Teddy JA: 65
Kottke, Leo BL: 224; FO: 63, **118**
Koussevitzky, Serge CL: xxiii–xxiv, **128–129**
 Leonard Bernstein CL: 26, 27
 Boston Symphony Orchestra CL: 35
 Aaron Copland CL: 56–57
 Irving Fine CL: 78
 Lukas Foss CL: 81
 Dimitri Mitropoulos CL: 157
 Charles Munch CL: 160
 Walter Piston CL: 178–179
 William Schuman CL: 202
Kovacevich, Stephen CL: **129**
Koyaanisqatsi (Philip Glass) CL: 89, **129**
Kozmic Blues Band RR: 123–124
KPHO (Phoenix, Arizona) CO: 176
Kraft, Victor CL: 57
Kraft, William CL: **129–130**
Kraftwerk RR: 158
Kragen, Ken CO: 202, 223
Krainis, Bernard CL: 93
Krall, Diana JA: **114,** 200
Kramer, Eddie RR: 109–111
Kramer, Joey RR: 1
Krasner, Louis CL: **130**
Krause, Bernie FO: 212
Krauss, Alison CO: **117–118,** *118*
 bluegrass music CO: 16
 Cox Family FO: 45–46
 Jerry Douglas FO: 55
 fiddle CO: 73; FO: 67
 Nickel Creek CO: 150
 Dolly Parton CO: 158
 Rounder Records BL: 186
 Shenandoah CO: 185
Kravitz, Lenny JA: 16
Krazy Kat (John Alden Carpenter) CL: **130**
Kreiger, Robbie RR: 62–64
Kreisler, Fritz CL: 21, **130,** 204
Kreissig, Hans CL: 63
Kreutzmann, Bill RR: 93
Krips, Josef CL: 40, **130,** 199
Kriss, Eric BL: 161
Kristal, Hilly RR: 188
Kristofferson, Kris CO: **118–119,** *119*
 Norman Blake FO: 16
 Johnny Cash CO: 35
 Dave Dudley CO: 65
 Glaser Brothers CO: 83–84
 Buck (Uncle Josh) Graves FO: 81
 "Help Me Make It through the Night" CO: 98
 Waylon Jennings CO: 110
 "Me and Bobby McGee" CO: 139
KRLA (Little Rock, Arkansas) CO: 25
Krog, Karin JA: 191
Krohn, R.J. *See* RJD2
Kroll, William CL: 5, **130**
Kronos Quartet CL: **131,** 189; BL: 75
Krosnick, Joel CL: 121
KRS-One RB: **157–158**
Krueger, Karl CL: 67, 204
Krupa, Gene JA: **114–115**
 Carnegie Hall JA: 28
 Cozy Cole RB: 46
 Roy Eldridge JA: 59–60
 Benny Goodman JA: 76
 Lionel Hampton JA: 81
 Buddy Harman CO: 94
 Gerry Mulligan JA: 141
Krusen, Dave RR: 168
K7 RB: **158**
K-Solo RB: **158**
Kubek, Smokin' Joe BL: **109**
Kubelik, Rafael CL: **131**
Kubik, Gail CL: **131**
Kubrick, Stanley RR: 30, 31
Kuerti, Anton CL: **131**
Kuhn, Steve JA: 192
Ku Klux Klan BL: 86, 121, 198–199, 201; FO: 34; JA: 181
Kulberg, Andy FO: 81
Kulick, Bruce RR: 131
Kunwald, Ernst CL: 51
Kupersmith, Noel JA: 32
Kurious RB: **158**
Kuykendall, Pete FO: 43
Kwamé RB: **158–159**
Kweskin, Jim FO: **119**
 Richard Greene FO: 81
 jug bands BL: 101
 Bill Keith FO: 114
 Geoff Muldaur BL: 142
 Maria Muldaur FO: 142
 vocal styles BL: 233
 Sippie Wallace BL: 237
KWKH (Shreveport, Louisiana) CO: 14, 123, 171, 212

L

"La Bamba" RR: 84, 239
LaBelle, Patti RB: **161**
labels. *See* record labels
Laboe, Art RB: 261
LaBour, Fred FO: 170, *171*
Lachmund, Carl Valentine CL: **133**
Lacy, Steve JA: **119**
Ladies Fresh RB: 215
Ladnier, Tommy BL: 177
"Lady Madonna" RR: 59, 60
La Farge, Peter FO: **121**

LaFaro, Scott JA: *37*, 71, 210
Lafayette, Louisiana BL: 111, **121**
Lahey, Larry FO: 43
Laine, Cleo JA: **119–120**
Laine, Frankie CO: 26, 217
Lair, John CO: 76, 87, 148; FO: 124, 155
Laird, Rick JA: 65, 99, 132
Lake, Greg RR: 184
Lake Charles, Louisiana BL: 122, 183
Lamb, Joseph BL: 152, 176
Lambert, Darrell "Pee Wee" CO: 190; FO: 193
Lambert, Dave JA: 120
Lambert, Hendricks, and Ross JA: **120**
Lambert, Mississippi BL: 94
Lamble, Martin FO: 64
Lampell, Millard BL: 168; FO: 87, 168, 182
Lampley, Claude FO: 73
Lance, Major RB: **161–162**
Landau, Jon RR: 224
Landau, Sigfried CL: 38
Landowska, Wanda CL: 127
Landress, "Uncle Bud" FO: 75, 76
Landreth, Sonny BL: **111;** FO: 95
Landry, George BL: 152
Lane, John RR: 104
Lang, Eddie BL: 3, 95; FO: 189; JA: 55, **120,** 206
Lang, Jonny BL: **111**
lang, k. d. CO: 21, 39, **121;** RR: 166
Lang, Michael RR: 248
Lange, Jessica CO: 39
Lange, Robert "Mutt" CO: 133, 204
Langhorne, Bruce BL: 250
Lanois, Daniel CO: 150; RR: 236, 237
Laquan RB: **162**
Laredo, Jaime CL: 37, *133,* **133–134,** 205, 214
Laredo, Ruth CL: **134**
Larkin, Milt BL: 228
Larkin, Nelson CO: 42
Larkin, Patty FO: 121
Lark Quartet CL: **134**
Larks, The BL: 213; RB: **162**
La Rocca, Nick JA: 149
Larsen, Libby CL: **134**
La Salle, Denise BL: **111;** RB: **162**
Lasky, Louie BL: 3
"Last Date" CO: 47, 55
Last Exit JA: 175
Laswell, Bill JA: 83, 165, 170, 175; RB: 110, **162–163**
Lateef, Yusef JA: 38, 71, 86, **121**
Lateiner, Jacob CL: **134,** 221
Latham, Billy Ray FO: 53, 115
Latin and Afro-Cuban jazz JA: xxiii–xxiv, 20, 57, 117, **121,** 252*t. See also specific artists*
Latinos RR: 239–240
Latin percussion. *See* percussion (Latin)
Latouche, John FO: 174
Lauderdale, Jim FO: 137
Laughing Stars JA: 115
Laurie, Annie RB: 104
LaVere, Steve BL: 138, 145
Lavigne, Avril RR: 176
Lavin, Christine FO: **121–122,** *122*
Law, Andrew CL: **134–135**
Law, Don BL: xxi, 97; CO: 168–169
"Lawdy Miss Clawdy" BL: 162, 164
Lawlar, Ernest. *See* Little Son Joe
Lawrence, Pete FO: 184
Lawrence, Tracy CO: 37
Laws, Ronnie RB: 77
Lawson, Doyle CO: 86; FO: 44, 47, **122**
Lawson, Henry FO: 94
Lawson, Jerry RB: 205
Lay, Sam BL: 16, 33, **111**
"Layla" BL: 6, 41
Layla (and Other Assorted Love Songs) (Derek and the Dominos) RR: 4, 40
Layman, Zora FO: 129
Lazy Lester BL: **111,** 240
lead JA: **121**
Lead Belly BL: *112,* **112–113;** FO: ix, **122–124**
  Animals, The RR: 9
  Archive of American Folk Song FO: 4
  Moses Asch BL: 8; FO: 7
  "Bourgeois Blues" BL: 28–29
  Dallas, Texas BL: 216
  folk revival FO: 70
  Fred Gerlach BL: 68
  "Goodnight, Irene" FO: 79
  guitar FO: 86
  Blind Lemon Jefferson BL: 93
  Leo Kottke FO: 118
  Alan Lomax BL: 118
  John Lomax BL: 120
  John and Alan Lomax FO: 127
  protest songs BL: 166, 168
  "Salty Dog Blues" FO: 179
  Sonny Terry and Brownie McGhee FO: 201
  12-string guitar BL: 224
  Weavers FO: 212
  Josh White BL: 242
  young black country blues artists BL: 248

Leaders of the New School RB: 223
Leadon, Bernie CO: 75, 151; FO: 36; RR: 73, 75
League of Composers/International Society for Contemporary Music CL: 57, 94, **135**
Leary Family, The FO: 41
Leavell, Chuck CO: 142; RR: 5, 6
"Leaving on a Jet Plane" CO: 56; FO: 31, 51
LeBlanc, Shorty CO: 150; FO: 148
Ledbetter, Huddie. *See* Lead Belly
Ledbetter, Tiny BL: 49–50
Ledford, Lily May CO: 33; FO: **124**
Ledford, Minnie Lena FO: 124
Ledford, Rosa FO: 124
Led Zeppelin BL: **113;** RR: **133–137,** *134*
  Atlantic Records BL: 9
  Willie Dixon RB: 63
  Memphis Minnie BL: 133
  music business and the blues BL: 144–145
  the Yardbirds BL: 247; RR: 253
Lee, Albert RR: 78
Lee, Barbara RB: 41
Lee, Beverly RB: 238; RR: 217
Lee, Bill FO: 31
Lee, Brenda CO: 21, 61, 94, **121;** RR: **137–138,** *138*
Lee, Johnny CO: 97, **121–122,** 123
Lee, Julia BL: 140; RB: **163**
Lee, Kate FO: 42
Lee, Peggy JA: 110, **121–122**
Lee, Rose CO: 133
Lee, Spike RB: 101, 213
Leffew, Tommy FO: 73
A Left Hand Like God: A History of Boogie-Woogie Piano (Peter J. Silvester) BL: 27, 85
Leftwich, Brad FO: 28
The Legacy of the Blues (TV series) BL: xvi, 12, 74, 94, 114, 252
Legendary Blues Band BL: 159
Legends night club (Chicago) BL: 69
Lehrman, Paul CL: 16
Leiber, Jerry, and Mike Stoller RB: **163–164;** RR: **138–139,** *139*
  Ruth Brown RB: 28
  Coasters, The RB: 45, 46
  Drifters, The RB: 72
  Ahmet Ertegun RB: 83
  "Kansas City Blues" BL: 103
  Elvis Presley RR: 181
  Phil Spector RR: 222
Leigh, Kerri BL: **113**
Leigh, Richard CO: 61
Leighton-Levy, Marian BL: 186
Leinsdorf, Erich CL: 35, 134, **135**
Lelee (Leanne Lyons) RB: 251
LeMaitre, Christian FO: 24
Lemann, Nicholas BL: 134, 190
Lembo, Ralph BL: 212
Lennon, John
  Beatles RR: 18, 21, 22
  David Bowie RR: 31
  Michael Brecker JA: 22
  Eric Clapton RR: 40
  Fats Domino RR: 59
  Lonnie Donegan FO: 55
  Donovan RR: 60
  Bob Dylan RR: 69
  Buddy Holly RR: 114
  Oasis RR: 163
  Carl Perkins RR: 169
  rock revival RR: 207
  Rolling Stones RR: 209
  Phil Spector RR: 221, 223
Lennox, Annie RR: 92, 158–159
Lenoir, J. B. BL: **114,** 170
Lenox School of Jazz JA: 36, 224
Lentz, Daniel CL: **135**
Leonora (William Henry Fry) CL: xxii, 83, **135**
Leppard, Raymond CL: **135**
Lerole, Elias JA: 187
Leroy's Buddy BL: 5
Lesh, Phil RR: 93
Leslie, Chris FO: 64
Les Paul guitar BL: 58; RR: 100, 137
Lessard, Stefan RR: 52
Lester, James JA: 194
Lester, Julius BL: 249; FO: 34
Lester, Robert RB: 41
Lesurf, Cathy FO: 102
Let It Be (the Beatles) RR: 21–22, 221, 223
Let's Dance (David Bowie) RR: 31, 32
Levant, Oscar CL: **135–136**
Leventhal, Harold FO: **124–125,** 212
Levert, Eddie RB: 199
Levi, Yoel CL: 13
Levine, James CL: 21, 35, **136,** 155, 186, 234
LeVox, Gary CO: 166
Lewenthal, Raymond CL: **136–137**
Lewis, Bobby RB: **164**
Lewis, Earl RB: 37
Lewis, Earlen BL: 187
Lewis, Furry BL: 89, 91, **114,** 131, 132, 229
Lewis, George (trombone) JA: **122**

Lewis, Jerry Lee CO: **122;** RB: **164;** RR: **139–140,** *140*
"Cowboy" Jack Clement CO: 38
"Crazy Arms" CO: 48
drums RR: 67
Mickey Gilley CO: 82
keyboards RR: 126
Nashville sound CO: 148
Roy Orbison RR: 165
Sam Phillips RR: 170, 171
rockabilly CO: 177
Lewis, John BL: 251; JA: 15, 36, 67, 138, 156
Lewis, Laurie FO: 68, 79, **125**
Lewis, Meade Lux BL: 27, 96, **114**
Lewis, Mel JA: 73, 110, **122,** 124. *See also* Jones, Thad—Mel Lewis Orchestra
Lewis, Noah BL: 72, **115**
Lewis, Pete RR: 138
Lewis, Ramsey JA: 218; RB: **165**
Lewis, Roy "Pop" FO: 125
Lewis, Smiley RB: **165**
Lewis, Terry. *See* Jam, Jimmy, and Terry Lewis
Lewis Family, The FO: **125**
Lhévinne, Josef CL: 91, 117, 137, 147
Lhévinne, Rosina CL: **137**
John Browning CL: 39
Van Cliburn CL: 53
Byron Janis CL: 117
James Levine CL: 136
Garrick Ohlsson CL: 168
John Williams CL: 239
Libea, Gene FO: 145
Liberace CL: **137–138**
Liberation Music Orchestra JA: 79
Library of Congress. *See also* the Archive of American Folk Song
Archive of American Folk Song FO: 4–5
E. C. and Orna Ball FO: 12
blind musicians and singers BL: 18
Willie Brown BL: 31
Dixon Brothers FO: 54
David "Honeyboy" Edwards BL: 57
Tom Glazer FO: 77
Woody Guthrie FO: 87
Son House BL: 82
Aunt Molly Jackson FO: 109
Juilliard String Quartet CL: 121
Lead Belly BL: 113
John Lomax BL: 119, 120
John and Alan Lomax FO: 127
Bascom Lamar Lunsford FO: 128
Jelly Roll Morton BL: 141
music business BL: 146
piano BL: 162
Hobart Smith FO: 190
Oscar Sonneck CL: 211
Sonny Terry BL: 215
Wade Ward FO: 210
lick JA: **122**
Lieberson, Peter CL: **138,** 205
Life Is a Dream (Lewis Spratlan) CL: **138**
Lifers Group RB: **166**
Lifetime (Tony Williams group) JA: 72, 131, 216
Liggins, Joe & His Honeydrippers RB: **166**
Light Crust Doughboys CO: 24, 65, 191, 214, 218; FO: 213
Lightfoot, Gordon CO: 93; FO: 28, 106, **125–126;** RR: 221
Lightnin' Slim BL: 74, **115,** 240; RB: 117
Likwit Crew RB: 287
Lilacs (George Walker) CL: **138**
Lil' Jon RB: 203
Lil' Kim RB: *166,* **166–167**
Lil' Louis RB: **167**
Lilly, B FO: 126
Lilly, Everett FO: 126
Lilly, Mark FO: 126
Lilly Brothers FO: **126**
Lillywhite, Steve RR: 236
Lil Romeo RB: 179
Lil Soldiers RB: **167**
Lincer, William CL: **138–139**
Lincoln, Abbey JA: 51, **122–123,** 200
Lincoln Center for the Performing Arts CL: **139**
Alice Tully Hall CL: 5
Avery Fisher Hall CL: 14
Schuyler Chapin CL: 48
Jazz at Lincoln Center JA: 106
New York State Theater CL: 165
Philharmonic Hall CL: 177
Lincoln Memorial CL: 9, 10
A Lincoln Portrait (Aaron Copland) CL: 57, 128, **139**
Lind, Jenny CL: 104, **139**
Linda, Solomon FO: 215, 216
Lindsey, Pink and Shorty FO: 53
Lindy Hop JA: 170
Lipkin, Seymour CL: **139–140**
Lipps, Inc. RB: **167**
Lipscomb, Mance BL: 7, *115,* **115–116,** 207; FO: 196
List, Eugene CL: **140**
Liston, Melba JA: **123**
Liszt, Franz CL: xxi–xxii, 76–77, 133, 146, 222
Little Ann BL: 213

Little Anthony and the Imperials CO: 13; RB: **167–168**
Little Beaver RB: **168**
Littlefield, Little Willie RB: **168;** RR: 59
Little Milton BL: **116**
"Little Old Log Cabin in the Lane" CO: 33, **123**
Little Richard RB: **168–169,** *169;* RR: **140–143,** *142*
the Beatles RR: 19
Bumps Blackwell RB: 18
Peacock Records BL: 158
Huey "Piano" Smith BL: 194
Little Son Joe BL: 3, 132, 133, 205
Little Walter BL: **116**
Carey Bell BL: 16
Paul Butterfield BL: 33
harmonica BL: 73
David Myers BL: 149
Muddy Waters BL: 239
Litton, Andrew CL: 63, **140**
Litwack, Leon F. BL: 133
Live Aid (1985) RR: 56, 136, 207, 235, 246
Live Evil (Miles Davis) JA: 131, 223
live recordings RR: 93–94, 96
Liverpool, England RR: 18, 19, 22
"Livery Stable Blues" JA: 116, **124,** 150, 162
Livingston, Bunny RB: 175; RR: 201
Llewellyn, Grant CL: 97
L. L. Cool J RB: 26, 55, **169–170,** *170*
Lloyd, A. L. FO: 78, **126–127,** 131
Lloyd, Bill CO: 77
Lloyd, Charles JA: 44, 51, 80, 104, **124**
Locker, Ann FO: 210
Locker, Joe FO: 148
Lockhart, Keith CL: 34, **140,** *140,* 231
Locklin, Hank CO: 4
Lockwood, Kathryn CL: 134
Lockwood, Robert Jr. BL: **116–117,** *117*
Arkansas BL: 7
Robert Johnson BL: 97, 98
Little Walter BL: 116
Lonnie Pitchford BL: 163
Jimmy Rogers BL: 184
Johnny Shines BL: 191
Otis Spann BL: 205
Sunnyland Slim BL: 209
Baby Boy Warren BL: 237
Loeffler, Charles Martin CL: 23, **140–141**
Loesser, Frank CL: 202
Lofgren, Nils RR: 225
Lofton, Cripple Clarence BL: **117**
Lofton, Keith RB: 11
Logan, Benjamin "Tex" FO: 126, 177
Logan, Horace CO: 162
Loggins, Dave CO: 144
Loggins, Kenny RR: 35
Loggins and Messina RR: 35
"Lola" RR: 91, 128
Lomax, Alan BL: xx, xxi, *118,* **118–119,** *119;* FO: ix, **127**
Animals, The RR: 9
Archive of American Folk Song FO: 4
E. C. and Orna Ball FO: 12
"Bourgeois Blues" BL: 28, 29
Willie Brown BL: 31
Clarksdale, Mississippi BL: 137
Shirley Collins FO: 40
Copper Family FO: 42
Cousin Emmy FO: 44
Bob Dylan FO: 57
David "Honeyboy" Edwards BL: 57
Forest City Joe BL: 65
Tom Glazer FO: 77
Woody Guthrie FO: 87
"Home on the Range" FO: 99
Son House BL: 82
Aunt Molly Jackson FO: 109
Bessie Jones FO: 112
Lead Belly BL: 112, 113; FO: 123
John Lomax BL: 120
Bascom Lamar Lunsford FO: 128
Fred McDowell BL: 128
J. E. Mainer CO: 131; FO: 132
Jelly Roll Morton BL: 141
piano BL: 162
Lonnie Pitchford BL: 163
protest songs BL: 167, 168
recording FO: 163
Almeda Riddle FO: 170
Pete Seeger FO: 182
Hobart Smith FO: 190
social history BL: 204
vocal styles BL: 229, 232
Wade Ward FO: 210
Muddy Waters BL: 239, 240
Bukka White BL: 241
"Wimoweh" FO: 215
Lomax, John BL: **119–120;** FO: viii, **127**
Archive of American Folk Song FO: 4
E. C. and Orna Ball FO: 12
folk revival FO: 70
Lead Belly FO: 123
Alan Lomax BL: 118

Bascom Lamar Lunsford FO: 128
Blind Willie McTell BL: 130
recording FO: 163
Wade Ward FO: 210
London, Edwin CL: 51, **141**
London, England
Black Radical MK II RB: 18
Sandy Denny FO: 51
Jimi Hendrix RR: 107, 108
Dave Holland JA: 92
Ashley Hutchings FO: 102
Andy Irvine FO: 107
Island Records RB: 133
A. L. Lloyd FO: 126
Ewan MacColl FO: 131
Billy Ocean RB: 197
psychedelic rock RR: 185
Ramones RR: 198
reggae RR: 200–201
Rolling Stones RR: 208
Sade RB: 233
ska/bluebeat revival RB: 241
Amii Stewart RB: 248
Yardbirds RR: 251
London, Jack RR: 228
London Jazz Festival JA: 192
London Palladium JA: 14, 64
"Lonely Weekends" CO: 173; RR: 171
Lonesome Pine Fiddlers CO: 194; FO: 78
Lonesome Sundown BL: **120**
Lone Star Ridaz RB: **170**
Long, J. B. BL: xxi, 65, **120–121,** 129, 212; FO: 201
Long, Shorty RB: **170**
"Looking for Love" CO: 122, **123**
Lopes, Lisa "Left-Eye" RB: 259, *259*
Lopez, Jennifer RB: 213
López-Cobos, Jesús CL: 51
Lord Finesse RB: 238
Lornell, Kip FO: 203
Los Angeles, California BL: **35**
country rock RR: 44
drums RR: 67, 68
folk rock RR: 85
Goldstar Studio RB: 107
jump blues and rhythm and blues BL: 101
Kentucky Colonels FO: 115
migration BL: 134
Monterey Pop Festival RR: 151, 152
Motown RR: 154
pop rock RR: 176
power pop RR: 177
psychedelic rock RR: 185–187
record labels BL: 178, 180–182
Phil Spector RR: 222
surf rock RR: 229–230
Los Angeles Chamber Orchestra CL: 50, **141,** 148
Los Angeles Master Chorale CL: **141,** 235
Los Angeles Philharmonic Orchestra CL: **141–142**
Lawrence Foster CL: 81
Carlo Maria Giulini CL: 89
Ferde Grofé CL: 94
Horacio Gutiérrez CL: 95
John Harbison CL: 98
Otto Klemperer CL: 127
William Kraft CL: 129
Zubin Mehta CL: 151
André Previn CL: 183
Artur Rodzinski CL: 190
Walter Rothwell CL: 192
Esa-Pekka Salonen CL: 197
Isaac Stern CL: 214
William Grant Still CL: 215
Steven Stucky CL: 217
Alfred Wallenstein CL: 235
Los Lobos RR: 239
Los Super Seven CO: 72
Loudermilk, Ira and Charlie. *See* Louvin Brothers
Loudermilk, John D. CO: 93
Lou Gehrig's disease (ALS) FO: 123
Louis, Joe BL: 202
Louisiana BL: **121**. *See also* Cajun music; New Orleans; zydeco
Louisiana Hayride CO: **123**
Armstrong Twins FO: 6
Bailes Brothers CO: 9; FO: 10
Floyd Cramer CO: 47
Johnny Horton CO: 104
David Houston CO: 104
Doug Kershaw CO: 116
Jerry Lee Lewis RR: 140
Rose Maddox CO: 130
Jimmy Martin FO: 134
Jimmy "C" Newman CO: 150; FO: 148
Webb Pierce CO: 162
Elvis Presley RR: 180
Jim Reeves CO: 171
Kitty Wells CO: 212
Hank Williams CO: 216–217
Faron Young CO: 225
Louisiana Red BL: **121**
Louisiana Story (Virgil Thomson) CL: **142**
Louisville, Kentucky BL: 126
Louisville Jug Band BL: 101, 184
Louisville (Kentucky) Orchestra CL: 55, 154, 167
Louvin, Charlie CO: 123, 124, 142
Louvin, Florence CO: 124

Louvin, Ira CO: 123, 124
Louvin Brothers CO: **123–124,** *124*
Lovano, Joe JA: **124**
Love, Airron RB: 248–249
Love, Andrew RB: 182
Love, Courtney RR: 160, 161
Love, Darlene RB: 21, 52
Love, Mike RR: 15, 17, 18
Lovelace, Terry CO: 125
Loveless, Patty CO: 84, 105, **124–125,** *125;* FO: 55
"Lovesick Blues" CO: 89, **125–126,** 217, 224; FO: 138
A Love Supreme (John Coltrane) JA: 39, **124,** 131
Lovett, Lyle CO: **126,** *149;* FO: 2, 114
Love Unlimited RB: 278
Lovin' Spoonful BL: 101, **121–122,** 153, 218; FO: 71
Lowe, Charlie FO: 37, 110
Lowe, Junior RB: 115, 189
Lowe, Nick FO: 95
Lower East Side (New York City) BL: 49–50; FO: 118, 219
Lowery, Bill CO: 171; RB: 189
Lowry, Pete BL: 213
LP record BL: xxi, 179; FO: 163
LSD RR: 172, 186
L.T.D. RB: **170–171,** 200
L'Trimm RB: **171**
Lubbock, Texas RR: 111
Luca, Sergiu CL: *142,* **142**
Lucas, George RR: 208
Lucas, Harold FO: 111
Lucas, Lazy Bill BL: 220
Lucas, Randy FO: 111
Lucas, Ruby JA: 47
Lucas, Trevor FO: 51, 64
Lucier, Alvin CL: **142**
"Lucille" CO: **126,** 178
Luckett, LaToya RB: 58, 59
Luck of the Draw (Bonnie Raitt) BL: 127, 177
Ludacris RB: **171,** 200
Luening, Otto CL: 55, **143,** 231
Lulu Belle and Scotty FO: **127–128**
Luman, Bob CO: 27, 210
Lunn, Robert FO: **128**
Lunny, Donal FO: 17, 24, 140, 141, 158
Lunsford, Bascom Lamar FO: 7, 13, 23, **128–129**
Lutcher, Nellie BL: **122;** RB: **171**
Luther, Frank FO: **129,** 175
Lydian Chromatic Concept of Tonal Organization, The (George Russell) JA: 138, 166
Lyle, Lainie FO: 23
Lyles, Pat RB: 49, 217
Lyman, Mel FO: 119
Lymon, Frankie, and the Teenagers RB: 36, 67, *68,* **171;** RR: 64
Lynch, David (director) RR: 165
Lynch, David (singer) RB: 207
Lynch, Laura CO: 58
Lynch, Stan RR: 177
lynchings BL: 23, 199
Lynn, Barbara RB: 182
Lynn, Loretta CO: viii, **126–127**
  Owen Bradley CO: 21
  Patsy Cline CO: 39
  "Coal Miner's Daughter" CO: 39
  "Don't It Make My Brown Eyes Blue" CO: 61
  Crystal Gayle CO: 80
  Patty Loveless CO: 125
  Dolly Parton CO: 158
  Conway Twitty CO: 206
Lynn, Oliver "Mooney" CO: 127
Lynne, Jeff RR: 75–77, 166
Lyon, James CL: **143**
Lyon, Mark BL: 113
Lyon and Healy BL: 125; CO: 89, 131; FO: 133
Lyons, Jimmy JA: 139
Lyric Opera of Chicago CL: 65, **143,** 208
lyrics. *See* blues lyrics
Lytle, Marshall RR: 104

M

Ma, Yo-Yo CL: *145,* **145**
  Stephen Albert CL: 5
  Baltimore Symphony Orchestra CL: 17
  Caramoor CL: 43
  Bobby McFerrin JA: 131
  Gregor Piatigorsky CL: 178
  André Previn CL: 184
  Leonard Rose CL: 191
  Isaac Stern CL: 214
Maazel, Lorin CL: 52–53, **145–146,** 179
Mabaso, Lemmy JA: 187
Mabie, Milt CO: 134
Mabon, Willie BL: 118
Mácal, Zdenek CL: **146,** 163
MacArthur, Dan, Gary and Megan FO: 131
MacArthur, Margaret FO: **131**
MacArthur Foundation grant JA: 38, 167
MacColl, Ewan FO: 6, 78, 112, **131,** 182
MacColl, Kirsty FO: 131
MacDowell, Edward CL: 88, **146**
MacDowell, Marian CL: 146–147
MacDowell Colony CL: 22, 146, **146–147,** 203
Macero, Teo JA: 158
Machito JA: xxiii–xxiv, **125**

Mack, Lonnie BL: **123,** 237; RR: 25, 116
Macon, Dorris CO: 129
Macon, Georgia RR: 140, 141
Macon, Uncle Dave CO: *129,* **129–130**
  banjo, five-string FO: 13
  Fruit Jar Drinkers FO: 73
  Grand Ole Opry CO: 86, 87
  Hay, George D. CO: 97
  Hot Mud Family FO: 99
  Sam McGee FO: 136, 137
  rube/hillbilly humor CO: 180
Macy, Robin CO: 58
Madden, Owney JA: 44
Maddox, Rose CO: 46, **130,** 156
Maddox Brothers and Rose CO: 130
Maderitz, Jim RB: 78–79
Madison Square Garden RR: 136, 156
Madonna RB: **173;** RR: 159
Magee, Sterling BL: 188
Magic Dick BL: 94
Magic Sam BL: **123,** 141, 248
Magil, Joseph CL: 182
Magnificent Montague, The RB: 174
Magnificents, The RB: **173–174**
Magoo RB: 258
Maguire, Barry FO: 146
Maguire, Sean FO: 24
Maguire, Tommy FO: 29
Mahal, Taj BL: **123–124,** *124;* FO: 82, **199**
Maharishi Mahesh Yogi RR: 17, 21, 60
Mahavishnu Orchestra
  Bitches Brew JA: 16
  Billy Cobham JA: 35
  European jazz JA: 65
  fusion JA: 72
  Jan Hammer JA: 80–81
  Inner Mounting Flame, The JA: **99**
  John McLaughlin JA: 131–132
  Jean Luc Ponty JA: 156
  Narada Michael Walden RB: 273
Mahler, Gustav CL: 128, **147,** 151, 192, 236
Maine FO: 17
Mainer, J. E. CO: **130–131;** FO: 110, **132,** 142
Mainer, Wade CO: 130, 131; FO: 132, 142
Maines, Lloyd CO: 58, 59
Maines, Natalie CO: 58
Main Source RB: 191
Makeba, Miriam FO: 33; JA: 187; RB: 178
Makem, Tommy FO: 35, 68
"Make the World Go Away" CO: **131**
Malaco Records BL: **124**
Malathini and the Mahotella Queens JA: 187
Malik B RB: 230
Malloy, Matt FO: 17, 33, 158–159
Malo, Raul CO: 155
"Mama He's Crazy" CO: **131**
Mamas and the Papas, The FO: 71; RR: *145,* **145–146,** 152, 153
"Mamas Don't Let Your Babies Grow up to Be Cowboys" CO: **131**
mambo JA: 125, **125,** 158
"Man, I Feel Like a Woman" CO: **133**
managers CL: 30, 48; FO: 83–84, 124–125
Manchester, Melissa BL: 141
Mandel, Harvey BL: **124–125**
Mandela, Nelson JA: 186
mandolin BL: xxii, *125,* **125–126;** CO: **131–132,** *132;* FO: *132,* **132–133**
Mandrell, Barbara BL: 111; CO: viii, 104, **132–133,** 133
Mandrell, Irlene CO: 133
Mandrell, Louise CO: 133, **133**
Maness, J. D. CO: 161
Manfred Mann RR: 33–34, 217
Mangano, Diana RR: 121
Mangione, Chuck JA: 70, **125–126**
Mangsen, Cindy FO: 94
Manhattans, The RB: **174**
Manhattan School of Music CL: **147**
Manhattan Transfer JA: **126,** 208
Mann, Aimee RR: 178
Mann, Barry RR: 204
Mann, Carl RR: 171
Mann, Herbie JA: 71, 85, **126,** 175, 224
Mann, Robert CL: 121
Mann, Woody BL: 32, 191, 192, 222
Mann Act RB: 17
Manne, Shelly JA: 91, 112
Mannes, David CL: 147
Mannes, Leopold CL: 147, 189
Mannes College of Music CL: **147**
Mantler, Michael JA: 18, **126–127,** 170
Manuel, Bobby RB: 24
Manuel, Richard RR: 11, 13
Manzarek, Ray RR: 62–64, 126
manzello JA: 114
Maphis, Joe CO: **133,** 200; FO: 81
"Maple Leaf Rag" JA: 110, **127**
Mapp, Eddie BL: 240

Marable, Fate JA: 18, 53
Marathons, The. *See* the Jayhawks
Marchan, Bobby RB: **174–175**
March on Washington (1963) FO: 34, 157
Marcus, Adele CL: 117, **147–148**
Marcus, Greil FO: 17; RR: 182
Margolin, Bob BL: **126**
Mariano, Charlie JA: 4
Maricle, Sherrie JA: 53
marijuana RR: 200
Marillion RR: 185
Marin County Blues Festival BL: 151
Mariner, Neville CL: 141, **148**
Mar-Keys, The RB: **175,** 182, 247
Markowitz, Phil JA: 52
Marks, David RR: 15, 18
Marl, Marley RB: 46, 132, 169, **176**
Marlboro Music School and Festival CL: **148**
Marley, Bob RB: 133, 134, **175–176,** 222–223; RR: 199, 201
Marley, Rita RB: 134
Marquees, The RB: 187
Marriott, Steve BL: 108
Marsalis, Branford JA: 17, **127;** RB: **176–177**
Marsalis, Ellis JA: 127
Marsalis, Wynton CL: **148–149;** JA: **127–129,** *128*
  Louis Armstrong JA: 6
  Art Blakey JA: 17
  Blood on the Fields CL: 31
  John Coltrane JA: 41
  JALC JA: 106
  Bobby McFerrin JA: 131
  Branford Marsalis RB: 176
  Chico O'Farrill JA: 147
Marsh, Dave FO: 124; RB: 23, 33
Marsh, Warne JA: 199
Marshall, Maithe RB: 19, 218
Marshall, Mike FO: 145
Marshall, Thurgood BL: 202
Marshall amplifiers RR: 111
Martha & the Vandellas RB: *123,* **177**
Martha White Flour CO: 73–74; FO: 100
Marthe, Linley JA: 223
Martin, Asa FO: 173
Martin, Benny FO: **133–134**
Martin, Billy JA: 133
Martin, Bogan & Armstrong BL: 62, 208
Martin, Carl BL: 8, 208
Martin, Christian Friedrich CO: 89; FO: 84, 86
Martin, Dewey RR: 34, 35
Martin, George RR: 19
Martin, Grady CO: **134**
Martin, Janis FO: 69
Martin, Jimmy FO: **134**
  J. D. Crowe FO: 47
  Bill Emerson FO: 61
  Hawkshaw Hawkins CO: 96
  Doyle Lawson FO: 122
  Osborne Brothers FO: 153
  truck-driving songs CO: 202
  "Uncle Pen" CO: 207
Martin, Sara BL: 1, 87, **126–127,** 240, 243
Martin, Stu JA: 191
Martinez, Cliff RB: 51
Martin Guitars BL: 41; CO: 89, 90, 92; FO: 84, 86
Martino, Donald CL: **149,** 166
Martino, Pat JA: **129**
Martinon, Jean CL: **149**
Marvelettes, The RB: **177,** 188
Marx, Groucho RR: 193
Marx Brothers RR: 191, 193
Marxer, Marcy FO: 68
Maryland FO: 166
Mary Lou Williams Women in Jazz Festival JA: **129**
Masada (John Zorn ensemble) JA: 224–225
Mase RB: **177–178,** 194
Mase, Raymond CL: 7
Masekela, Hugh JA: 16, 97, **129,** 186; RB: **178;** RR: 152
Mashiyane, Spokes JA: 187
Mason, Daniel Gregory CL: **149**
Mason, Dave RR: 84
Mason, Harvey JA: 88
Mason, Molly FO: 68
Mason, Nick RR: 172, 174
Mason, William CL: 143, 223
Massachusetts Institute of Technology CL: 76, 98
Masse, Laurel JA: 126
Masselos, William CL: **150**
Massey, Cal JA: 177
Massey, Curt CO: 134
Massey, Louise CO: 58
Massey, Louise, and the Westerners CO: **134**
Massi, Nick RR: 86
Mass (Leonard Bernstein) CL: 27, 125, **149–150**
Master of Puppets (Metallica) RR: 107, 146
Master P RB: **178–179,** 189
Masters, The (bluegrass band) FO: 11
Masters of Ceremony RB: 110
Masur, Kurt CL: 149, **150**
Mata, Eduardo CL: 63
Matassa, Cosimo BL: 121
"Matchbox Blues" BL: 93, 158
Material RB: 162

Mathers, Marshall RB: 80–81. *See also* Eminem
Mathis, Johnny JA: 73
Matrix (San Francisco club) RR: 228
Mattacks, Dave FO: 64
Mattea, Kathy CO: 16, **134–135,** 203; FO: 2, 82, 125
Matthews, Dave RR: 52, 53. *See also* Dave Matthews Band, The
Matthews, Denise RB: 270
Matthews, Iain FO: 64
Matthews, Julie FO: 102
Mauldin, Joe B. RR: 113, 114
Maupin, Bennie JA: 15, 83, 88
Max's Kansas City RR: 2
Maxwell Street Market (Chicago) BL: 40, 74, 148, 247, 252
May, Brian RR: 191, 193
May, Derrick RB: 95
Mayall, John BL: 41, 124, **127;** RR: 39, 81
"Maybelline" BL: 16; RR: 24
Mayfield, Curtis BL: **127;** RB: *131,* **179**
  blues lyrics BL: 25
  Jan Bradley RB: 24
  Billy Butler RB: 30
  Jerry Butler RB: 30, 31
  electric guitar BL: 59
  Fascinations, The RB: 87
  Impressions, The RB: 130–132
  Major Lance RB: 161, 162
  social history and the blues BL: 203
Mayfield, Percy BL: **127;** RB: **179**
Maynard, Ken CO: 7
Mayo, John "Gypie" RR: 253
Mays, Lyle JA: 72, 134, 187
Maytals RB: 222
Mazia, Marjorie FO: 88
Mazur, Bret RB: 162
Mazurek, Rob JA: 32
M-Base collective JA: 217
Mbulu, Letta JA: 187McAuliffe, Leon CO: 160, 218; FO: **134**
McBride, John CO: 135
McBride, Martina CO: **135**
McCabe's (Los Angeles, California) BL: 35
McCall, Bill CO: 170
McCall, C. W. CO: **135,** 203
McCall, Louis RB: 48
McCandless, Fiddlin' Al FO: 164
McCann, Les JA: 92, 195
McCarthy, Eugene FO: 157
McCartney, Paul
  bass RR: 15
  Beatles RR: 18, 20, 22
  Fats Domino RR: 59
  Donovan RR: 60
  Everly Brothers CO: 70; RR: 78
  Lawrence Foster CL: 81
  Buddy Holly RR: 111, 114
  Carl Perkins BL: 158; RR: 169
  power pop RR: 177
  Rolling Stones RR: 209
  James Taylor FO: 200
  Allen Toussaint BL: 220
  Stevie Wonder RB: 283
McCarty, Jim RR: 251, 253
McCary, Michael RB: 24
McClain, Billy BL: 137
McClennan, Tommy BL: 57, **127,** 159, 210
McClintock, Harry. *See* Haywire Mac
McClinton, Delbert BL: **127–128**
McClinton, O. B. CO: **135–136**
McClure, Kit JA: **129–130**
McClure, Ron JA: 52
McComiskey, Billy FO: 29
McConnell, Cathal FO: 18, 75
McConnell, Page RR: 118
McConnell, Rob JA: **130**
McCoo, Marilyn RB: 88
McCormick, Mack BL: 7, 81, 115, 190
McCoury, Del CO: 16, 67; FO: 83, **134–135,** 217
McCoury, Jerry FO: 83
McCoury, Rob FO: 135
McCoury, Ronnie FO: 135
McCoy, Charles (Papa Charlie) BL: 125, **128**
McCoy, Charlie CO: 98, **136**
McCoy, Joseph (Kansas Joe) BL: 3, 125, **128,** 132
McCoy, Papa Charlie, and Kansas Joe BL: **128,** 215
McCoy, Van RB: **179**
McCracklin, Jimmy BL: **128,** 181
McCrae, George RB: 149
McCrea, Ethel "Earl-Jean" RB: 49, 217
McCready, Mike RR: 167, 168
McCreesh, Tom FO: 99
McCrimmon, Dan FO: 73
McCurdy, Ed FO: 99, **135**
McCusker, John FO: 13
McCutcheon, John FO: 113
McDaniel, Ellas. *See* Diddley, Bo
McDaniel, Mel CO: **136**
McDaniels, Daryll RB: 231
McDermott, P. J. FO: 39
McDonagh, Johnny "Ringo" FO: 50
McDonald, Country Joe FO: **135–136,** 196; RR: 247–248
McDonald, Skeets CO: **137**
McDonough, Megon FO: 122

McDowell, Mississippi Fred BL: 32, **128,** 139, 154, 177; FO: 196
McDowell, Wilcil FO: 106
MC Eiht RB: 47
McElroy, Thomas RB: 82
McEnery, Red River Dave CO: **137**
McEntire, Pake CO: 137
McEntire, Reba CO: 20, **137–138**
McEuen, Bill FO: 136
McEuen, John CO: 151; FO: **136**
McFadden, Larry CO: 88
McFarland, Lester FO: 168
McFarlane, Spanky RR: 146
McFerrin, Bobby JA: 20, **131;** RB: **180**
MC5 RR: 188
McGann, Andy FO: 23, 24
McGarrigle, Kate and Anna FO: **136**
McGee, David RR: 169
McGee, Dennis CO: 29; FO: 5, 27
McGee, Kirk CO: 86, 97, 129; FO: 73, 136, 189
McGee, Sam FO: **136–137**
  Fruit Jar Drinkers FO: 73
  Grand Ole Opry CO: 86
  Theron Hale and Daughters FO: 90
  Hay, George D. CO: 97
  Steve James BL: 91
  Uncle Dave Macon CO: 129
  Fiddlin' Arthur Smith FO: 189
McGegan, Nicholas CL: 177
McGhee, Brownie BL: **128–129;** FO: *201*
  acoustic guitar BL: 4
  aliases BL: 5
  Champion Jack Dupree BL: 55
  Blind Boy Fuller BL: 65
  harmonica FO: 92
  holy blues BL: 77
  Larry Johnson BL: 95
  J. B. Long BL: 120, 121
  Stick McGhee BL: 129; RB: 180
  Buddy Moss BL: 142
  New York City BL: 152, 153
  protest songs BL: 166–167
  record labels BL: 181
  social history BL: 202
  Sonny Terry BL: 215, 216
  Terry, Sonny and Brownie McGhee FO: 200, 201
  Happy Traum BL: 221
  Happy and Artie Traum FO: 204
  Van "Piano Man" Walls BL: 237
  Josh White BL: 242
  Ralph Willis BL: 245
McGhee, Howard JA: 86
McGhee, Stick BL: 95, **129;** RB: 83, **180**
McGlynn, Arty FO: 24
McGovney, Ron RR: 145
McGraw, Tim CO: 100, *138,* **138–139,** 139
McGraw, Tug CO: 138
McGregor, Chris JA: 186, 187, 217
McGriff, Jimmy JA: 92; RB: **181**
McGuinn, Roger (Jim)
  Byrds FO: 25; RR: 35, 37
  Chad Mitchell Trio FO: 31
  Gene Clark FO: 36
  folk rock RR: 85
  folk-rock FO: 71
  Frank Hamilton FO: 90
  power pop RR: 177
  12-string guitar BL: 224–225
MC Hammer RB: 72, **116,** 197
McIntosh, Andra Faye BL: 187
McIntosh, Nat JA: 221
MC Isis RB: 287
McJohn, Goldy RR: 228
McKenna, Barney FO: 55
McKenzie, Scott RR: 146, 152
McKernan, Ron "Pigpen" RR: 93
McKibbon, Al JA: 15
McKinney, Pet FO: 110
McKinney's Cotton Pickers JA: 59, 163
McKuen, Rod CO: 116
McLaughlin, David FO: 111
McLaughlin, John JA: **131–133,** *132. See also* Mahavishnu Orchestra
  Bitches Brew JA: 15, 16
  Billy Cobham JA: 35
  Miles Davis JA: 49
  Joey DeFrancesco JA: 51
  Al Di Meola JA: 52
  European jazz JA: 64–65
  fusion JA: 72
  guitar synthesizer JA: 78
  Jan Hammer JA: 80–81
  The Inner Mounting Flame JA: **99**
  Carlos Santana RR: 214
  In a Silent Way JA: 98
  John Surman JA: 191
  Miroslav Vitous JA: 207, 208
  Narada Michael Walden RB: 273
  Tony Williams JA: 216
  Larry Young JA: 219
McLean, Don FO: **137;** RR: 165
McLean, Jackie JA: 19
MC Lyte RB: **179–180,** 209
McMahon, Ed CO: 99

McMichen, Clayton CO: 200; FO: 187
McMurry, Lillian BL: 90, **129–130,** 139, 181
McNair, Sylvia CL: **150,** 184
McNeely, Big Jay RB: **181**
McNeill, Brian FO: 13
McNett, Bob CO: 63
McPartland, Jimmy JA: 133
McPartland, Marian JA: **133**
McPhatter, Clyde RB: 16, 71, **181,** 281
McRae, Carmen JA: 120, 126, *130,* **130**
M.C. Ren RB: 196
McReynolds, Jesse FO: 11. *See also* Jim and Jesse
McShann, Jay BL: **130,** 140, 183, 245; JA: 69, 152
McShee, Jaqui FO: 109, 156
MC Shy D RB: **180**
McTell, Blind Willie BL: **130**
  Allman Brothers Band, The BL: 6
  Atlanta BL: 9
  blind musicians and singers BL: 19
  Buddy Moss BL: 142
  Piano Red BL: 163
  "Statesboro Blues" BL: 206
  12-string guitar BL: 224, 225
  Curley Weaver BL: 240
MC Treach RB: 192
McVey, Cameron RB: 40
McVie, Christine BL: 41, 63; RR: 82–84
McVie, John BL: 62, 127; RR: 81–84
MC Vinne RB: 192
Meadon, Pete RR: 244
"Me and Bobby McGee" CO: 118–119, **139;** RR: 124
Meat Puppets RR: 161
Meaux, Huey P. BL: 187; CO: 72; RB: **181–182**
mechanical royalties BL: 144
Meco RB: **182**
Medeski, John JA: **133**
Medeski, Martin and Wood JA: 133
medicine shows FO: 7, 140, 180
Medley, Bill RB: 225–226; RR: 204, 205
Medlin, Julian "Greasy" FO: 111
Megadeth RR: 146
Megahertz RB: 226
Mehta, Zubin CL: 125, 142, **151,** 207
Meisner, Randy RR: 73, 75
Mel, Melle RB: 108
mellotron RR: 127, 183
melodeon FO: 2
melody JA: 88
Melrose, Lester BL: **130–131**
  Chicago BL: 40
  Lonnie Johnson RB: 144
  Tommy McClennan BL: 127
  "That's All Right" BL: 218
  Big Joe Williams BL: 243
  Sonny Boy Williamson I BL: 244
Melton, Barry FO: 135
Melvin, Harold & the Blue Notes RB: 204–205
Melvins, Maxwell RB: 166
"Memphis" (Chuck Berry) BL: 123; RR: 116
Memphis, Tennessee BL: xix, **131–132;** JA: 95
  W. C. Handy BL: 72
  Sam Phillips RR: 169, 170
  Elvis Presley BL: 164; RR: 179–180, 182
  social history BL: 203
"Memphis Blues" BL: xvii, 72, 131; JA: 84
Memphis Horns, The RB: 153, 175, **182**
Memphis Jug Band BL: 81, 101, 125, **132,** 132–133, 241
Memphis Minnie BL: xix, **132–133**
  acoustic guitar BL: 3
  Big Bill Broonzy BL: 29
  McCoy Brothers BL: 128
  Memphis BL: 131
  Memphis Jug Band BL: 132
  Jimmy Rogers BL: 184
  Walls, Mississippi BL: 140
  Casey Bill Weldon BL: 241
  Robert Wilkins BL: 243
Memphis Recording Service RB: 25; RR: 170, 179
Memphis rockabilly RR: ix
Memphis Rock 'n' Soul Museum BL: 132
Memphis Slim BL: 53, 118, 142, 161, 241
Mendez, Sergio JA: 163
Mendoza, Lydia FO: 202
Meneses, Antonio CL: 23
Mengelberg, Willem CL: **151,** 226
Mennin, Peter CL: 64, 70, 121, **151**
Menotti, Gian Carlo CL: xxv, **152**
  Amahl and the Night Visitors CL: **6**
  Samuel Barber CL: 17
  Consul, The CL: **56**
  Festival of Two Worlds CL: **77**
  Lee Hoiby CL: 105
  Christopher Keene CL: 124
  Otto Luening CL: 143
  George Rochberg CL: 189
  Saint of Bleecker Street, The CL: **197**

Menotti, Gian Carlo (continued)
- Thomas Schippers CL: 200
- Spoleto Festival CL: 213
- *Vanessa* CL: 233
- Charles Wadsworth CL: 235
- Efrem Zimbalist CL: 245

Menuhin, Hephzibah CL: 152
Menuhin, Yehudi CL: 16, **152–153**
Mercier, Peadar FO: 33
Mercury, Freddie RR: 125, 191, 193
"Mercury Blues" BL: 7, 145
Mercury Phoenix Trust RR: 193
"Mercy, Mercy, Mercy" JA: 3, 223
Meridian, Mississippi BL: **139**
Merola, Gaetano CL: **153–154,** 198
Merrill, Robert CL: **154**
Merritt, Jymie JA: 137
Merriweather, Maceo. *See* Big Maceo
Merry Blackbirds JA: 186
Merry Pranksters RR: 93, 249
Mersey beat RR: 33
Mesner, Eddie BL: 30; RB: 4, 90
"The Message" RB: 108, 249
Messiaen, Olivier CL: 161
Messina, Jim RR: 34, 35
Messina, Jo Dee CO: 138, **139**
Mester, Jorge CL: **154**
Metallica RR: 107, **145–149**
Metallica (The Black Album) RR: 145, 146
Meters, The RB: **182–183**
Metheny, Pat JA: *133*, **133–134**
- Richard Bona JA: 20
- Michael Brecker JA: 22
- Gary Burton JA: 26
- guitar synthesizer JA: 78
- Jim Hall JA: 80
- Dave Holland JA: 92
- Jaco Pastorius JA: 152
- *Still Life Talking* JA: **187**
- Tony Williams JA: 216
- Attilla Zoller JA: 224

Method Man RB: 284, 285
Metropolitan Opera CL: xxiii, xxiv, **154–155**
Metropolitan Opera House CL: **155,** 199, 200
Mexico RR: 103, 213. *See also* border radio; Tex-Mex music
Meyer, Edgar FO: 55, 69
Meyers, Augie CO: 72
Mhaonaigh, Mairéad Ní FO: 4
Miami RB: 247–248
Michael, Walt FO: 99–100
Michaels, Lee RR: 125
Michigan BL: 19, 185. *See also* Detroit
Mickey and Sylvia RB: 228
Microsoft RR: 210
microtonality CL: xv, 173–174
Midday Merry-Go-Round CO: 124; FO: 133, 144
MIDI (Musical Instrument Digital Interface) CL: 16; JA: **134**
Midler, Bette CO: 89
Miedél, Rainer CL: 204
migration BL: xv, xix, 35, 39–40, **133–135**
Milburn, Amos BL: **135;** RB: **183**
Miles, Buddy BL: 20; RB: **183;** RR: 110, 214
Miles, Lizzie BL: **135**
Miley, Bubber JA: 16, 184
Milhaud, Darius CL: **155**
- Stephen Albert CL: 5
- Arthur Berger CL: 25
- William Bolcom CL: 32
- Dave Brubeck JA: 24
- Michael Colgrass CL: 54
- Philip Glass CL: 89
- Ben Johnston CL: 119
- Robert Moran CL: 159
- Peter Schickele CL: 199
- Seymour Shifrin CL: 208
- Lester Trimble CL: 227

Milk and Gizmo RB: 179
"Milk Cow Blues" BL: 8, 144
Millar, George, Joe, and Will FO: 106
Miller, Arthur CL: 236
Miller, Buddy and Julie CO: 220; FO: **137–138**
Miller, Emmett CO: 89, 125, 224; FO: **138**
Miller, Gene "Bowlegs" RB: 204
Miller, Glenn JA: 55, **134,** 195
Miller, J. D. BL: **135**
- Nathan Abshire FO: 1
- Slim Harpo BL: 74
- Lazy Lester BL: 111
- Lightnin' Slim BL: 115
- Lonesome Sundown BL: 120
- Katie Webster BL: 240

Miller, Jimmy RR: 210
Miller, "Lost" John CO: 73
Miller, Marcus JA: 50, 74, **134–135,** 152
Miller, Mark CO: 183
Miller, Mitch BL: 179; FO: 146
Miller, Ned CO: 184
Miller, Percy. *See* Master P
Miller, Rice. *See* Williamson, Sonny Boy II
Miller, Roger CO: 118, 139, **139–140,** 181
Miller, Rose RB: 226
Miller, Steve RR: 152
Miller, Tommy RB: 33
Miller, Zell CO: 39
Millinder, Lucky RB: **183–184**
- Annisteen Allen RB: 5
- Ruth Brown RB: 28
- Bill Doggett RB: 64

Wynonie Harris BL: 74; RB: 118
Bull Moose Jackson RB: 135
Million Dollar Quartet CO: 122
Milli Vanilli RB: **184**
Mills, Irving CO: 125
Mills, Mike RR: 201, 202
Mills, Stephanie RB: **184**
Mills Blue Rhythm Band RB: 183
Milnes, Sherrill CL: **156**
Milsap, Ronnie CO: **140**
Milstein, Nathan CL: 16, 106, **156**
Milton, Roy RB: **184–185**
Milwaukee, Wisconsin BL: 248; FO: 179
Min, Elizabeth Seja CL: 241
Mingus, Charles JA: **135–137,** *136*
Pepper Adams JA: 3
Toshiko Akiyoshi JA: 4
Jimmy Blanton JA: 18
Blues and Roots JA: **19**
Eric Dolphy JA: 54, 55
double bass JA: 56
Duke Ellington JA: 61
Chico Hamilton JA: 80
Lionel Hampton JA: 81
Illinois Jacquet JA: 101
Rahsaan Roland Kirk JA: 114; RB: 155
Yusef Lateef JA: 121
Mingus Ah Um JA: **135**
Joni Mitchell FO: 140
Red Norvo JA: 145
Charlie Parker JA: 151, 152
Gunther Schuller JA: 172
John Scofield JA: 172
third stream jazz JA: 197
Mingus, Sue Graham JA: 135
Mingus Ah Um (Charles Mingus) JA: **135**
Mingus Big Band JA: 107, **135,** 137
Minimoog JA: 192
Minneapolis Symphony Orchestra CL: 2, 157–158, 169, 209
Minnesota FO: 118; RR: 69
Minnesota Orchestra CL: **156,** *157*
Edo de Waart CL: 68
Aaron Jay Kernis CL: 125
Libby Larsen CL: 134
Neville Mariner CL: 148
Peter Serkin CL: 205
Osmo Vänskä CL: 233
minstrel/traveling shows BL: xv, **135–137,** 176, 193; FO: **138–140,** *139*
Minton, Henry JA: 137
Minton's Playhouse JA: 18, 34, 48, 85, **137,** 139, 156
Minus, Rene RB: 38
Miracles, The RB: 188, 228, *228*. *See also* Robinson, Smokey
Mirrorball (Neil Young and Pearl Jam) RR: 168, 254
"Miserlou" RR: 229, 230
Mississippi BL: **137–139**. *See also* Delta blues; Mississippi Delta; *specific cities and towns, e.g.:* Clarksdale
acoustic guitar BL: 1
Civil Rights movement FO: 34
crossroads BL: 47
field hollers BL: 62
migration BL: 133
sharecropping BL: 190
slide guitar BL: 192
young black country blues artists BL: 252
Mississippi Blues Highway Association BL: 137
Mississippi Delta BL: xix. *See also* Delta blues
Chicago BL: 40
Highway 61 BL: 75
Memphis BL: 131
migration BL: 134
protest songs BL: 166
vocal styles BL: 229
Mississippi River BL: 11
Mississippi Sheiks BL: **140**
Texas Alexander BL: 4
Bo Carter BL: 36
fiddle BL: 61
"Sittin' on Top of the World" BL: 191
string bands BL: 208
Walter Vinson BL: 228
Missouri BL: **140–141**. *See also* Kansas City, Missouri; St. Louis
"Mr. Tambourine Man" FO: 25; RR: 35–36, 84
"Misty" JA: 73, 92
Mitchell, Billy RB: 44
Mitchell, Blue JA: 42
Mitchell, Chad CO: 56; FO: 30, 31, 140. *See also* Chad Mitchell Trio
Mitchell, Charles CO: 224
Mitchell, Howard CL: 162
Mitchell, Howie FO: 191
Mitchell, James RB: 182
Mitchell, Joni FO: **140**
Michael Brecker JA: 22
Judy Collins FO: 39
Robben Ford BL: 64
Herbie Hancock JA: 83
Ian and Sylvia FO: 106
Furry Lewis BL: 114
Jaco Pastorius JA: 152
Tom Rush FO: 178
Wayne Shorter JA: 178
singer/songwriter movement FO: 185

Mitchell, Joni (*continued*)
- singer-songwriters RR: 220, 221
- tunings BL: 223
- Dave Van Ronk BL: 227
- Woodstock RR: 249

Mitchell, Mitch CO: 24; RR: 68, 109, 110
Mitchell, Red JA: 31
Mitchell, Roscoe JA: 6, 20, 21, 122, **137**
Mitchell, "Satch" RB: 198
Mitchell, Willie RB: 111, **185,** 204
Mitropoulos, Dimitri CL: 156, **156–158,** 185
Mitterhoff, Barry FO: 188, *188*
Mix-Master Ice RB: 268
Mizell, Jay. *See* Jam Master Jay
Mo', Keb BL: 14, 26, **141,** 204, 251, 252
Moanin' (Art Blakey and the Jazz Messengers) JA: **137–138**
Mobb Deep RB: 142, **185**
Mobley, Hank JA: 86, 180, 219
Moby Grape RR: 119
modal jazz JA: xxiv, 113, **138,** 252*t*
Modarelli, Antonio CL: 179
Modeliste, Joseph "Zigaboo" RB: 182
modern jazz JA: xxiv–xxv
Modern Jazz Quartet JA: 34, **138,** 172, 197
Modern Sounds in Country and Western Music (Ray Charles) CO: viii, 36, 107
mods RR: 244–245
Moffett, Charnett JA: 83, 175
mohawk haircut RR: 187
Moholo, Louis JA: 187
Moloney, Mick FO: 29, 112, **140–141**
Moloney, Paddy FO: 32–33
Molsky, Bruce FO: 28
Moments, The RB: **185–186**
Monarch, Michael RR: 228
Monarchs, The RB: 249
Monica RB: **186**
Monick, Susie FO: 23
Monie Love RB: 192
Monk, Meredith CL: **158**
Monk, Thelonious JA: **138–139**
- bebop JA: 12
- Birdland JA: 15
- Ed Blackwell JA: 16
- Art Blakey JA: 17
- *Brilliant Corners* JA: **23**
- Donald Byrd JA: 26
- Kenny Clarke JA: 34
- John Coltrane JA: 40
- "Epistrophy" JA: **62–63**
- Dizzy Gillespie JA: 75
- Barry Harris JA: 86
- Coleman Hawkins JA: 87
- Steve Lacy JA: 119
- Minton's Playhouse JA: 137
- Charlie Parker JA: 151, 152
- Oscar Pettiford JA: 154
- Bud Powell JA: 156
- Sonny Rollins JA: 165
- "Stompin' at the Savoy" JA: 188
- "Straight, No Chaser" JA: **188**
- tone cluster JA: 198
- McCoy Tyner JA: 200
- Mary Lou Williams JA: 216
- Shadow Wilson JA: 218

Monkees, The FO: 145; RR: **149–151,** *150*
Monkey, The RB: 161
Monogram Theater (Chicago) JA: 7
Monroe, Bill CO: xvii, **140–141**
- Kenny Baker FO: 11
- Byron Berline FO: 14–15
- bluegrass music CO: 15, 16
- "Blue Moon of Kentucky" CO: 16
- Vassar Clements FO: 37
- John Cohen FO: 38
- Country Gentlemen FO: 43
- Jim Eanes FO: 59
- five string banjo CO: 11
- Flatt and Scruggs CO: 73
- Emory Gordy, Jr. CO: 84
- gospel music CO: 85
- *Grand Ole Opry* CO: 87
- Bill Grant and Delia Bell FO: 80
- Richard Greene FO: 81
- Bill Keith FO: 114
- Kentucky Colonels FO: 115
- Del McCoury FO: 134
- Sam McGee FO: 137
- Rose Maddox CO: 130
- mandolin BL: 125; CO: 132; FO: 133
- Benny Martin FO: 133
- Jimmy Martin FO: 134
- minstrel/traveling shows FO: 140
- Muleskinner FO: 144
- Nashville sound CO: 148
- Osborne Brothers FO: 153
- railroad songs CO: 166
- Don Reno FO: 168
- Ralph Rinzler FO: 170
- rockabilly RR: 205
- Peter Rowan FO: 177
- Stanley Brothers FO: 193
- Stanley Brothers, The CO: 191
- Carl Story FO: 195
- Stringbean CO: 194
- Sullivan Family FO: 197
- "Uncle Pen" CO: 207
- Doc Watson FO: 211
- Chubby Wise FO: 216

Mac Wiseman FO: 216
yodeling CO: 224
Monroe, Birch CO: 140
Monroe, Charlie CO: 140, 141, 194; FO: 142, 180
Monroe, Clark JA: 85
Monroe, James CO: 141
Monroe Brothers CO: 85, 132; FO: 126, 133
Montana, Patsy CO: 46, 108, **141–142,** 224; FO: 125
Montana Slim. *See* Carter, Wilf
Monterey Bay Blues Festival BL: 269
Monterey Jazz Festival BL: 151; JA: 4, 139, **139,** 156
Monterey Pop Festival RR: **151–152**
Animals, The RR: 9
Beach Boys, The RR: 18
Buffalo Springfield RR: 34
Byrds, The RR: 37
Jimi Hendrix BL: 75; RR: 108, 109
Janis Joplin BL: 100; RR: 123
Mamas and the Papas, The RR: 145–146
pop rock RR: 176
Otis Redding RB: 220
rock festivals RR: 206
Simon and Garfunkel RR: 218
Who, The RR: 243, 245
Monterey Pop (movie) RR: 109, 123, 152
Monteux, Claude CL: 159
Monteux, Pierre CL: **158–159**
Boston Symphony Orchestra CL: 35
Seiji Ozawa CL: 171
André Previn CL: 183
San Francisco Symphony Orchestra CL: 199
Robert Shaw CL: 208
Montgomery, Bob CO: 57, 101; RR: 111
Montgomery, Buddy RB: 186
Montgomery, Eddie CO: 142
Montgomery, Eurreal "Little Brother" BL: 15, 26, **141,** 160, 247
Montgomery, John Michael CO: 142
Montgomery, Melba CO: 52, 111, 124, **142**
Montgomery, Monk RB: 186
Montgomery, Wes JA: **139;** RB: **186**
Paul Chambers JA: 30
Bill Frisell JA: 72
Lionel Hampton JA: 81
Incredible Jazz Guitar of Wes Montgomery, The JA: 98
Pat Martino JA: 129
Montgomery Gentry CO: **142–143,** *143*
Montgomery Ward CO: 19
Montoya, Craig RR: 99
Montreal Jazz Festival JA: 166
Montreux Jazz Festival BL: 214; JA: **139,** 166, 191
Moody, C. E. FO: 75
Moody, Clyde FO: 216
Moody Blues RR: 183
Moog, Robert CL: 43, 218
Moog synthesizer CL: 43; JA: 192
Moon, Keith RR: 68, 133–134, 243–246
Moon Band, The RB: 291
Mooney, John BL: **141**
Moonglows, The RB: 103, **186–187,** 245
Moonshine Kate (Rosa Lee Carson) CO: 33; FO: **141**
Moonsie, Susan RB: 270
Moore, Ben RB: 213
Moore, Bob CO: 147
Moore, Christy FO: 24, **141,** 158
Moore, Dorothy RB: **187–188**
Moore, Douglas CL: 15, 88, **159**
Moore, Frankie FO: 44
Moore, J. B. RB: 21
Moore, Johnny BL: 30; RB: 143. *See also* Johnny Moore's Three Blazers
Moore, Leroi RR: 52
Moore, Melba RB: **188**
Moore, Oscar BL: 101; RB: 143
Moore, Sam RB: 234
Moore, Scotty BL: 209; RB: 209; RR: 179, 205
Moore, Tiny CO: 132, 214, 219; FO: 133, **141–142,** 213
Moore, Whistlin' Alex BL: **141,** 162, 216
Moran, Robert CL: **159**
Moravians CL: xxi, 11
Moreira, Airto JA: 43, 52; RB: 275
Morel, Jean CL: **159,** 210
Morello, Joe JA: 24
Moreve, Rushton RR: 228
Morgan, Edwin JA: 185
Morgan, George CO: **143**
Morgan, J. P. CL: 146
Morgan, Lee JA: 19, 86, 137, 138, **140**
Morgan, Lorrie CO: 143, 215
Morgan City, Mississippi BL: **139**
Mormon Tabernacle Choir CL: **159**
Moroder, Giorgio RB: 61, 249, 250; RR: 27
Morris, Chuck CO: 32

Morris, Dale CO: 47
Morris, Gary CO: **144**
Morris, Joe RB: 3
Morris, Wiley FO: 142
Morris, Zeke FO: 142
Morris Brothers, The FO: **142,** 168
Morris dancing FO: 102, 117, 173
Morris On FO: 102, 117
Morrison, Jim RR: 62, 64
Morrison, Sterling RR: 240, 242
Morrison, Van BL: 233; FO: 33; RR: 211, 219
Morse, Kevin RB: 265
Morton, Jelly Roll BL: **141;** JA: *140,* **140–141**
  Archive of American Folk Song FO: 4
  "Black Bottom Stomp" JA: **16**
  Cozy Cole RB: 46
  definition of jazz JA: xxii
  Baby Dodds JA: 53
  Scott Joplin JA: 110
  Alan Lomax BL: 118
  Lester Melrose BL: 131
  New Orleans jazz JA: 143
  Kid Ory JA: 150
  Ralph Peer BL: 158
  piano BL: 160; JA: 155
  ragtime JA: 161
  Jimmy Rushing BL: 186
  Stuff Smith JA: 184
Morton, Robin FO: 18, 75
Morton, Shadow RR: 91
Morvan, Fabrice RB: 184
Mosby, Johnny and Jeanie CO: 105
Moser, Cactus CO: 32
Moses, Bob JA: 26
Moss, Buddy BL: 120, 121, **142,** 240, 245
Moss, Mark FO: 187
Most, Andrew RB: 261
Most, Mickie RB: 125; RR: 9, 61, 252
Mostly Mozart Festival CL: 79, **160,** 203, 204
Moten, Bennie BL: 186; JA: 10, 111, **141,** 212–213
Mother Blues (Chicago) RR: 122–123
Mother Earth BL: 151
Motherfolkers, The BL: 63
Mother Love Bone RR: 167
Mother McCree's Uptown Jug Stompers RR: 93
Mothers of Invention RR: 257
Motian, Paul JA: 65, 104, 124, 210
Motörhead RR: 106
Motown BL: **180–181;** RB: xvi, **188–189;** RR: **152–154**
  Luther Allison BL: 5
  Ashford & Simpson RB: 6
  J. J. Barnes RB: 11
  Contours, The RB: 48
  DeBarge RB: 55
  Detroit BL: 52
  drums RR: 68
  Four Seasons RR: 87
  Four Tops, The RB: 94
  Marvin Gaye RB: 103
  Georgio RB: 104
  girl groups RB: 106; RR: 90
  Holland-Dozier-Holland RB: 122
  Michael Jackson RB: 137
  Rick James RB: 139
  Marv Johnson RB: 144
  Eddie Kendricks RB: 151
  Shorty Long RB: 170
  Martha & the Vandellas RB: 177
  Marvelettes, The RB: 177
  Amos Milburn BL: 135
  Moonglows, The RB: 187
  reggae RR: 199–200
  rhythm and blues combos BL: 182
  Lionel Richie RB: 223, 224
  Smokey Robinson RB: 228
  Diana Ross RB: 231
  Spinners, The RB: 245
  Edwin Starr RB: 246
  Switch RB: 251
  Temptations, The RB: 255
  Vanity 6 RB: 270
  Junior Walker & the All Stars RB: 273
  Robert Ward BL: 237
  Mary Wells RB: 276
  Kim Weston RB: 277
  Stevie Wonder RB: 282–283
Mott the Hoople RR: 31
Mountain Dance and Folk Festival (Asheville, North Carolina) FO: 23, 128
Mountaineers, The CO: 130; FO: 132
"Mountain Music" CO: **144**
Mountain Music Blue Grass Style (Folkways anthology) CO: 15; FO: 7
Mount Airy, North Carolina FO: 67
mouthbow CO: 63–64
Mouzon, Alphonse RB: 275
Move, The RR: 75
"Move It On Over" CO: **144,** 216
movies (soundies) JA: **185**
Moving Hearts FO: 141
Mowatt, Judy RB: 134
Moynihan, Johnny FO: 50, 158
Mozart, Wolfgang Amadeus CL: 160
mp3 format RR: xi

MTV
  Paula Abdul RB: 1
  alternative rock RR: 8
  Neneh Cherry RB: 40
  Missy "Misdemeanor" Elliott RB: 80
  J. Geils Band BL: 94
  Monkees RR: 151
  Michael Nesmith FO: 145
  new wave RR: 157
  Pearl Jam RR: 167
  rockabilly RR: 206
  Sheila E. RB: 237
  George Thorogood BL: 220
  ZZ Top BL: 255
MTV Unplugged in New York (Nirvana) RR: 97, 161
Muck, Carl CL: 35, **160**
Mud Acres FO: 176, 204
Muddywood guitar BL: 138, 255
Mudhoney RR: 167
Muir, Ann Mayo FO: 17
Muldaur, Geoff BL: **142;** FO: **142–143,** *143*
  Paul Butterfield BL: 33
  Jim Kweskin FO: 119
  Maria Muldaur BL: 142
  vocal styles BL: 233
Muldaur, Maria BL: **142;** FO: **142–143,** *143*
  Jim Kweskin FO: 119
  Happy and Artie Traum FO: 204
  young black country blues artists BL: 251
Muldow, Barbara BL: 194
Mule Bone (musical) BL: 51, 124, 151, 251; FO: 199
Muleskinner FO: 81–83, 114, 115, **143–144,** 177
Mullen, Larry RR: 235, 236
Mullican, Moon CO: 51, **144–145,** 202; FO: 177; RR: 139
Mulligan, Gerry JA: *141,* **141–142**
  Pepper Adams JA: 3
  Chet Baker JA: 9
  Birth of the Cool JA: 15
  Dave Brubeck JA: 25
  Gil Evans JA: 67
  Art Farmer JA: 69
  Chico Hamilton JA: 80
  Mel Lewis JA: 122
  Gunther Schuller JA: 172
  John Scofield JA: 172
  Lester Young JA: 220
Mulligan, Gerry—Chet Baker Quartet JA: 80
multiphonics JA: **142**
multi-tracking RR: 100
multitrack recording BL: 179; FO: 181
Munch, Charles CL: 35, **160,** 171
Munde, Alan FO: 43, 115
Muni, Nicholas CL: 51
Munz, Mieczyslaw CL: 14
Murdoch, Colin CL: 198
Murmur (R.E.M.) RR: 201, 202
Murphey, Joaquin CO: 43
Murphey, Michael Martin CO: 46, **145;** FO: 73
Murphy, Al FO: 176
Murphy, Eddie RB: **189**
Murphy, Jess JA: 173
Murphy, Jimmy FO: **144**
Murphy, Matt "Guitar" BL: **142**
Murray, Anne CO: **145–146**
Murray the K RB: 229
Muscle Shoals, Alabama CO: 185; RB: 115, **189;** RR: 4. *See also* FAME Studio
museums JA: 4
Musica Electronica Viva JA: 119
Musical America (magazine) CL: **160,** 222, 227
Musical Quarterly (journal) CL: **160,** 211
music business and the blues BL: **142–148.** *See also* recording industry
Music from Big Pink (the Band) RR: 11, 211
Music Maker BL: 68, **148**
Music Maker Foundation BL: 148
music promoter FO: 83–84, 124–125
music theory CL: xix, 15
Musselwhite, Charlie BL: 108, 124, **148**
Mussorgsky, Modest RR: 184
Mustaine, Dave RR: 145–147
mute JA: 51, **142**
Muti, Riccardo CL: **160,** 176
Mutter, Anne-Sophie CL: 183
Mutual Broadcasting System FO: 100
"My Babe" BL: 73, 116
"My Days Have Been So Wondrous Free" CL: xx–xxi, 105, **160**
Mydland, Brent RR: 93
Myers, Billy RB: 203
Myers, David BL: 116, **148.** *See also* the Aces
Myers, James E. RR: 102
Myers, Louis BL: 116, **149.** *See also* the Aces
Myers, Sam BL: 66
"My Favorite Things" JA: 40, **142**
Myles, Willie RB: 174
Mynah Birds, The RB: 139; RR: 253–254
"Mystery Train" BL: 157, 164

Mystikal RB: **189–190,** 203
"My Toot Toot" BL: 183; RB: 182

N

Naftalin, Mark BL: 33, **151**
Nagano, Kent CL: **161**
Nagler, Paul CL: 51
Nancarrow, Conlon CL: 78, **161**
Nance, Ray JA: 189
Napalm Death RR: 107
Napoleon, Cedric RB: 207
Napster RR: 147
Naropa Institute FO: 190
Nas RB: 26, 142, 185, **191**
Nash, Graham RR: 120
Nash, Johnny RB: 175, **191–192,** 222; RR: 201
Nashville Bluegrass Band CO: 16; FO: 43, 115, **145**
Nashville Grass CO: 75, 194
Nashville Network. *See* TNN
Nashville Skyline (Bob Dylan)
  Norman Blake FO: 16
  Johnny Cash CO: 35
  country rock CO: 45
  Charlie Daniels CO: 53
  Bob Dylan FO: 57
  Charlie McCoy CO: 136
  roots rock RR: 211
Nashville sound CO: xvii–xviii, 21, **147–148,** 161, 169
Nathan, Syd BL: 106, 107; CO: 43, 169
National Association of Jazz Educators JA: 163
National Barn Dance CO: **148**
  Rex Allen CO: 3
  Arkie the Arkansas Woodchopper FO: 5
  Bob Atcher FO: 8
  Dinning Sisters, The CO: 58
  Red Foley CO: 76
  Girls of the Golden West CO: 83
  Grand Ole Opry CO: 86
  Hay, George D. CO: 96–97
  Hoosier Hot Shots CO: 103
  Bradley Kincaid FO: 116
  Lily May Ledford FO: 124
  Lulu Belle and Scotty FO: 127, 128
  Joe Maphis CO: 133
  Louise Massey and the Westerners CO: 134
  Patsy Montana CO: 141
  Linda Parker FO: 155
  "Fiddlin'" Doc Roberts FO: 173
National Conservatory of Music CL: **161**
National Folk Festival (1966) FO: 5, 128
National Folklife Festival. *See* Festival of American Folklife
National Medal of Arts JA: 29, 81
National Old-Time Fiddler's Contest FO: 44, 152
National Public Radio (NPR) BL: 143; FO: 166, 170; JA: 23, 218
National Quartet Convention CO: 15
National steel guitar CO: 60, 160; FO: 54
National Symphony Orchestra CL: **162**
Nation of Islam RB: 209, 235
Native American music CL: 41, 76
Native Americans CL: vii, xxiv, 129, 237; FO: 121, 179
Native Tongues Posse RB: **192**
Natural Four RB: **192**
Naughty by Nature RB: **192**
Navarro, Esther RB: 33, 34
Navarro, Fats JA: 81
Nazty RB: 4
NBC CL: 6; CO: 76, 87, 103, 148; JA: 196
NBC Symphony Orchestra CL: xxiii, **162**
Neal, Kenny BL: **151**
Near, Holly FO: 125, 185
Neff, Pat BL: 112; FO: 123
Nelly RB: **192–193,** *193,* 194
Nelson, Billy RB: 43
Nelson, Earl RB: 54
Nelson, George RB: 200
Nelson, Harriet RR: 155
Nelson, Ken CO: 170
Nelson, Nate RB: 93, 94
Nelson, Nikki CO: 32
Nelson, Oliver JA: 19
Nelson, Ozzie RR: 155
Nelson, Ricky RR: *155,* **155–156**
  Albert Brumley CO: 26
  country rock CO: 44
  Fats Domino RR: 59
  Joe Maphis CO: 133
  Roy Orbison RR: 165
Nelson, Sandy RR: 115
Nelson, Tracy BL: **151**
Nelson, Willie CO: **148–150,** *149*
  Johnny Cash CO: 35
  Ray Charles BL: 38
  Patsy Cline CO: 39
  Jessi Colter CO: 41, 42
  cowboy songs CO: 46
  "Crazy" CO: 47, 48
  Harold "Pappy" Daily CO: 52
  Steve Frumholz FO: 74
  Johnny Gimble CO: 82; FO: 77
  Merle Haggard CO: 92
  "Hello Walls" CO: 98

"In the Jailhouse Now" CO: 108
Waylon Jennings CO: 110
Toby Keith CO: 116
Kris Kristofferson CO: 119
"Mamas Don't Let Your Babies Grow up to Be Cowboys" CO: 131
Grady Martin CO: 134
"On the Road Again" CO: 154
Webb Pierce CO: 162
Ray Price CO: 163
Jeannie Seely CO: 184
Townes Van Zandt FO: 208
Hank Williams, Jr. CO: 217
Faron Young CO: 225
Neptunes, The RB: 177, **193–194**
N.E.R.D. RB: 194
Nesby, Ann RB: 195
Nesmith, Michael FO: **145**
Nesmith, Mike RR: 149, 151
Neuendorff, Adolf CL: 34
Nevermind (Nirvana) RR: 97, 160
Neville, Aaron BL: 151; CO: 224
Neville, Art BL: 151, 152; RB: 182, 183
Neville, Charles BL: 151
Neville, Cyril BL: 151, 152
Neville, Ivan BL: 152
Neville Brothers, The BL: **151–152,** 220; RB: 183
Nevins, Marian. *See* MacDowell, Marian
Nevins, Richard BL: 153; FO: 38
New Air JA: 217
New Birth Brass Band JA: **143**
Newborn, Phineas RB: 15
Newbury, Mickey BL: 44
New Christy Minstrels, The CO: 178; FO: **145–146**
"new country" CO: xviii, 16
New Deal BL: 201–202
New Deal String Band FO: 148
New Edition RB: 25, **194**
New England CL: xx; FO: 192
New England Conservatory of Music CL: **162**
New England Psalm-Singer, The (William Billings) CL: 29, **162–163**
Newfield, Heidi CO: 201
New Grass Revival CO: 16; FO: 68, **146–147,** 161
New Jack Swing RB: 25, 194. *See also* swingbeat
New Jersey BL: 153; JA: 10; RR: 85, 224
New Jersey Symphony Orchestra CL: 146, **163,** 240
New Jill Swing RB: 82, 251
New Lost City Ramblers FO: *147,* **147–148**
Moses Asch FO: 7
Cajun music CO: 29; FO: 27
John Cohen FO: 38
Cousin Emmy FO: 45
Bill Cox FO: 45
fiddle FO: 67
folk revival FO: 70
Newport Folk Festival FO: 149
Mike Seeger FO: 181
Newman, Buster RB: 120
Newman, Jimmy "C" CO: 92, **150;** FO: **148–149**
Newman, John FO: 18
Newman, Paul (folklorist) FO: 210
New Nashville Cats (Mark O'Connor) CO: 186; FO: 152
New Orleans, Louisiana BL: **121,** 134, 161–162, 176, 182
New Orleans Jazz and Heritage Festival BL: 55, 165, 244, 269; JA: **143**
New Orleans jazz (classic) JA: xxii–xxiii, **143**. *See also specific artists*
Chicago jazz JA: 32
Dixieland jazz JA: 53
hot jazz JA: 94–95
jazz firsts JA: 116
Preservation Hall JA: 157–158
prominent artists JA: xxxii
recordings of early jazz JA: 162
Storyville JA: 188
time line JA: 252*t*
traditional jazz JA: 198
New Orleans jazz (contemporary) JA: 16, 127, 143
Newport Folk Festival FO: **149**
Joan Baez FO: 9
Michael Bloomfield BL: 20
Dock Boggs FO: 17
Johnny Cash CO: 35
Rev. Gary Davis BL: 50
Willie Dixon BL: 53
Bob Dylan BL: 55; FO: 57; RR: 71
folk rock RR: 84
Jesse Fuller BL: 65–66
Bob Gibson FO: 76
Albert Grossman FO: 83
Son House BL: 82
Mississippi John Hurt BL: 83; FO: *101*
Skip James BL: 90
Sam Lay BL: 111
Fred McDowell BL: 128
Morris Brothers FO: 142
New Lost City Ramblers FO: 148
Ralph Rinzler FO: 170

Newport Folk Festival (*continued*)
Jean Ritchie FO: 172
Rooftop Singers FO: 175
Jim Rooney FO: 176
Sing Out! magazine FO: 186
Skillet Lickers FO: 187
vocal styles BL: 232
Robert Pete Williams BL: 242
Newport Jazz Festival JA: **143–144**
Dave Brubeck JA: 25
Coleman Hawkins JA: 88
Helen Humes BL: 83
Abdullah Ibrahim JA: 97
jazz firsts JA: 117
Charles Mingus JA: 136
Cecil Taylor JA: 194
Joe Venuti JA: 206
New Riders of the Purple Sage CO: 46; RR: 120
New River Ranch FO: 166–167
Newsome, Bobby RB: 271
the New South (J. D. Crowe band) CO: 186, 215; FO: 3, 47, 169
Newsted, Jason RR: 146, 147
Newton, Abby FO: 38, 148
Newton, Wayne CO: 22
Newton, Wendy FO: 4
new wave RR: 92, 127–128, **156–159,** 176, 189, 199. *See also* Blondie; Talking Heads
New Wave of British Heavy Metal RR: 106
New World Singers FO: 204
New World Symphony Orchestra CL: 223
New York City CL: xxiv; BL: **152–153;** FO: xvi; JA: **144.** *See also* Greenwich Village; Harlem
New York City Opera CL: **163–164**
New York Contemporary Five JA: 31, 177
New York Dolls RR: 188
New York Herald Tribune CL: 36, 99, 224
New York Philharmonic Orchestra CL: xxii, **164–165**
New York Pro Musica Antiqua CL: 93, **165**
New York Ramblers FO: 83
New York State Theater CL: 163–164, **165**
New York Symphony Society CL: **165–166**
An American in Paris CL: 7
Concerto in F CL: 55
Leopold Damrosch CL: 64
Walter Damrosch CL: 64
New York Philharmonic Orchestra CL: 164
Philharmonic Symphony Society of New York CL: 177
New Zealand RR: 157
Next RB: **195**
Ngqawana, Zim JA: 187
the Nice RR: 184
Nice, Gregg RB: 195
Nice, Pete RB: 158
Nice & Smooth RB: **195**
Nicholas, Hayden CO: 14
Nichols, Red JA: 206
Nicholson, Jack RR: 151
Nickel Creek CO: 16, **150–151;** FO: **149**
Nicks, Stevie BL: 63; RR: 75, 82–84, 177–178
Nico RR: 241–242
Nicol, Simon FO: 64, 102
Nigeria RB: 70
A Night at the Opera (Queen) RR: 191, 193
nightclubs and ballrooms JA: 14–15, 43–44, 170–171
Night Flyers BL: 163
Nighthawk, Robert BL: **153–154**
Willie Dixon RB: 63
"Kansas City Blues" BL: 103
Charlie Musselwhite BL: 148
Pinetop Perkins BL: 159
Jimmy Rogers BL: 184
Houston Stackhouse BL: 206
Peetie Wheatstraw BL: 241
Nighthawk Syncopators JA: 59
Night Owl Coffeehouse BL: 153
Nike RR: 182
Niles, John Jacob FO: **150**
Nirvana RR: 97, **159–161**
Nite Shift RB: 273
Nitty Gritty Dirt Band CO: **151**
Carter Family CO: 35
country rock CO: 45
Jimmy Martin FO: 134
John McEuen FO: 136
Michael Nesmith FO: 145
Jerry Jeff Walker FO: 209
Nix, Don RB: 175
Nixon, Hammie BL: 60, 175
Nixon, Richard M. CL: 175; CO: 87, 175
Noack, Eddie CO: **152**
"Nobody Knows You When You're Down and Out" BL: **154**
Nocentelli, Leo RB: 182
Nolan, Bob CO: 189, 204
nonet JA: 15, 49, 67, **144**
No Nukes concerts RR: 221
Noone, Jimmie BL: 76
Norma Jean CO: **152,** 209
Norman, Bob FO: 186
Norris, Fate FO: 75
Norris, Land FO: 187
North Carolina Ramblers FO: 159
North Mississippi All Stars BL: **154;** RR: 211

Northumbrian pipes FO: 10
Norvo, Red BL: 83; JA: 136, **144–145,** 224
Norway JA: 73; RR: 157
nostalgia CO: vii, viii
Notorious B. I. G., The (Biggie Smalls) RB: 7, 54, 166, **195–196,** 213
Notturno (Donald Martino) CL: **166**
Novosel, Steve JA: 98
Novoselic, Krist RR: 159–161
Nowlin, Bill BL: 186
NPR. *See* National Public Radio
NRBQ CO: 55, 162
Nudie suits CO: 46
Numan, Gary RR: 158
Nunley, Louis CO: 116
Nunn, Bobby RB: 45, 227
N.W.A. RB: 54, 71, 78, 130, **196**
Nyro, Laura RR: 152

O

Oakenfold, Paul RR: 182
Oakland, California
  Lowell Fulson BL: 66
  Bob Geddins BL: 67
  Alvin Youngblood Hart BL: 74
  migration BL: 134
  San Francisco Bay Area BL: 35
  Katie Webster BL: 240
  young black country blues artists BL: 252
Oakley, Berry BL: 6; RR: 4, 5
Oak Publications BL: 215; FO: 186
Oak Ridge Boys CO: **153–154**
Oaktown's 3-5-7 RB: **197**
Oasis RR: **163–164**
Oberlin Conservatory of Music CL: **167**
Oberstein, Eli FO: 142
Oborin, Lev CL: 26
O'Briain, Garry FO: 18
O'Brien, Ed RR: 195
O'Brien, Molly FO: 151
O'Brien, Tim FO: 100, **151**
O Brother, Where Art Thou? (movie)
  Emry Arthur FO: 6
  Norman Blake FO: 16
  Albert E. Brumley FO: 22
  Cox Family FO: 46
  Jimmie Davis CO: 54
  John Hartford FO: 93
  Haywire Mac FO: 94
  "I Am a Man of Constant Sorrow" CO: 107
  Alison Krauss CO: 118
  Stanley Brothers FO: 194
  The Stanley Brothers CO: 191
  Gillian Welch FO: 213
  "You Are My Sunshine" CO: 225
O'Bryant, Alan FO: 145
Ocasek, Ric RR: 158
Ocean, Billy RB: **197**
Oceans, Lucky CO: 5
Ochs, Larry JA: 166
Ochs, Phil FO: 19, 34, 76, 99, **151**
O'Connell, Helen CO: 192
O'Connell, Maura FO: 50
O'Connell, Robbie FO: 35
O'Connor, Mark FO: **151–152**
  "Devil Went Down to Georgia, The" CO: 56
  fiddle CO: 73; FO: 67
  Johnny Gimble CO: 83; FO: 77
  Doug Kershaw CO: 116
  Ricky Skaggs CO: 186
O'Day, Molly FO: 126, **152–153,** 216
O'Day, Skeets FO: 152
"O Death" CO: 191; FO: 194
O'Dell, Kenny CO: 131
Oden, Jimmy (St. Louis Jimmy) BL: **155**
"Ode to Billie Joe" CO: 80, **154**
Odetta BL: 249; FO: 34, **153,** 207
O'Domnhaill, Michael FO: 17, 24
O'Donnell, Eugene FO: 141
Odum, Howard BL: xvii
Oertle, Ernie BL: 97, 98
Oestriech, James R. CL: 211
O'Farrill, Chico JA: **147**
O'Flynn, Liam FO: 158
Of Reminiscences and Reflections (Gunther Schuller) CL: **167**
"Oh, Pretty Woman" RR: 164, 165
Oh Boys, The FO: 151
Ohio Players, The BL: 237; RB: **197–199,** *198,* 265
Ohlsson, Garrick CL: xxv, *167,* **167–168**
O'Jay, Eddie RB: 199
O'Jays, The RB: **199**
"Okie from Muskogee" CO: viii, 91, **154**
Okies CO: 10, 41; FO: 190
Oklahoma Blues Society BL: 113
Oklahoma City, Oklahoma BL: 190
Okun, Milton FO: 30, 157
Olaine, Jason JA: 3
Olander, Jimmy CO: 56
Olatunji, Babatunde RR: 213

Old and In the Way CO: 45; FO: **153,** 177; RR: 96
Old and New Dreams JA: 16, 79
Old Dogs, The CO: 12
Oldham, Andrew Loog RR: 208, 209
Oldham, Spooner RB: 115, 189
Ol' Dirty Bastard RB: 283, 285
Old Reliable String Band FO: 148
Old Songs, Inc. FO: 191
old-time country CO: xvii
Old Town School of Folk Music FO: 90
O'Leary, Christy FO: 18
Olive, Patrick RB: 124, 125
Oliveira, Elmar CL: **168**
Oliver, Joseph "King" JA: **147–148,** *148*
  Louis Armstrong JA: 6
  in Chicago JA: xxiii
  cornet JA: 43
  "Dipper Mouth Blues" JA: **52–53**
  Baby Dodds JA: 53, 54
  Johnny Dodds JA: 54
  Lil Hardin JA: 84
  Lil Hardin and JA: xxx
  Bertha "Chippie" Hill BL: 76
  Alberta Hunter JA: 95
  Lizzie Miles BL: 135
  New Orleans jazz JA: 143
  Kid Ory JA: 150
  recordings of early jazz JA: 162
Oliver, Paul BL: xxi, 5; FO: 195
Olliver, Perry CL: 29
Olson, Carla FO: 36
Onassis, Jacqueline Kennedy CL: 149
O'Neal, Jim BL: 51
One-derful Records RB: **199**
114 Songs (Charles Ives) CL: 114, **168**
"One Kind Favor." *See* "See That My Grave Is Kept Clean"
one-man band BL: 65–66, 185, 188
Ono, Yoko RR: 40
On the Corner (Miles Davis) JA: 2, 50
"On the Other Hand" CO: **154,** 201
"On the Road Again" CO: 150, **154**
On the Road (Jack Kerouac) RR: 93, 251
On the Transmigration of Souls (John Adams) CL: 3, **168–169**
Onyx Club JA: 184
"Ooby Dooby" RR: 112, 164–165
Opals, The RB: 239
Open House FO: 24
open strings BL: 2–3
open-throat singers BL: 118, 229, 232
open tunings BL: 222
opera CL: xvi, xxii, 154–155; CO: 52. *See also specific artists and works*
operetta CL: 101–102
Oppens, Ursula CL: **169,** 212
Opryland USA CO: 1, 56, 87–88, 99
O'Raida, Sean FO: 32–33
oral transmission FO: xv
"Orange Blossom Special" CO: 166; FO: 177
Orbison, Roy RR: **164–166,** *165*
  Electric Light Orchestra RR: 76–77
  Buddy Holly RR: 112
  Charlie McCoy CO: 136
  Don McLean FO: 137
  Carl Perkins CO: 162
  Bruce Springsteen RR: 225
  U2 RR: 237
orchestra CL: xvi, xix–xx, xxvi. *See also specific orchestras*
Organized Noize RB: **199–200**
organ/organists JA: **148**
Original Dixieland Jazz Band JA: **148–150,** *149*
  Dixieland jazz JA: 53
  jazz JA: 105
  jazz firsts JA: 116
  "Livery Stable Blues" JA: **124**
  recordings of early jazz JA: 162
Original Tuxedo Jazz Band JA: 10
Orioles, The RB: *66,* **200;** RR: 65
Orlons, The RB: **200**
Ormandy, Eugene CL: **169–170**
  Young Uck Kim CL: 126
  Jacob Lateiner CL: 134
  Minnesota Orchestra CL: 156
  Philadelphia Orchestra CL: 176
  Francis Thorne CL: 224
Ornstein, Leo CL: *170,* **170–171**
Orpheus (chamber orchestra) CL: **171**
Ory, Kid JA: **150**
  Hot Five and Hot Seven JA: 94
  jazz firsts JA: 116
  Charles Mingus JA: 136
  King Oliver JA: 147
  recordings of early jazz JA: 162
  Hociel Thomas BL: 219
Orzabal, Roland RB: 3
Osborn, Joe RR: 14

Osborne, Bobby FO: 134, 153, 154, 217
Osborne, Jeffrey RB: 170, 171, **200**
Osborne, Sonny FO: 134, 153, 154
Osborne Brothers, The FO: 3, 44–45, 134, **153–154**
Osbourne, Ozzy RR: 106
Oscar Awards JA: 121
Oscela, Arkansas BL: 189
Oscher, Paul BL: **155**
Oskar, Lee RB: 273, 274
Oslin, K. T. CO: **154–155**
Osmond, Donnie CO: 155
Osmond, Marie CO: **155**
Ossman, Vess L. CO: 11; FO: 12
Oster, Harry
  blues lyrics BL: 20, 22, 25
  Snooks Eaglin BL: 57
  Jenkins and Sherrill FO: 111
  Chris Strachwitz BL: 207
  Robert Pete Williams BL: 244
Oswald, Bashful Brother CO: 60, 209; FO: 54
Other Ones, The RR: 96
Otis, Clyde RB: 16, 276
Otis, George RB: 247
Otis, Johnny BL: **155;** RB: **200**
  Hank Ballard and the Midnighters RB: 8
  Etta James BL: 90; RB: 138
  Leiber and Stoller RR: 138
  Little Richard RR: 141
  Esther Phillips RB: 206
  Robins, The RB: 227
  Big Mama Thornton BL: 219
Otis, Shuggie BL: 155
Ottenberg, Simon BL: 19
Ottley, Jerold CL: 159
Ousley, Curtis. *See* King Curtis
"Outbound Plane" CO: 18; FO: 82
OutKast RB: 199, 200, **201**
outlaw country CO: xviii; FO: 73–74. *See also specific artists*
Outlaws, The (anthology) CO: 83, 110, 149
Outskirts, The FO: 199
Out There (Eric Dolphy) JA: 55, **150**
Out to Lunch (Eric Dolphy) JA: 55, 216
Ovation guitar FO: 86
Ovations, The RB: **201**
overdubbing JA: **150**
Overstake, Lucille CO: 83
Owen, Fuzzy CO: 91, 155
Owen, Jackie CO: 3
Owen, Randy Yuell CO: 3
Owens, Bonnie CO: 91, 155, **155**
Owens, Buck CO: **155–156**
  "Act Naturally" CO: 1
  Bakersfield Sound CO: 10
  Albert Brumley CO: 26
  Albert E. Brumley FO: 22
  Tommy Collins CO: 41
  country rock RR: 44
  Hee Haw CO: 97, 98
  Rose Maddox CO: 130
  Bonnie Owens CO: 155
  Dwight Yoakam CO: 224
Owens, Jack BL: 137, **155,** 230
Owens, Jesse BL: 202
Owens, Marshall BL: 166
Owens, Monte RB: 243
Owens, Richard RB: 141
Owens, Shirley RB: 238; RR: 216, 217
Owens, Tex CO: 36
Oxford, Mississippi BL: **139**
Oxley, Tony JA: 131
Ozark Jubilee CO: 25, 76
Ozawa, Seiji CL: **171–172**
  Marin Alsop CL: 6
  Boston Symphony Orchestra CL: 35
  Peter Lieberson CL: 138
  Ravinia Festival CL: 186
  San Francisco Symphony Orchestra CL: 199
Ozuna, Sunny RB: 250

P

P. Diddy. *See* Puff Daddy
Pablo, Petey RB: **203**
Pace, Harry Herbert BL: 178, 187; JA: 116, 162
Paderewski, Ignacy CL: 21, 187
Paepcke, Walter CL: 13
Paganini, Niccolò CL: 188
Page, Jimmy
  Donovan RR: 60
  Fred Gerlach BL: 68
  heavy metal RR: 106
  Led Zeppelin BL: 113; RR: 133–137
  Yardbirds, The BL: 247; RR: 251–253
Page, Oran "Hot Lips" JA: 15, 109
Page, Patti CO: 117, 140, 197
Paine, John Knowles CL: **173**
  Azara CL: **14**
  John Alden Carpenter CL: 45
  Centennial Hymn CL: **47**
  Louis Coerne CL: 54
  Arthur Foote CL: 80
  Edward Burlingame Hill CL: 102
  Daniel Gregory Mason CL: 149
Paine, Zack FO: 110
Paisley, Brad CO: **157,** *157*
Paisley Park RB: 212
Paisley Underground RR: 187, 211

Paley, Tom FO: 38, 148, 181
Palmer, Bruce RR: 34, 35, 254
Palmer, Carl RR: 69, 184
Palmer, Clarence. *See* the Jive Bombers
Palmer, Clive FO: 106
Palmer, Earl RB: 150; RR: 58, 67
Palmer, Robert (writer) BL: 104; RR: 220
Palomar Ballroom, Los Angeles JA: 76
"Pan American Blues" BL: 72; CO: 10, 166; FO: 92
Pappalardi, Felix FO: 28; RR: 46
Paradise in Harlem (movie) JA: 184; RB: 184
Paradons, The RB: **203**
Paray, Paul CL: 68
Parchman Penitentiary (Farm) BL: 74–75, 81, 138, 241
Parents' Music Resource Center (PMRC) BL: 37; RR: 259
Paris, France
  Eddie Boyd BL: 29
  Jimi Hendrix RR: 109
  Son House BL: 82
  Steve Lacy JA: 119
  Lizzie Miles BL: 135
  Bud Powell JA: 157
  Archie Shepp JA: 177
Paris, Texas (movie) BL: 43, 79, 94, 193
Parke, Nathaniel CL: 34
Parker, Byron FO: 110, 111
Parker, Charlie JA: xxiv, *151*, **151–152**
  Cannonball Adderley JA: 3
  American Jazz Museum JA: 4
  Chet Baker JA: 9
  bebop JA: 11
  Birdland JA: 15
  Art Blakey JA: 17
  Ray Brown JA: 24
  Kenny Clarke JA: 34
  Ornette Coleman JA: 36
  cutting contest JA: 45
  Miles Davis JA: 48, 49
  Dizzy Gillespie JA: 75
  Dexter Gordon JA: 77
  Earl "Fatha" Hines JA: 91
  JATP JA: 106
  jazz and the blues BL: 92
  Hank Jones JA: 109
  Kansas City jazz JA: 111
  Machito JA: 125
  Jay McShann BL: 130
  Charles Mingus JA: 136
  Minton's Playhouse JA: 137
  Red Norvo JA: 145
  Chico O'Farrill JA: 147
  Pleasant Joe BL: 163
  Bud Powell JA: 156, 157
  Max Roach JA: 165
  "Salt Peanuts" JA: 169
  saxophone JA: 171
  Sonny Stitt JA: 188
  Sir Charles Thompson JA: 197
  Sarah Vaughn JA: 205
  the Yardbirds RR: 251
Parker, Horatio CL: **173**
  Hora Novissima CL: **106**
  Charles Ives CL: 113
  Clara Anna Korn CL: 128
  Douglas Moore CL: 159
  Roger Sessions CL: 206
Parker, Jeff JA: 32
Parker, Junior BL: **157,** 209, 241; RB: **203–204**
Parker, Linda FO: **155**
Parker, Maceo JA: 217; RB: 276
Parker, Ray, Jr. RB: **204**
Parker, Richard RB: 39
Parker, Colonel Tom RB: 210; RR: 180, 181
Parks, Rosa FO: 33
Parks, Van Dyke FO: 28; RR: 17
Parlan, Horace JA: 19
Parlet RB: 274
Parliament/Funkadelic RB: 43–44, 98–99, 274, 276
Parris, Fred RB: 90, 91
Parry, Dick RR: 174
Parry, John CL: 159
Parsons, Alan RR: 174
Parsons, Gene CO: 75; RR: 37
Parsons, Gram
  Byrds FO: 25; RR: 37
  country rock CO: 44, 45; RR: 45
  Flying Burrito Brothers CO: 75
  Emory Gordy, Jr. CO: 84
  Emmylou Harris CO: 94
  pedal steel guitar CO: 161
  Barry and Holly Tashian FO: 199
Partch, Harry CL: 119, **173–174**
Parton, Dolly CO: **158**
  Suzy Bogguss CO: 18
  "Coat of Many Colors" CO: 39
  countrypolitan CO: 44
  Cox Family FO: 46
  Jerry Douglas FO: 55
  Emmylou Harris CO: 95
  Nickel Creek CO: 150; FO: 149
  Porter Wagoner CO: 209, 210
Passarelli, Kenny BL: 214
Pastorius, Jaco JA: 11, 15, 20, **152;** RB: 275; RR: 15
patent medicines FO: 180
Paton, Caroline FO: 155, 164
Paton, Sandy FO: **155–156,** 164
Patrick, Pat JA: 190
Patrick Street FO: 24, 107
patriotism CO: viii

patronage CL: vii, xxi, xxv, xxvi
Patton, Charley BL: **157**
aliases BL: 5
Willie Brown BL: 31
Cleveland, Mississippi BL: 138
country blues BL: 45
John Fahey BL: 61; FO: 63
Holly Ridge, Mississippi BL: 138
holy blues BL: 77, 79
Son House BL: 82
Howlin' Wolf BL: 82
Tommy Johnson BL: 99
"Pony Blues" BL: 164
Bukka White BL: 241
Joe Willie Wilkins BL: 243
Paul, Alan JA: 126
Paul, Les BL: 58, 179; CO: 6; RR: 100
Paul, Woody FO: 170, *171*
Paul Butterfield Blues Band. *See* Butterfield, Paul
Pauling, Clarence RB: 90
Pauling, Lowman RB: 90
Paur, Emil CL: 179
Paxton, Tom BL: 84; FO: 19, 95, **156,** 185
Paycheck, Johnny CO: 40, **158–159,** 197
Payne, Benny JA: 212
Payne, Rufe CO: 216
Payton, Lawrence RB: 94, 95
Peabody Conservatory (Peabody Institute) CL: **174**
"Peace in the Valley" BL: 54; CO: 76, **159**
Peaches & Herb RB: **204**
Peacock Records BL: **157–158.** *See also* Robey, Don
Peak, Donald RB: 39
Pearl, Minnie CO: 87, 117, 140, *159,* **159–160,** 180–181
Pearl Beer CO: 101
Pearl Harbor BL: 202; FO: 168
Pearl Jam RR: 97, **167–168,** *168,* 254
Pearl (Janis Joplin) BL: 100; RR: 122, 124
Pearlman, Martin CL: 34
Pearl Wranglers CO: 101
Pebbles RB: 223, 258
pedal steel guitar CO: 45, 90, **160–161,** 212; FO: 54
Pedersen, Herb FO: 43, 53, 169
Peebles, Ann RB: **204**
Peekskill, New York FO: 174, 185
Peer, Ralph BL: xxi, **158;** CO: vii
Carter Family CO: 34
Kelly Harrell FO: 92
Hill Billies FO: 97
"Little Old Log Cabin in the Lane" CO: 123
record labels CO: 167
Blind Alfred Reed FO: 166
Jimmie Rodgers BL: 182; CO: 177
rube/hillbilly humor CO: 180
Ernest "Pop" Stoneman FO: 194
Robert Wilkins BL: 243
Peerce, Jan CL: 227
Pegg, Dave FO: 64
Pelham, Dick FO: 139
Pendergast, Tom BL: 131, 140
Pendergrass, Teddy RB: **204–205**
Penelope's Children FO: 69
Penguins, The RB: **205,** 207; RR: 64
Penn, Dan RB: 115
Pennario, Leonard CL: **174**
Pennebaker, D. A. RR: 31
Pennington, J.P. FO: 124
Pennsylvania FO: 134–135, 166–167
Penny, Hank CO: 26, 43
pennywhistles FO: 69
Pentangle FO: 109, **156,** 167
Peoples, Tommy FO: 17, 19, 24
People's Choice RB: **205**
People's Songs FO: 174, 182, 185
Perahia, Murray CL: **174–175**
percussion. *See* drums; *specific percussion instruments, e.g.:* vibraphone
percussion (Latin) JA: 125, 157, 158, 170; RR: 213
Perfect, Christine. *See* McVie, Christine
Perick, Christof CL: 141
period instruments. *See* early music
Perkins, Al CO: 75
Perkins, Carl BL: **158;** CO: **161–162;** RR: **168–169**
Johnny Cash CO: 35
Jerry Lee Lewis CO: 122
Nashville sound CO: 148
Roy Orbison RR: 165
Sam Phillips RR: 170, 171
rockabilly CO: 176–177; RR: 205
U2 RR: 237
Perkins, Clayton CO: 161, 162; RR: 169
Perkins, Greg RR: 169
Perkins, Jay CO: 161, 162; RR: 169
Perkins, Luther CO: 35
Perkins, Pinetop BL: **158–159,** *159,* 239
Perkins, Stan RR: 169
Perle, George CL: **175**
Perlis, Vivian CL: 171
Perlman, Itzhak CL: 153

Perls, Nick BL: 153; FO: 164
Perry, Joe RB: 232; RR: 1–3
Perry, Lee "Scratch" RB: 175
Perryman, William Lee. *See* Piano Red
Persichetti, Vincent CL: **175–176**
  Richard Danielpour CL: 64
  James DePreist CL: 67
  Jacob Druckman CL: 70
  Philip Glass CL: 89
  Steve Reich CL: 186
  Peter Schickele CL: 200
Persinger, Louis CL: **176**
personal management CO: 64
Persuaders, The RB: **205**
Persuasions, The RB: 2, **205–206**
Perverett, Dave BL: 155
Peter, Paul and Mary FO: **156–157**
  Hamilton Camp FO: 28
  Civil Rights movement FO: 34
  Rev. Gary Davis BL: 50
  Bob Dylan FO: 57
  folk revival FO: 70
  Bob Gibson FO: 76
  Albert Grossman FO: 83
  "If I Had My Way" FO: 106
  Gordon Lightfoot FO: 125
  Phil Ochs FO: 151
Peterson, Oscar JA: *153*, **153–154**
  Toshiko Akiyoshi JA: 3
  Ray Brown JA: 24
  Roy Eldridge JA: 60
  Herbie Hancock JA: 82
  Japanese jazz JA: 103
  JATP JA: 106
  Clark Terry JA: 196
Peterson, Wayne CL: **176**
Petri, Egon CL: 118, **176**
Petrucciani, Michel JA: 124, **154**
Pet Shop Boys RR: 158
Pettiford, Oscar JA: 18, 23, **154**
Petty, Norman CO: 19, 101; FO: 95; RR: 112, 113, 164
Petty, Tom RR: 76, 166, 177–178, 216
Petty, Tom, and the Heartbreakers RR: 177, 178
Petty, Vi RR: 125
Petway, Robert BL: 57, 127, **159**
P-Funk All Stars RB: 44
Phelps, Arthur. *See* Blake, Blind
Phelps, Kelly Joe BL: 4, **159**
Phife RB: 260
Philadelphia Orchestra CL: xxiv, **176**
philanthropy CL: xxi
Philharmonia Baroque Orchestra CL: **177**
Philharmonia Virtuosi CL: **177**
Philharmonic Hall CL: **177**. *See also* Avery Fisher Hall
Philharmonic Symphony Society of New York CL: **177**
Philip Glass Ensemble CL: 89, **177**
Phillips, Barre JA: 191
Phillips, Brewer BL: 213
Phillips, Bruce "U. Utah" FO: **157–158,** 191
Phillips, Dewey RR: 179
Phillips, Esther CO: 61; RB: **206**
Phillips, John FO: 71; RR: 145–146, 152
Phillips, Julianne RR: 225
Phillips, Mackenzie RR: 146
Phillips, Michelle RR: 145, 146
Phillips, Phil BL: 240
Phillips, Robert RB: 33, 34
Phillips, Sam RR: ix, **169–172,** *171*
  "Blue Moon of Kentucky" CO: 16
  Jackie Brenston RB: 25
  Martha Carson CO: 33
  "Cowboy" Jack Clement CO: 38
  Howlin' Wolf BL: 82
  Jerry Lee Lewis CO: 122; RB: 164
  Little Milton BL: 116
  Memphis BL: 131
  Carl Perkins CO: 161, 162; RR: 169
  Elvis Presley BL: 164; RB: 209; RR: 179, 180
  record labels CO: 170
  Sun Records BL: 209
  Ike and Tina Turner RB: 262
Phillips, Todd FO: 47, 122
Phillips International CO: 169
Phillips's Louisville Jug Band BL: 101
Phish FO: 135; RR: 118
Phoenix Singers, The BL: 249
phrase JA: **154,** 165
Phuture RB: 125
Pianet RR: 126
piano accordion FO: 2
piano/pianists BL: xxii, xxiii, **159–163;** JA: **155**. *See also* boogie-woogie; *specific pianists*
Piano Red (Willie Perryman) BL: **163**
Piatigorsky, Gregor CL: 134, **177–178**
Piazza, Rod BL: **163,** 194
Pickard, Obed, and Leila May FO: 158
Pickard Family, The FO: **158**
Pickett, Wilson RB: *206*, **206–207**
  Duane Allman BL: 6
  Falcons, The RB: 87

King Curtis BL: 106
Memphis BL: 132
Buddy Miles RB: 183
Muscle Shoals RB: 189
Pickow, George FO: 172
Pieces of a Dream RB: **207**
Piedmont blues BL: xix, xxii. *See also specific artists*
acoustic guitar BL: 1–2
Etta Baker FO: 10–11
blind musicians and singers BL: 18
blues revival BL: 26
country blues BL: 45
harmonica BL: 73–74
migration BL: 134
ragtime BL: 176
vocal styles BL: 229, 232
young black country blues artists BL: 253
Pierce, Don CO: 51, 52, 170; FO: 125
Pierce, Maryland RB: 89–90
Pierce, Webb CO: **162**
Bailes Brothers CO: 9
Bill Cox FO: 45
"In the Jailhouse Now" CO: 108
Louisiana Hayride CO: 123
pedal steel guitar CO: 161
"Slowly" CO: 186
Mel Tillis CO: 198
Faron Young CO: 225
Pigg, Billy FO: 10
Piggot, Charlie FO: 50
Pigpen. *See* McKernan, Ron "Pigpen"
Pilatus, Rob RB: 184
Pilgrim Travellers, The RB: 219
Pinder, Mike RR: 127
Pine, Courtney JA: **155–156,** 217; RB: 3
"Pine Top's Boogie" BL: 27, 195
Pink Floyd BL: 7; RR: **172–175,** *173,* 184, 187
Pinkham, Daniel CL: **178**
Pinson, Rev. Louis BL: 78
"Pistol Packin' Mama" CO: **162–163**
Piston, Walter CL: **178–179,** *179*
Samuel Adler CL: 4
Arthur Berger CL: 25
Leonard Bernstein CL: 26
Elliott Carter CL: 46
Irving Fine CL: 78
Joseph Fuchs CL: 83
John Harbison CL: 98
Gail Kubik CL: 131
Conlon Nancarrow CL: 161
recommended listening CL: 250
Harold Shapero CL: 207
Pitchford, Lonnie BL: **163**
Pitney, Gene CO: 142
Pittsburgh Symphony Orchestra CL: 101, **179–180,** *180*
Plant, Robert BL: 108, 113; RR: 133–137, 180
Planxty FO: 19, 107, 141, **158–159**
Plastic Ono Band RR: 40, 207
Platters, The RB: 205, **207–208,** *208*
player piano CL: 16, 161
Pleasant Joe BL: **163**
Pleasant Valley Boys FO: 175
PMRC (Parents' Music Resource Center) BL: 37; RR: 259
pocket trumpet JA: 32, **156**
Poco CO: 45, 161; RR: 35
Poe, Bobby CO: 61
Poe Cats CO: 61
Pogues, The FO: 55
Pohlig, Karl CL: 176
Pointer, Anita CO: 42; RB: 208, 209
Pointer, Bonnie RB: 208, 209
Pointer, June RB: 208, 209
Pointer, Ruth RB: 208
Pointer Sisters RB: **208–209**
Police, The RR: 158, 199
Polisi, Joseph W. CL: 121
politics CO: 54
Pollock, Ben JA: 102, 163
Pollock, Jackson CL: 38
polyrhythm JA: xxiv, 12, 108, **156,** 190
Pompilli, Rudy RR: 104
Pomus, Doc BL: **164,** 185; RR: 181
Ponce, Daniel JA: 165
Ponselle, Rosa CL: **180–181,** *181*
Ponti, Michael CL: **181**
Pontoja, Victor JA: 83
Ponty, Jean Luc JA: 52, **156**
"Pony Blues" BL: 157, **164**
Poole, Barry CO: 113
Poole, Charlie FO: *159,* **159–160**
Pop, Iggy RR: 31, 32, 188
pop punk RR: 189
pop rock RR: **175–176,** 214–216
Popwell, Robert RB: 218
Porgy and Bess (George Gershwin opera) CL: 87, **181–182,** 184
Porgy and Bess (Miles Davis and Gil Evans album) JA: 49, 68
Port Arthur, Texas BL: 99, **217,** 235; RR: 122, 124
Porter, Arthur RB: 8
Porter, Cole CL: 25
Porter, David RB: 119, 234, 244
Porter, George RB: 182
Porter, Quincy CL: 55, **182**
Porter, Roy JA: 55
Porterfield, Nolan BL: 120

Portland, Oregon BL: 51, 63, 188; FO: 24
Portland Waterfront Blues Festival BL: 269
Posies, The RR: 178
Positive-K RB: **209**
Posner, Bruce CL: 16
Poss, Barry CO: 170
Posselt, Ruth CL: **182**
post-punk RR: 157
Potts, Bob FO: 96
Potts, John FO: 35
Potts, Sean FO: 33
Potts, Sylvester RB: 48
Powdermaker, Hortense BL: 190
Powell, Bud JA: **156–157,** *157*
- bebop JA: 12
- Birdland JA: 15
- Barry Harris JA: 86
- Charles Mingus JA: 136
- Minton's Playhouse JA: 137
- Thelonious Monk JA: 138
- Oscar Pettiford JA: 154
- Sonny Rollins JA: 165
- Sonny Stitt JA: 188
- tone cluster JA: 198
- McCoy Tyner JA: 200
- Mary Lou Williams JA: 216

Powell, Dirk FO: 12
Powell, Maud CL: **182**
Powell, Mel CL: 71, **182–183**
Powell, Michael CL: 7
Powell, Monty CO: 207
Powerhouse RR: 39–40
power pop RR: xx, 157, 159, 176, **176–178**
power trio RR: 45–46
Pozo, Chano JA: 75, 117, 147, **157**
Pozo Seco Singers CO: 215
A Prairie Home Companion CO: 181; FO: 166
Prairie Ramblers CO: 141, 142
Pras Michel RB: 97, 98
Prater, Annadeene FO: 72
Prater, Dave RB: 234
Prater, Samuelle RB: 44, 45
Pratt, Matthew RB: 261
Pratt City, Alabama BL: 185
Precision Bass RR: 14
Premier RB: 191
Preminger, Otto FO: 14
prepared piano CL: 41–42
Preservation Hall, New Orleans JA: **157–158**
Preservation Hall Jazz Band JA: 10
Presley, Elvis BL: **164;** RB: **209–211;** RR: x, *138,* **178–182**
- Kokomo Arnold BL: 8
- Chet Atkins CO: 6
- Blackwood Brothers CO: 14
- "Blue Moon of Kentucky" CO: 16
- Roy Brown RB: 27–28
- Floyd Cramer CO: 47
- Arthur "Big Boy" Crudup BL: 47; RB: 52
- Mac Davis CO: 54
- Thomas A. Dorsey BL: 54
- drums RR: 67
- Emory Gordy, Jr. CO: 84
- gospel music CO: 86
- Peter Guralnick BL: 69
- Buddy Harman CO: 94
- Wynonie Harris BL: 74; RB: 118
- Buddy Holly CO: 101
- honky-tonk music CO: 102
- Jordanaires CO: 112
- Leiber and Stoller RB: 163
- Jerry Lee Lewis CO: 122
- Smiley Lewis RB: 165
- *Louisiana Hayride* CO: 123
- Memphis BL: 131
- Nashville sound CO: 147
- Roy Orbison RR: 164
- Junior Parker BL: 157
- "Peace in the Valley" CO: 159
- Carl Perkins BL: 158; CO: 161; RR: 169
- Sam Phillips RR: 170
- Doc Pomus BL: 164
- record labels CO: 170
- Jerry Reed CO: 171
- rockabilly CO: 176; RR: 205, 206
- Buffy Sainte-Marie FO: 179
- "She Thinks I Still Care" CO: 185
- "That's All Right" BL: 218
- Big Mama Thornton BL: 219; RB: 258
- Conway Twitty CO: 205

Presley, Lisa Marie RR: 181
Pressler, Menahem CL: 23
Preston, Billy RB: 25, **211;** RR: 125, 140
Preston, Terry CO: 106
Prestopino, Paul FO: 31
Pretenders, The RR: 128, 157
Previn, André CL: 142, 179, *183,* **183–184**
Price, Alan BL: 7; RR: 9
Price, Fred FO: 8
Price, Leontyne CL: 18, **184**
Price, Lloyd BL: **164–165;** RB: **211**
- Fats Domino RR: 58
- "Kansas City Blues" BL: 103
- Little Richard RB: 168; RR: 141
- Wilson Pickett RB: 206
- Huey "Piano" Smith BL: 194
- Paul Williams RB: 279

Price, Ray CO: **163;** FO: 77
- "Whispering" Bill Anderson CO: 4
- "Crazy Arms" CO: 48

Johnny Gimble CO: 82
Buddy Harman CO: 94
"Make the World Go Away" CO: 131
Roger Miller CO: 140
Willie Nelson CO: 149
Johnny Paycheck CO: 158
Price, Sammy BL: **165,** 216, 217; RB: 262
Pride, Charley CO: viii, 39, 79, **163**
Primes, The RB: 254
Prime Time JA: 37–38
Prince RB: **212**
Andre Cymone RB: 52
Miles Davis JA: 51
funk punk RB: 99
Jimmy Jam and Terry Lewis RB: 138
Sheila E. RB: 237, 238
Vanity 6 RB: 270
Prince, Wesley BL: 101
Prince Buster RB: 18
Prince Paul RB: 110
Prine, John FO: 51, 79, **160**
Prior, Maddy FO: 131, 194
prison. *See* jail
Procol Harum RR: 183
Prodigy RB: 185
producer. *See* record producer
Professor Griff RB: 212
Professor Longhair BL: 12, 54, 57, **165,** 221; RR: 67
Professor X RB: 287
Proffitt, Frank FO: 155, **160,** 203–204, 210
Profit, Sam RB: 247
progressive bluegrass CO: 15–16; FO: **160–161**
progressive jazz JA: xxiv, 111–112, **158**
progressive metal RR: 185
progressive rock RR: x, xx, **182–185**
instrumental rock RR: 116
keyboards RR: 126
new wave RR: 157
psychedelic rock RR: 187
Prohibition BL: 8; CO: 102
Prokofiev, Sergey CL: 26, 156–157, 215
Promised Land, The (Nicholas Lemann) BL: 134, 190
promoter. *See* music promoter
protest songs BL: **165–171,** *170*
blues lyrics BL: 22, 25
censorship BL: 37
Civil Rights movement FO: 34
social history BL: 197, 201, 202
Pruett, Sammy CO: 63, 187
Pryor, Snooky BL: 80, 125, **171**
Prysock, Arthur RB: 181
pseudonyms BL: 147
psychedelic RR: xx, 182, **185–187**
public domain material FO: 129
Public Enemy RB: 56, 102, **212–213**
Public Television FO: 98, 157
Public Works Administration (PWA) BL: 167
publishing CL: xxii; BL: xviii. *See also* recording royalties
Boosey & Hawkes CL: **33**
Albert Brumley CO: 25–26
Leonard Chess BL: 39
Ted Daffan CO: 51
G. Schirmer CL: **95**
W. C. Handy BL: 72
J. B. Long BL: 121
Lester Melrose BL: 131
music business BL: 143–147
Nashville sound CO: 147
New York City BL: 152
Ralph Peer BL: 158
ragtime BL: 176
talent scouts BL: 211
J. Mayo Williams BL: 244
publishing rights RR: 154, 169
Puckett, Riley CO: 90, 167, 224; FO: **161–162,** 187
Puente, Tito JA: **158,** 170; RR: 213
Puff Daddy RB: 177, 195, 196, **213,** 266
Pugh, Joe Bennie. *See* Forest City Joe
Pugh, Mike FO: 30
Pukwana, Dudu JA: 186, 187
Pullen, Don JA: 16, 101
punk blues BL: 99
punk funk RB: 139–140
punk rock ('60s) RR: 89
punk rock ('70s-'80s) RR: xx, **187–189**
alternative rock RR: 6
Neneh Cherry RB: 40
garage rock RR: 89
glam rock RR: 92
grunge RR: 97
new wave RR: 156, 157
reggae RR: 199
roots rock RR: 211
ska/bluebeat revival RB: 241
Purchase, New York CL: 177
Purify, James and Bobby RB: 189, **213**
Purim, Flora JA: 43
Purple Onion FO: 116
Putnam County String Band FO: 38
Puzey, Leonard RB: 218
PWA. *See* Public Works Administration

Q

Q-Tip RB: 191, 260
Quaife, Peter RR: 128
Quarrymen, The FO: 55; RR: 18, 114
quartet JA: **159**
Quartet West JA: 79
Quattlebaum, Doug BL: **173**
Queen RR: **191–193,** *192*
Queen Latifah RB: 192, **215**
Queens, New York RB: 231–232; RR: 198, 217
Queler, Eve CL: **185**
Quick, Clarence RB: 57, 58
Quicksilver FO: 122
Quicksilver Messenger Service BL: 52; FO: 28; RR: 151
Quinones, Marc RR: 6
quintet JA: **159**
Quintet of the Hot Club of France JA: 164
Quito, Mississippi BL: 139

R

Rabbit, Eddie CO: 20, 44, **165**
Rabbit Foot Minstrels BL: 177, 193, 219; RB: 146
Rabin, Michael CL: **185**
Rabson, Ann BL: 187
race music JA: **161,** 164
race records JA: **161**
race riots BL: 135, 184, 199
Rachell, Yank BL: 60, 125, **175**
Rachmaninoff, Sergey CL: 49, 107, 128, 134, 216
racism BL: 37–38, 118, 136, 201, 202; JA: 186
radio CL: 33; FO: viii; RB: viii, 61
radio (blues) BL: **175**
radio (country music). *See Grand Ole Opry; Louisiana Hayride; National Barn Dance; specific radio stations*
radio (jazz) JA: 10, 56, 76
Radio Caroline FO: 55
Radiohead RR: 175, **195–196**
Rae, Tanya CO: 24
Raeletts, The RB: 49, **217**
Rafelson, Bob RR: 149
Ragovoy, Jerry RB: 240
Ragsdale, Howard FO: 73
ragtime BL: xv, xvii, **176;** JA: xxvi, **161**
  Scott Joplin JA: **110**
  "Maple Leaf Rag" JA: **127**
  social history BL: 199–200
  syncopation JA: 192
railroad songs CO: 10, **165–166,** 209, 220–221
Rainbows, The RB: 51, 248
Raines, Annie BL: 183
Raines, Sue FO: 23
Rainey, Ma BL: xv, xvii–xviii, **176–177;** JA: **161**
  Louis Armstrong BL: 8
  Lovie Austin JA: 7
  Blind Blake BL: 18
  blues lyrics BL: 24
  classic blues BL: 42
  Thomas A. Dorsey BL: 54
  field hollers BL: 62
  Bertha "Chippie" Hill BL: 76
  Papa Charlie Jackson BL: 89
  Nellie Lutcher BL: 122
  music business BL: 143
  recording vs. live performance BL: 177–178
  saxophone, trombone, trumpet, and clarinet BL: 189
  Bessie Smith BL: 193; JA: 182
  Pine Top Smith BL: 195
  vocal styles BL: 229
Rains, Chick CO: 97
Rainwater, Cedric CO: 15, 63
Raitt, Bonnie BL: xxi, **177**
  Paul Brady FO: 19
  Charles Brown BL: 30
  John Hiatt FO: 95
  "Spider" John Koerner FO: 118
  Delbert McClinton BL: 127
  Fred McDowell BL: 128
  music business BL: 148
  John Prine FO: 160
  slide guitar BL: 193
  Chris Smither BL: 195
  Sippie Wallace BL: 237
  "Women Be Wise" BL: 245
Ram, Buck RB: 94, 205, 207
Ramey, Roger CO: 124–125
Ramey, Samuel CL: **185**
Ramone, Dee Dee RR: 198
Ramone, Joey RR: 198
Ramone, Johnny RR: 198
Ramone, Marky RR: 198
Ramone, Tommy RR: 198
Ramones, The RR: 188, **196–198,** *197,* 223
Ramsey, Frederick, Jr. BL: 9, 64; FO: 123, 164
Ran, Shulamit CL: **185–186**
Randall, Bobby CO: 183
Randall, Eddie JA: 48
Randolph, Boots CO: 147; RB: 210
Rands, Bernard CL: 43, **186**
rap RB: vii–viii, xvii, **217–218;** RR: xi
  Blondie RR: 27
  censorship BL: 36
  punk rock RR: 188
  reggae RR: 201
  rhythm and blues combos BL: 182
  social history and the blues BL: 203–204

"Rapper's Delight" RB: xvii, 122, 217, 229, 249
Rascal Flatts CO: **166**
Rascals, The RB: **218;** RR: **198–199**
Raskin, John JA: 166
Raspberries RR: 177
Rastafarianism RB: 18, 222; RR: 200
Rathebe, Dolly JA: 187
Ravel, Maurice CL: 240; RR: 119
Ravens, The RB: 19, **218–219;** RR: 65
raves RB: 254
Ravinia Festival CL: 171, **186**
Rawlings, David FO: 213
Rawls, Lou RB: **219;** RR: 152
Ray, Dave "Snaker" BL: 108, 233; FO: 118
Ray, Goodman, and Brown RB: 186
Raybon, Marty CO: 185
Raydio RB: 204
Razaf, Andy JA: 210
Reagon, Bernice Johnson BL: 249; FO: 34, 197
Real Roxanne, The RB: **219**
Rebennack, Mac. *See* Dr. John
Record, Eugene RB: 41, 42, 53
record distribution BL: 106–107
recording FO: **163–164;** JA: 150, 158. *See also* session
recording, live performance vs. BL: **177–178**
recording ban BL: 178–179
recording contracts BL: 147
recording industry BL: xxi. *See also specific record industry executives and producers; specific record labels*
  aliases BL: 5
  Chicago BL: 39–40
  Grand Ole Opry CO: 87
  Jackson, Mississippi BL: 138
  music business BL: 142–148
  talent scouts BL: 211–212
recording royalties BL: xviii, **146–148**. *See also* publishing
  aliases BL: 5
  music business BL: 143–145
  talent scouts BL: 211
recordings of early jazz JA: **161–162**
record labels BL: xxi, **178–182;** CO: **166–171,** *168;* FO: ix; RB: xvi–xvii. *See also specific record labels*
record producer JA: **158**
Rector, Red FO: 37, 195
Red Clay Ramblers, The FO: **164–165,** *165*
Redding, Dexter RB: 220
Redding, Noel RR: 109
Redding, Otis RB: **220,** *220*
  Bar-Kays RB: 10
  Eddie Kirkland BL: 107
  Monterey Pop Festival RR: 151, 152
  Stax Records RB: 247
  Carla Thomas RB: 256
  Irma Thomas RB: 257
  Katie Webster BL: 240
Reddings, The RB: **220–221**
Redford, Robert CO: 67, 72
Red-Headed Stranger (Willie Nelson) CO: 46, 149
Red Hot and Blue (radio program). *See* Phillips, Dewey
Red Hot Peppers (Jelly Roll Morton band) JA: 53, 140
Red Knuckles and the Trailblazers CO: 182; FO: 100
Redman, Dewey JA: 79, 104, 134, 169, 195
Redman, Don JA: 11, 30, 89, **162–163**
Redpath, Jean FO: **166**
Reed, Alex FO: 166, 167
Reed, Blind Alfred FO: **166**
Reed, Bud FO: 166
Reed, Dave FO: 167
Reed, Jerry CO: 12, 64, **171**
Reed, Jimmy BL: **182;** RB: **221**
  Fred Below BL: 16
  Lonnie Brooks BL: 29
  Eddie Taylor BL: 213
  Vee-Jay Records BL: 180; RB: 270
Reed, Lou JA: 173; RR: 31, 91, 240–242
Reed, Ola Belle FO: **166–167**
Reese, Della RB: **221**
Reeve, Phil FO: 75
Reeves, Del CO: 88
Reeves, Diane JA: **163**
Reeves, Jim CO: **171–172**
  "Whispering" Bill Anderson CO: 4
  Browns, The CO: 25
  Floyd Cramer CO: 47
  Johnny Horton CO: 104
  Louisiana Hayride CO: 123
  Roger Miller CO: 140
  "Welcome to My World" CO: 212
  Dottie West CO: 213
Reeves, Martha RB: 87
Reeves, Shirley Alston RR: 217
reggae RB: 73, **221–223;** RR: **199–201**. *See also specific artists*
Reich, Steve CL: 89, **186–187**
Reid, Alan FO: 13
Reid, Brenda RB: 85
Reid, Don CO: 192
Reid, Harold CO: 192
Reid, L. A. and Babyface RB: 25, **223,** 259

Reid, Lou FO: 183
Reinagle, Alexander CL: **187**
Reiner, Fritz CL: **187**
  Leonard Bernstein CL: 26
  Jorge Bolet CL: 33
  Cincinnati Symphony Orchestra CL: 51
  Pittsburgh Symphony Orchestra CL: 179
  Felix Slatkin CL: 209
  Janos Starker CL: 213
Reinhardt, Django JA: **163–164**
  Philipe Brun JA: 25
  Benny Carter JA: 28
  European jazz JA: 64
  Coleman Hawkins JA: 87
  Hot Club de France JA: 94
  Eddie Lang JA: 120
Reisenberg, Nadia CL: 91, 140, 185–186, **187–188**
Reiser, Harry FO: 189
reissues BL: xxi, 8, 35
Relf, Jane RR: 253
Relf, Keith RR: 251, 253
R.E.M. RR: 196, **201–203**
Remains, The FO: 199, 200
remixes JA: 2; RB: 1, 34, 53, 102; RR: 182
Renaissance RR: 253
Renbourn, John FO: 79, 84, 109, 156, *167,* **167**
Reneau, George FO: **167–168**
Renfro Valley Barn Dance CO: 33, 65, 76, 87, 148; FO: 124
Reno, Don CO: 73; FO: **168**
rent parties BL: 27, 117, 152, 155
Replacements RR: 177
Respighi, Ottorino CL: 118
Restless Heart CO: 64
Return to Forever JA: 34, 35, 43, 52
"Reuben James" FO: **168**
Revard, Jimmie CO: 100
Revellers, The FO: 129
Rex, Al RR: 104
Reynolds, Allen CO: 23, 80, 215
Reynolds, Burt CO: 171, 216
Reynolds, Malvina FO: 19, **168–169**
Reynolds, Nick FO: 116
Reynolds, Roger CL: **188**
Reynolds, Tim RR: 52, 53
"Rhapsody in Blue" JA: 213, 214
Rhapsody in Blue (George Gershwin) CL: xxiv, 86–87, **188,** 239; JA: 213, 214
"Rhinestone Cowboy" CO: **172**
Rhoad, Herbert "Tubo" RB: 205
Rhodes, Ed BL: 130
Rhodes, Harold RR: 126
Rhodes, Phyllis RB: 233
Rhodes, Red CO: 161; FO: 74, 145
Rhodes, Samuel CL: 121
Rhymes, Busta RB: **223**
Rhyme Syndicate RB: 84
rhythm
  improvisation BL: 85
  listening for JA: xxviii
  polyrhythm JA: **156**
  ride rhythm JA: **165**
  shuffle rhythm JA: **179**
  syncopation JA: **192**
rhythm and blues (R&B) BL: xvi, xx, xxii–xxiii, **101;** JA: **164;** RB: 1–311
  Big Al Downing CO: 62
  earliest use of term RB: xv
  as market designation RB: xvi
  race music JA: 161
  record labels BL: 180–181
  reggae RR: 199–200
  rhythm and blues combos BL: 182
  social history BL: 203
Rhythm & Blues Foundation BL: 31, 148, 177, 269
rhythm section BL: ix; JA: **164**
  bass and drums BL: 15–16
  big band JA: 14
  double bass JA: **56**
  drums JA: **57**
  guitar JA: **78**
  piano JA: **155**
  quartet JA: 159
  quintet JA: 159
Ricci, Ruggerio CL: **188**
Rice, Larry FO: 47, 169
Rice, Mack RB: 87
Rice, Sylvester JA: 47
Rice, Thomas D. BL: 136; FO: 138
Rice, Tony CO: 186; FO: 47, 55, 122, *169,* **169**
Rich, Buddy JA: **164**
  Benny Carter JA: 29
  Buddy Harman CO: 94
  Gene Krupa JA: 115
  Chico O'Farrill JA: 147
  Charlie Parker JA: 152
  Oscar Peterson JA: 153
  Zoot Sims JA: 182
  Mel Torme JA: 198
Rich, Charlie CO: 13, 77, *172,* **172–173;** RR: 171
Rich, Don CO: 10
Rich, Margaret CO: 173
Richard, Roy RB: 227
Richards, Dick RR: 104
Richards, Keith BL: 98, 152, 185; RB: 182; RR: 25, 208–210
Richardson, Chuck BL: 207
Richardson, Dave FO: 18
Richardson, Johnnie Louise RB: 141
Richardson, Tich FO: 18
Richbourg, John ("John R") RB: 120

Richie, Lionel CO: 44, 178; RB: **223–225,** *224,* 231
Richmond, Dannie JA: 19
Richmond, Fritz FO: 119
Richmond, Indiana BL: **86,** 178
Ricks, Jerry BL: **182–183,** 233, 250–253
Ricks, Jimmy RB: 19, 218, 219; RR: 65
Riddle, Almeda FO: **169–170**
Riddle, H. P. FO: 170
ride cymbal JA: 34, **164–165,** 179
ride rhythm JA: **165**
Riders in the Sky CO: 46, *181,* 182; FO: **170,** *171*
Ridgley, Tommy RB: 257
Riegger, Wallingford CL: 77, **188–189**
riff JA: xxiii, 111, **165;** RR: 15
Rifkin, Joshua BL: 176; FO: 39
Rigg, Jane FO: 210
Righteous Brothers, The RB: **225–226;** RR: *204,* **204–205,** 223
"Right Next Door (Because of Me)" BL: **183**
Riley, Ben JA: 30
Riley, Jeannie C. CO: 43, 92, **173**
Riley, Jim JA: 15
Riley, Leo FO: 141
Riley, Teddy RB: 25, 194, 250, 251
Riley, Terry CL: 131, **189**
Rimes, LeAnn CO: 36, **173–174,** *174,* 223
Rimes, Wilbur CO: 173, 174
Rinzler, Ralph FO: **170–171**
  Tom Ashley FO: 7–8
  Folkways Records BL: 64
  Greenbriar Boys FO: 81
  Bill Monroe CO: 141
  Doc Watson FO: 211
  Izzy Young FO: 219
Riperton, Minnie RB: 217, **226**
Rishell, Paul BL: **183**
Rising Sons, The BL: 43, 123–124; FO: 199
Rising Star Fife and Drum Band BL: 139, 224
Ritchie, Jean FO: 56, 99, **171–172,** *172,* 211
Ritter, John CO: 175
Ritter, Tex CO: **174–175,** *175*
  Johnny Bond CO: 19
  cowboy songs CO: 46
  Harlan Howard CO: 105
  Hank Thompson CO: 197
Ritz, David BL: 39
Rivers, Jerry CO: 63
Rivers, Johnny RR: 25, 152
Rivers, Sam JA: 41, 44, 92
Riverside Ramblers FO: 89
RJD2 RB: **226–227**
RKO circuit FO: 189
Roach, Max JA: **165**
  Muhal Richard Abrams JA: 1
  bebop JA: 12
  Birth of the Cool JA: 15
  Dee Dee Bridgewater JA: 23
  Brilliant Corners JA: 23
  Clifford Brown JA: 23
  Donald Byrd JA: 26
  Benny Carter JA: 29
  Duke Ellington JA: 61
  Rufus Harley JA: 85
  Coleman Hawkins JA: 87
  Abdullah Ibrahim JA: 97
  Gene Krupa JA: 115
  Abbey Lincoln JA: 123
  Charlie Parker JA: 152
  Sonny Rollins JA: 165–166
  George Russell JA: 166, 167
  Stanley Turrentine JA: 200
Roach, Max—Clifford Brown Quintet JA: 23, 165
Robbins, Marty CO: **175–176**
  "El Paso" CO: 68
  Glaser Brothers CO: 83
  Jordanaires CO: 112
  Robert Earl Keen FO: 114
  rockabilly RR: 205
Robbinsville, Mississippi BL: **139**
Roberson, LaTavia RB: 58, 59
Robert, Richard CL: 219
Roberts, Dink BL: 13
Roberts, "Fiddlin'" Doc FO: **172–173**
Roberts, Howard RR: 222
Roberts, J. A. JA: 105–106
Roberts, James Carson CO: 33
Roberts, John RR: 248
Roberts, John, and Tony Barrand FO: **173,** 191–192
Roberts, Julia CO: 126
Roberts, Liebert FO: 172
Roberts, Luckey BL: 176
Roberts, Rick CO: 75
Robert Shaw Chorale CL: **189,** 208
Robertson, Don CO: 47, 58
Robertson, Eck CO: 72, 167, *168;* FO: 67, **173**
Robertson, Robbie RR: 11, 13
Robeson, Paul FO: **174**
  Alberta Hunter BL: 83
  protest songs BL: 170
  Earl Robinson FO: 174
  Sing Out! magazine FO: 185
  social history and the blues BL: 201
  Josh White BL: 242
  young black country blues artists BL: 251
Robey, Don BL: 157–158, 217; RB: 26, 121, **227**

Robichaux, John JA: 45
Robillard, Duke BL: 61, **183,** 185
Robins, The RB: 45, **227**
Robinson, Bobby BL: 152, 181, **183;** RB: 42
Robinson, Earl FO: **174**
Robinson, Jeff RB: 151
Robinson, Oscar RB: 92
Robinson, Smokey RB: **228,** *228*
High Inergy RB: 121
Moonglows, The RB: 187
Motown RB: 188; RR: 153
Mary Wells RB: 276
Robinson, Sylvia RB: 120, **228–229,** 249
Robison, Carson J. CO: 52, 103; FO: 129, **174–175,** 189
Robison, Fabor CO: 104, 170, 171
Rob Roys, The RB: **229**
Robyn, Paul CL: 105
Rochberg, George CL: 5, 135, **189–190**
Rochester, New York BL: 31, 82
Rochester Philharmonic CL: 135, 215
rock (as distinct from "rock 'n' roll") RR: x, 21
Rock, Bob RR: 146, 147
rockabilly CO: **176–177;** RR: ix, 188, **205–206,** 211
rock and roll BL: viii; RR: 1–298. *See also* blues rock; fusion
rock and roll revival RR: **207–208,** 211
"Rock Around the Clock" RR: 101–103, 208
"Rocket 88" BL: 223; RB: 24; RR: 170
rock festivals RR: 108, 118, 151–152, **206–207,** 246–250. *See also* Monterey Pop Festival; Watkins Glen festival; Woodstock
"Rockin' Around the Christmas Tree" CO: 121; RR: 138
Rockin' Sidney BL: **183;** FO: 27; RB: 182
"Rockit" JA: 83, 165, **165;** RB: 162
rock steady RR: 200
Rockwell, John CL: 58
Rockwilder RB: 185
Roderick, Judy BL: **184,** 221
Rodgers, Jimmie (country singer) BL: **184;** CO: vii, *177,* **177–178**
Carlisle Brothers CO: 31
cowboy songs CO: 46
guitar CO: 90
"In the Jailhouse Now" CO: 108
Meridian, Mississippi BL: 139
Emmett Miller FO: 138
Moonshine Kate FO: 141
Ralph Peer BL: 158
railroad songs CO: 165–166
recording FO: 163
record labels CO: 167
Hank Snow CO: 188
Jimmie Tarlton BL: 213
"T for Texas (Blue Yodel Number One)" CO: 197
Ernest Tubb CO: 203
vocal styles BL: 232
yodeling CO: 224
Rodgers, Jimmy RR: 237
Rodgers, Nile RB: 41, 162, 173; RR: 27, 136
Rodgers, Paul RR: 136
Rodzinski, Artur CL: **190**
Leonard Bernstein CL: 27
Los Angeles Philharmonic Orchestra CL: 141
NBC Symphony Orchestra CL: 162
Leonard Rose CL: 191
Robert Shaw CL: 208
Roe, Marty CO: 56
Roe, Tommy CO: 84
Rogers, Claudette RB: 228
Rogers, Cy CO: 194
Rogers, Emerson and Bobby RB: 228
Rogers, Garnet FO: 68, 175
Rogers, Jimmy (blues guitarist) BL: **184,** 239
Rogers, Kenny CO: *178,* **178–179**
countrypolitan CO: 44
"Lucille" CO: 126
New Christy Minstrels FO: 146
Lionel Richie RB: 223
Mel Tillis CO: 199
Travis Tritt CO: 202
Dottie West CO: 213
Rogers, Lelan CO: 61
Rogers, Roy (blues guitarist) BL: 151, **185**
Rogers, Roy (country singer) CO: **179**
Gene Autry CO: 7
cowboy songs CO: 46
Stuart Hamblen CO: 93
"Happy Trails" CO: 94
Sons of the Pioneers CO: 189
Rogers, Sally FO: **175**
Rogers, Stan FO: **175**
Rojak, John CL: 7
Roland, Walter BL: 161, 166, 167, **185**
Rolie, Gregg RR: 213
"Roll 'em Pete" BL: 96, 223

Rolling Stone magazine RR: 3, 130, 160, 201
Rolling Stones, The BL: xx, **185;** RB: ix; RR: **208–210,** *209*
Solomon Burke RB: 29–30
Ry Cooder BL: 43
country rock RR: 45
Slim Harpo RB: 117
Little Walter BL: 116
Fred McDowell BL: 128
Mamas and the Papas RR: 146
Harvey Mandel BL: 124
Motown RR: 152
Roy Orbison RR: 165
Robert Petway BL: 159
reggae RR: 201
rock festivals RR: 206
David Sanborn JA: 169
Irma Thomas RB: 257
Rufus Thomas BL: 219
Ike and Tina Turner RB: 263
vocal styles BL: 233
Junior Wells BL: 241
Robert Wilkins BL: 243
young black country blues artists BL: 250
Rolling Thunder Revue FO: 9, 25, 60
Rollins, Sonny JA: **165–166**
Muhal Richard Abrams JA: 1
Dee Dee Bridgewater JA: 23
Brilliant Corners JA: 23
Donald Byrd JA: 26
Don Cherry JA: 31
Jim Hall JA: 80
Rufus Harley JA: 85
Coleman Hawkins JA: 88
Courtney Pine JA: 155
Saxophone Colossus JA: **171**
Lester Young JA: 220
Rome, Ritchie RB: 239
Romney, Hugh (Wavy Gravy) RR: 249
Ron C RB: **229**
Ronettes, The RB: **229;** RR: 91, 223
Ronson, Mick RR: 31
Ronstadt, Linda
Eagles, The RR: 73–74
Emmylou Harris CO: 95
George Jones CO: 111
Kate and Anna McGarrigle FO: 136
Gary Morris CO: 144
Michael Nesmith FO: 145
Roy Orbison RR: 165
Dolly Parton CO: 158
Rooftop Singers BL: 36, 224, 236; FO: 70, **175**
Roomful of Blues BL: 57, 183, **185,** 188, 228
Rooney, Herbert RB: 85
Rooney, Jim BL: 234, 239; FO: 51, 114, **176**
Rooney, Joe Don CO: 166
Roosevelt, Eleanor CL: 10; BL: 201–202; FO: 77, 174, 190
Roosevelt, Franklin D. CL: 224; BL: 166, 167, 201, 202; CO: 22
Roosevelt, Theodore FO: 127
Roots, The RB: 142, **230**
roots music BL: xvi
roots rock RR: xx, 84, 187, **210–211**
Rorem, Ned CL: 4, 36, **190–191**
Rorer, Posey FO: 92, 159
Rosas, Cesar CO: 72
Rose, Artie FO: 148
Rose, Fred CO: **179**
Roy Acuff CO: 1
Boudleaux and Felice Bryant CO: 26
"Cold, Cold Heart" CO: 40
record labels CO: 170
Hank Williams CO: 216, 217
Rose, Irving "Slim" RB: 91
Rose, Leonard CL: 50, 98, 113, 145, **191,** 214
Rose, Vincent RR: 59
Rose, Wesley CO: 26, 70, 170, **179**
Rose City Hipsters FO: 77
"Rose Garden" CO: 4, 44, **180**
Rosen, Charles CL: **191–192**
Rosen, Walter and Lucille CL: 43
Rosenbaum, Art BL: 17; FO: 164, **176**
Rosenman, Joel RR: 248
Rosenstock, Joseph CL: **192**
Rosenthal, Phil FO: 183
Rose Royce RB: 263
Ross, Annie JA: 120
Ross, Diana JA: 123; RB: 224, *230,* **230–231;** RR: 153
Ross, Doctor BL: 139, **185**
Rosselson, Leon FO: 30
Rostropovich, Mstislav CL: 85, 162, **192**
Roth, Kevin FO: 56
Rothchild, Paul A. RR: 63
Rothwell, Walter Henry CL: 141, **192**
Rotten, Johnny RR: 187
Rough Stock CO: 245
Rounder Records BL: **186;** FO: 164
'Round Midnight (movie) JA: 77, 82
Rouse, Christopher CL: **192–193**
Rouse, Earl B. FO: 176–177
Rouse, Ervin FO: 176, 177, 216
Rouse, Gordon FO: 176, 177
Rouse Brothers CO: 166; FO: **176–177,** 216

Roussakis, Nicholas CL: 7
Rova Saxophone Quartet JA: 51, **166**
Rowan, Peter FO: **177**
  Richard Greene FO: 81
  David Grisman FO: 83
  Kentucky Colonels FO: 115
  Muleskinner FO: 143, 144
  Mark O'Connor FO: 152
  Old and in the Way FO: 153
Rowans, The FO: 177
Rowland, Bruce FO: 64
Rowland, Kelly RB: 58, *59*
Rowsome, Leo FO: 10
"Roxanne Roxanne" RB: 219, 267–268
Roxy Music RR: 158
royalties. *See* recording royalties
Roy C RB: **231**
Rubalcaba, Gonzalo JA: 52, 124, **166**
rube/hillbilly humor CO: **180–182,** *181,* 194
Rubin, Rick
  Johnny Cash CO: 35, 36
  Def Jam Records RB: 55, 56
  Donovan RR: 61
  L. L. Cool J RB: 169
  Public Enemy RB: 212
Rubinstein, Arthur CL: xxiii, 19, **193–194**
Rubinstein, Beryl CL: 52
Rudel, Julius CL: **194**
Rudolph, Max CL: 51, 63, 118, **194,** 212
"Rudolph, the Red-Nosed Reindeer" CO: 7, **182**
Ruffhouse RB: **231**
Ruffin, David RB: 255
Ruffino, Joe RB: 257
Rufus RB: 152
Ruggles, Carl CL: 61, 189, **194–195**
Rundgren, Todd FO: 106
Run-D.M.C. RB: 102, 122, **231–232**
Runnells, Rochelle RB: 245
Rupe, Art RR: 141
rural blues BL: xvi. *See also* country blues; Delta blues; folk blues
Rush, Bobby BL: **186**
Rush, Otis BL: 141, 149, **186,** 248; RB: **232**
Rush, Tom FO: 39, **177–178,** *178,* 185
Rushing, Jimmy BL: 83, 92, 140, **186**
Russell, Curly JA: 169
Russell, Doc RB: 107
Russell, George JA: **166–167**
  Don Ellis JA: 62
  Bill Evans JA: 65
  Jan Garbarek JA: 73
  modal jazz JA: 138
  Courtney Pine JA: 155
  Gunther Schuller JA: 172
  Andy Sheppard JA: 177
  Steve Swallow JA: 191
  third stream jazz JA: 197
Russell, Leon FO: 36; RR: 127
Russell, Tony BL: 231
Russian Revolution CL: 106; FO: 7
Russo, William BL: 191
Rutherford, Leonard FO: 25
Ryan, Marc BL: 130
Ryman Auditorium (Nashville, Tennessee) CO: 87; FO: 93; RR: 79
RZA RB: 110, 284, 285

S

sacred music CL: xx, 24
sacred steel BL: 207
Sade RB: **233**
Saffire—The Uppity Blues Women BL: **187**
Sahm, Doug BL: **187;** CO: 72
St. Cyr, Johnny BL: 14; JA: 94
St. John, Mark RR: 130, 131
St. Louis, Missouri BL: **140**
"St. Louis Blues" BL: 72, **187–188;** JA: 84, 187
St. Lunatics RB: 193
St. Nicholas, Nick RR: 229
Sainte-Marie, Buffy FO: **179,** 187
Saint of Bleecker Street, The (Gian Carlo Menotti) CL: 124, **197**
Saint Paul Chamber Orchestra CL: **197**
sales chart. *See* chart, sales
Salgado, Curtis BL: **188**
Salkind, Milton CL: 198
"Sally Goodin" CO: 72; FO: 14–15, 173
Salomon, Frank CL: 37
Salonen, Esa-Pekka CL: 142, **197**
Salsoul Orchestra, The RB: **233**
Salt-N-Pepa RB: **233–234**
"Salt Peanuts" JA: 34, 63, 75, 152, **169**
"Salty Dog" BL: 89; FO: 3, **179**
Salzman, Eric CL: **197–198**
Sam and Dave RB: 170, **234,** 247
Samaroff, Olga CL: 136, 228
sampling RR: xi, 137
Samwell-Smith, Paul RR: 251, 252
San Antonio, Texas BL: 96, 97, 187; FO: 97
"San Antonio Rose" CO: **183,** 219

Sanborn, David BL: 33; JA: 135, **169**
Sandburg, Carl FO: viii, 76, **179–180**
Sanders, Pharoah JA: 16, 34, 41, **169–170,** 175, 219
Sanders, Ric FO: 64
Sanders, Steve CO: 153, 154
Sándor, György CL: **198**
Sandoval, Arturo JA: **170**
Sane, Dan BL: 206, 207
San Francisco Bay Area BL: **35**
  Grateful Dead RR: 92–97
  Jefferson Airplane RR: 118–121
  Janis Joplin BL: 99–100; RR: 121–123
  Monterey Pop Festival RR: 151, 152
  Old and in the Way FO: 153
  psychedelic rock RR: 185
  Santana (band) RR: **213–214**
"San Francisco Bay Blues" BL: 35, 65, **188**
"San Francisco (Be Sure to Wear Some Flowers in Your Hair)" RR: 145, 152
San Francisco Chamber Orchestra CL: **198**
San Francisco Conservatory of Music CL: **198**
San Francisco Opera CL: xxiv, **198–199**
San Francisco Symphony Orchestra CL: **199**
San Quentin prison CO: 21
Santa Fe School BL: 160, 190, 217
Santamaria, Mongo JA: 42, **170**
Santana (band) RR: **213–214**
Santana, Carlos JA: 178; RR: **213–214,** *214*
Santelli, Robert BL: 115
Santiago, Maria RR: 113
Saperton, David CL: 81, 139, 150, **199,** 209
Sargeant, Winthrop JA: 106
Satan & Adam BL: **188**
Satherly, Art BL: xxi, **188;** CO: 190; FO: 45, 193
"A Satisfied Mind" CO: **183,** 209
Saturday Night Fever (soundtrack) RB: 13, 61
Saud, Sulaimon. *See* Tyner, McCoy
Saunders, Merle RR: 96
Savoy, Ann Allen FO: 180
Savoy, Marc BL: 121; FO: 2, **180**
Savoy Ballroom JA: 27, 45, **170–171,** 212
Savoy Brown BL: **188–189**
Sawallisch, Wolfgang CL: 176, **199**
Sawtelle, Charles FO: 100
Sawyer Brown CO: **183**
saxophone BL: xxiii, 100, 182, **189;** JA: 142, **171**
Saxophone Colossus (Sonny Rollins) JA: 166, **171**
Sayles, John CO: 119
scale JA: **171**
Scarlett, Will BL: 81
scat singing JA: **171**
  Louis Armstrong JA: 6
  Cab Calloway JA: 27
  Betty Carter JA: 29
  Ella Fitzgerald JA: 70
  "Heebie Jeebies" JA: 88–89
  jazz firsts JA: 115
  recordings of early jazz JA: 162
Schandler, Hyman CL: 53
Schatz, Mark FO: 151
Schickele, Peter CL: 134, **199–200**
Schiff, Daryl CO: 135
Schifrin, Lalo JA: 9
Schippers, Thomas CL: 4, 51, **200,** 213
Schirmer. *See* G. Schirmer
Schirmer, Gustav CL: 95
Schloten, Jim CO: 183
Schmit, Timothy B. RR: 75
Schnabel, Arthur CL: 67, 82, 128, 177
Schneider, Alexander CL: 4, 37, **200–201**
Schneider, Bert RR: 149
Schneider, Maria JA: 107, **171**
Schoenberg, Arnold CL: xxii, xxv
  Marc Blitzstein CL: 30
  John Cage CL: 41
  Lou Harrison CL: 99
  Leon Kirchner CL: 126
  Louis Krasner CL: 130
  Nathan Milstein CL: 156
  Leo Ornstein CL: 171
  Rudolf Serkin CL: 205
Scholander, Sven FO: 56
Schon, Neal RR: 213
Schonberg, Harold C. CL: **201**
  Maria Callas CL: 44
  Paul Hindemith CL: 104
  Mass (Bernstein) CL: 150
  Arthur Rubinstein CL: 194
  William Steinberg CL: 214
  Paul Zukofsky CL: 245
Schooly D RB: 231, 253
Schuller, Gunther CL: **201–202;** JA: xxiv, **171–172**
  Birth of the Cool JA: 15
  Early Jazz JA: 59
  French horn JA: 72
  Edwin London CL: 141
  Of Reminiscences and Reflections CL: **167**
  Gerard Schwarz CL: 203

Schuller, Gunther (*continued*)
third stream jazz JA: 197
Treemonisha CL: 227
Schuman, Mort BL: 164
Schuman, William CL: *202*, **202–203**
American Brass Quintet CL: 6
American Festival Overture CL: **7**
Chamber Music Society of Lincoln Center CL: 48
A Free Song CL: **82**
Juilliard School CL: 121
Juilliard String Quartet CL: 121
André Kostelanitz CL: 128
recommended listening CL: 250–251
Leonard Rose CL: 191
Seymour Shifrin CL: 208
Charles Wadsworth CL: 235
Schuur, Diane JA: **172**
Schwall, Jim BL: 191
Schwantner, Joseph CL: 4, 7, **203**
Schwartz, Tracy FO: 76, *147*, 148, 181
Schwarz, Gerard CL: 141, **203–204,** 204
Schwerner, Michael FO: 34
Scialfa, Patti RR: 225
Scofield, John JA: **172–173,** *173*
Gary Burton JA: 26
Anthony Cox JA: 44
Bill Frisell JA: 72
John Medeski JA: 133
Steve Swallow JA: 192
Scorsese, Martin BL: xvi, xxi, 143, 252; RR: 13. *See also The Legacy of the Blues*
Scott, Bobby BL: 184
Scott, Bud BL: 14
Scott, Darrell FO: 151
Scott, Frank BL: 7
Scott, Frankie FO: 180
Scott, Jack RB: **234–235**
Scott, James BL: 176
Scott, Jimmy JA: 35, **173**
Scott, Joe BL: 18
Scott, Mabel RB: 25
Scott, Ronnie JA: 92
Scott, Shirley JA: 148, **173–174,** 200
Scott, Tom (saxophonist) BL: 64; FO: 140
Scott, Tommy (folk artist) FO: **180**
Scott, Tony JA: 30, 65
Scott-Heron, Gil RB: **235**
Scott-Hill, Joel CO: 75
scratching RB: 122, 287
Screaming Sirens, The FO: 69
Screwed Up Click RB: 64
Scriabin, Aleksandr CL: 26, 134
Scruggs, Earl
five string banjo CO: 11
banjo, five-string FO: 12
bluegrass music CO: 15
Vassar Clements FO: 37
Flatt and Scruggs CO: 73, 75
"Foggy Mountain Breakdown" CO: 75
Buck (Uncle Josh) Graves FO: 81
Tom T. Hall CO: 92
Doug Kershaw CO: 116
Bill Monroe CO: 141
Don Reno FO: 168
Pete Seeger FO: 182
Stanley Brothers FO: 193
Stanley Brothers, The CO: 190
Chubby Wise FO: 216
Scruggs, Gary CO: 75
Scruggs, Randy CO: 42, 75; FO: 16, 93
Sea Islands. *See* Georgia Sea Islands
Seals, Son BL: **189**
"Sea of Love" RR: 136, 216
Searchers, The FO: 169
Sears, Roebuck Co. BL: 192; CO: 148, 167; FO: 116
Seatrain FO: 81, 177
Seattle Symphony CL: 5, 204, **204,** 208
Sebastian, John
autoharp CO: 6
folk-rock FO: 71
Steve Frumholz FO: 74
Lovin' Spoonful BL: 121–122
New York City BL: 153
Happy and Artie Traum FO: 204
Woodstock RR: 247, 248
Sechler, Curly FO: 180
Second Fiddle to a Steel Guitar CO: 27, 187
Second Fret folk club BL: 182–183
secular music CL: viii, xx–xxi, 105, 160
Sedaka, Neil RR: 175–176
Seeds, The RR: 89
Seeger, Charles CL: 61; BL: 44; FO: 42, 121, 180
Seeger, Mike FO: *17*, **180–182,** *181*
Moses Asch FO: 7
autoharp CO: 6
bluegrass music CO: 15
Dock Boggs FO: 17
Bill Clifton FO: 37
John Cohen FO: 38
Elizabeth "Libba" Cotton FO: 42
Country Gentlemen FO: 44

"Freight Train" FO: 72
Alice Gerrard FO: 76
Bill Keith FO: 114
Sam McGee FO: 137
New Lost City Ramblers FO: 147
recording FO: 164
Eck Robertson FO: 173
Fiddlin' Arthur Smith FO: 189
Wade Ward FO: 210
Seeger, Peggy FO: **182**
Elizabeth Cotton BL: 44
Elizabeth "Libba" Cotton FO: 42
"Freight Train" FO: 72
Ewan MacColl FO: 131
New Lost City Ramblers FO: 148
Mike Seeger FO: 181
Izzy Young FO: 219
Seeger, Pete FO: **182–183**
Moses Asch FO: 7
banjo BL: 13
banjo, five-string FO: 12–13
Broadside magazine FO: 19
Byrds FO: 25
Len Chandler FO: 31
Civil Rights movement FO: 34
Cousin Emmy FO: 45
Ruth Crawford Seeger CL: 61
Bob Dylan FO: 57
Flatt and Scruggs CO: 74
folk revival FO: 70
folk rock RR: 84
Manny Greenhill FO: 82
Arlo Guthrie FO: 87
Woody Guthrie FO: 87
Cisco Houston FO: 100
Lead Belly BL: 112, 113; FO: 123, 124
Harold Leventhal FO: 124
Gordon Lightfoot FO: 125
Don McLean FO: 137
Uncle Dave Macon CO: 130
Newport Folk Festival FO: 149
Peter, Paul and Mary FO: 157
protest songs BL: 167, 168
"Reuben James" FO: 168
Malvina Reynolds FO: 169
Ralph Rinzler FO: 170
Paul Robeson FO: 174
Mike Seeger FO: 180
Sing Out! magazine FO: 185
Sonny Terry and Brownie McGhee FO: 201
"Waist Deep in the Big Muddy" FO: 209
Weavers FO: 212
Josh White BL: 242
"Wimoweh" FO: 215
young black country blues artists BL: 248, 251
Seeger, Ruth Crawford BL: 44; FO: 42, 180
Seely, Jeannie CO: 88, **183–184**
"See That My Grave Is Kept Clean" BL: 94, **189**
Segar, Chas. BL: 104
Seger, Bob CO: 48
segregation
"Bourgeois Blues" BL: 28–29
Harlem JA: 85
social history and the blues BL: 199, 201, 202
South African jazz JA: 186
vocal styles BL: 231
Segundo, Compay JA: **174**
Sehorn, Marshall RB: 70
Seidl, Anton CL: 82
Seldom Scene FO: 44, **183**
Sellers, Jason CO: 219
Selway, Phil RR: 195
Semien, Sidney. *See* Rockin' Sidney
Senatobia, Mississippi BL: **139**
September 11, 2001, terrorist attacks CL: 168–169; CO: 24, 109, 115, 200; RR: 226
Sgt. Pepper's Lonely Hearts Club Band (Beatles album) RR: 16, 20–21, 183
serialism CL: ix, xxv, 61, 119, 201, 242. *See also* 12-tone composition
Serkin, Peter CL: 37, 138, **204–205,** 221
Serkin, Rudolf CL: **205**
Adolf Busch CL: 40
Richard Goode CL: 91
Ruth Laredo CL: 134
James Levine CL: 136
Seymour Lipkin CL: 139
Marlboro Music School and Festival CL: 148
Murray Perahia CL: 174
Peter Serkin CL: 204
George Walker CL: 235
sermons BL: 78
SESAC BL: 145
session JA: **174,** 193
Sessions, Roger CL: **205–206**
John Adams CL: 2
Milton Babbitt CL: 15
Columbia-Princeton Electronic Music Center CL: 55
Concerto for Orchestra CL: **55**
Aaron Copland CL: 57
David Diamond CL: 68
John Eaton CL: 73
Vivian Fine CL: 78
Ross Lee Finney CL: 78
Andrew Imbrie CL: 111

Sessions, Roger (*continued*)
Jacob Lateiner CL: 134
Daniel Lentz CL: 135
Donald Martino CL: 149
Peter Mennin CL: 151
Conlon Nancarrow CL: 161
Eric Salzman CL: 197
Ellen Taafe Zwilich CL: 246
set JA: **174**
Settle, Mike CO: 178
Setzer, Brian RR: 42
78 (78 RPM record) CO: 167–168; FO: 164; JA: 6, 61, 99
Severance, John Long CL: 206
Severance Hall CL: 52, 53, 70, *206,* **206–207**
Seward, Alec BL: 95, **189**
Sex Pistols RR: 187, 188
sexuality RR: 91
sexually explicit lyrics BL: 24, 37, 238
Shabazz, Lakim RB: **235**
Shade, Will BL: 89, 125, 132, 148, 211
Shadows, The RR: 115
Shaggy RB: **235–236**
Shaham, Gil CL: **207**
Shahan, Wanda Lucille CO: 41
"Shake, Rattle and Roll" BL: 223; RR: 102
Shakti JA: 132
Shakur, Tupac RB: 7, 54, 60, 195, *236,* **236–237**
Shalamar RB: **237**
Shamblin, Eldon FO: 134
Sha Na Na RR: 207
Shane, Bob FO: 116, 117
Shankar, L. JA: 132
Shankar, Ravi CL: 153; RR: 152
Shannon, Del RR: 178, **214–216,** *215*
shape-note singing CO: 85; FO: **183–184**
Shape of Jazz to Come, The (Ornette Coleman) JA: **174–175**
Shapero, Harold CL: 2, 25, **207,** 238
Shapey, Ralph CL: 185, **207**
sharecropping BL: 115, **189–190,** 199; FO: 5, 122–123
Sharp, Alexander RB: 200
Sharp, Cecil FO: viii
Sharp, Dee Dee RB: **237**
Sharrock, Sonny JA: **175**
Shaver, Billy Joe CO: 110
Shaw, Artie JA: 91, **175–176,** *176,* 182, 197, 198
Shaw, Robert (blues pianist) BL: **190,** 216
Shaw, Robert (choral director) CL: 13, 52, 103, 189, **207–208**
Shaw, Woody JA: 73, 219
Sheahan, John FO: 55
Shear, Jules RR: 178
Shearing, George JA: 26, 170
Shedd, Harold CO: 115
sheet music BL: xxi, 143–145
"She Got the Goldmine (I Got the Shaft)" CO: 64, 171
Sheila E. RB: **237–238**
Shelasky, Paul FO: 79
Shelor, Harry "Ebo Walker" FO: 147
Shelton, James, Jr. RB: 41
Shelton, Ricky Van CO: **184–185**
Shelton, Ronnie CO: 184
Shelton Brothers FO: 77
Shenandoah CO: **185;** FO: 87
Shenandoah Cutups FO: 59
Shenandoah Valley Boys FO: 59
Sheng, Bright CL: **208**
Shepherd, Jean CO: 106; FO: 165
Shepherd, Kenny Wayne BL: **190**
Shepp, Archie JA: 31, **177,** 217
Sheppard, Andy JA: **177,** 192
Sheppard, Bob JA: 43
Sheppards, The RB: 92
Sheridan, Tony RR: 19
Sherrill, Billy
"Behind Closed Doors" CO: 13
Ray Charles BL: 38
Lacy J. Dalton CO: 53
Janie Fricke CO: 77
"Hello Darlin'" CO: 98
George Jones CO: 111
Johnny Paycheck CO: 159
record labels CO: 169, 170
Charlie Rich CO: 173
Marty Robbins CO: 176
"Stand by Your Man" CO: 190
Tanya Tucker CO: 204
Tammy Wynette CO: 221
Sherrill, Homer Lee "Pappy" FO: 59, 110–111, 142
Sherry, Fred CL: 221
"She Thinks I Still Care" CO: 111, **185**
Shifrin, Seymour CL: **208**
Shindig! (TV show) RB: 21, 211; RR: 204
Shiner, David FO: 165
Shines, Johnny BL: 97, 98, 117, **191**
Shirelles, The RB: 105, **238,** *238;* RR: 90, *216,* **216–217**
Shirley & Company RB: 244
Sho-Bud steel guitars CO: 161
Shocked, Michelle BL: 163; FO: **184**
Shocklee, Hank RB: viii, 212
Shocklee, Keith RB: 103
Sholes, Steve CO: 168

Short, J. D. BL: 243
Shorter, Wayne JA: *50,* **177–179,** *179*
"Birdland" JA: 15
Bitches Brew JA: 15
Art Blakey JA: 17
Miles Davis JA: 49
"E.S.P." JA: 63
Maynard Ferguson JA: 70
Herbie Hancock JA: 82, 83
Bobby McFerrin JA: 131
Jaco Pastorius JA: 152
saxophone JA: 171
In a Silent Way JA: 98
Horace Silver JA: 180
Weather Report RB: 275
Tony Williams JA: 216
Joe Zawinul JA: 223
Shostakovich, Dmitry CL: 140
Showbiz and AG RB: **238**
Showstoppers, The RB: **239**
Shreveport, Louisiana BL: 160, 219
Shrieve, Michael RR: 69, 213
Shuffler, George CO: 191; FO: 193
shuffle rhythm JA: **179,** 192
Shumsky, Oscar CL: **208–209**
Shure, Paul CL: 105
Sibelius, Jean CL: 10
Sibert, Johnny CO: 187
sideman JA: **179**
Sidewinder, The (Lee Morgan) JA: 86, 140
Siegel, Carol FO: 23
Siegel, Corky BL: 191
Siegel, Janis JA: 126
Siegel-Schwall Band BL: 111, **191**
Sigler, Bunny RB: 132, **239**
Silber, Irwin FO: 49, 185–186
silence CL: 41, 82
Silhouettes, The RB: **239–240**
Silk Road Project CL: 145, 208
Sill, Lester RR: 222
Sills, Beverly CL: 164, **209,** 235
Silly Wizard FO: **184–185**
Silver, Horace JA: **179–181,** *180*
Art Blakey JA: 17
Randy Brecker JA: 22
Paul Chambers JA: 30
Stanley Clarke JA: 34
Billy Cobham JA: 35
Art Farmer JA: 69
Joe Henderson JA: 90
King Curtis RB: 154
Oscar Peterson JA: 154
Wayne Shorter JA: 177–178
Song for My Father JA: **185–186**
Silver, Stan CO: 71
Silver Dollar City CO: 22
Silverman, Jerry BL: xxi
Silvers, Jim FO: 217
Silverstein, Joseph CL: 231
Silverstein, Shel CO: 12, 21, 35; FO: 107
Silvester, Peter J. BL: 27, 85
Simmonds, Kim BL: 188
Simmons, Daryl RB: 259
Simmons, Gene RR: 130, 131
Simmons, John JA: 62
Simmons, Joseph "Run" RB: 21, 231
Simmons, Russell RB: 21, 55, 158, 266
Simon, Abbey CL: **209**
Simon, Joe RB: **240**
Simon, Paul RR: **217–219**
Michael Brecker JA: 22
Davey Graham FO: 80
Hugh Masekela JA: 129
Oak Ridge Boys CO: 153
Mark O'Connor FO: 152
singer-songwriters RR: 219
Simon and Garfunkel FO: 28; RR: 78, 152, **217–219,** *218,* 219
Simone, Nina JA: *181,* **181–182;** RB: **240**
Simpkins, Ronnie FO: 183
Simpson, Valerie RB: 6
Sims, Jody RB: 251
Sims, Son BL: 157
Sims, Zoot JA: 13, 77, 90, 112, **182,** 192
Sinatra, Frank CL: 154; JA: 56, 102, 110, 164; RR: 237
Sinatra, Nancy CO: 199
Singer, Eric RR: 130, 131
singer-songwriters FO: ix, xvi, **185;** RR: xx, 85, 152, **219–221**
"Singing Christian, The" BL: 5, 77, 242
singing cowboys CO: xvii
Jules Verne Allen FO: 2
Rex Allen CO: 3
Gene Autry CO: 7
"Back in the Saddle Again" CO: 9
Elton Britt CO: 22
Wilf Carter CO: 34
cowboy songs CO: 46
Jimmie Davis CO: 54
Don Edwards CO: 67–68
Stuart Hamblen CO: 92–93
Tex Ritter CO: 174–175
Roy Rogers CO: 179
Carl T. Sprague CO: 189
yodeling CO: 224
"Singin' the Blues" JA: **182,** 199
singles chart RR: 178–179
Singleton, Shelby CO: 40, 169, 170, 173; RR: 171
Singleton, Zutty JA: 57
Sing Out! magazine FO: **185–187,** *186*
Michael Cooney FO: 41
Tom Paxton FO: 156

Sing Out! magazine (*continued*)
Pete Seeger FO: 182
Happy Traum BL: 221
Happy and Artie Traum FO: 204
Izzy Young FO: 219
Sir Douglas Quintet BL: 187
Sir Dyno RB: **240**
Sissle, Noble BL: 137, 201; JA: 93
Sister Sledge RB: **240**
Sister Souljah RB: **240**
sit-ins FO: 33
"Sittin' on Top of the World" BL: 140, **191,** 228–229
"Six Days on the Road" CO: 65, **185,** 202
"Sixteen Tons" CO: 76, **185,** 200
Sixth Street (Austin, Texas) BL: 216
"Six White Horses." *See* "See That My Grave Is Kept Clean"
ska RB: 175, 222; RR: 158, 200
ska/bluebeat revival RB: **240–241**
Skaggs, Ricky CO: **186**
bluegrass music CO: 16
Guy Clark FO: 36
Country Gentlemen FO: 44
J. D. Crowe FO: 47
Jerry Douglas FO: 55
Jim Eanes FO: 59
Vince Gill CO: 81
Emmylou Harris CO: 95
Bill Monroe CO: 141
Jimmy Murphy FO: 144
Dolly Parton CO: 158
Tony Rice FO: 169
Stanley Brothers FO: 193
Stanley Brothers, The CO: 191
"Uncle Pen" CO: 207
Whites FO: 214
Keith Whitley CO: 214
Lee Ann Womack CO: 219
Tammy Wynette CO: 221
Skee-Lo RB: **241**
Sketches of Spain (Miles Davis, Gil Evans) JA: 49, 68; RR: 119
skiffle FO: 54–55; RR: 28
Skillet Lickers, The FO: 161, **187**
Skinner, Jimmy FO: 99
Skrowaczewski, Stanislaw CL: 197, **209**
Sky, Patrick CO: 154; FO: 61, **187–188**
Skyline FO: *188,* **188,** 204–205
Skyscrapers (John Alden Carpenter) CL: **209**
Slack, Freddie RB: 262
slack-key tuning BL: 222–223; CO: 60; FO: 21–22, 54
slapback (echo) RR: 67, 180
slap bass JA: 56
Slatkin, Felix CL: 5, 105, **209–210**
Slatkin, Leonard CL: 39, 162, 185, **210**
slaves and slavery BL: vii, xv
banjo BL: 13; JA: 9
Thomas Bethune CL: 28
Blood on the Fields CL: 31
blues JA: 19
fiddle BL: 61–62
minstrel shows BL: 136
sharecropping BL: 189
social history and the blues BL: 195–196
Sledge, Percy CO: 13; RB: **241**
Slick, Darby RR: 119–120
Slick, Grace RR: 119–121, 206
slide guitar BL: xxii, 1, 2, **191–193.** *See also specific slide guitarists*
slide trombone JA: 199
"Slipping Around" CO: **186**
Sloan, Bobby FO: 47, 115
Sloane, Steven CL: 7
"Slowly" CO: 161, 162, **186**
Sly and the Family Stone RB: 98, **241–242**
Slye, Leonard (Roy Rogers) CO: 179, 189. *See also* Rogers, Roy (country singer)
Small, Millie RB: 222; RR: 200
Smalls, Biggie. *See* Notorious B.I.G., The
Small's Paradise JA: 85
Smashing Pumpkins RR: 98–99
Smear, Pat RR: 161
Smeck, Roy FO: **189**
"Smells Like Teen Spirit" RR: 97, 160
Smiley, Red FO: 59, 168
Smirnoff, Joel CL: 121
Smith, Arlene RB: 38, 105
Smith, Arthur BL: 26; RR: 115
Smith, Arthur "Guitar Boogie" FO: 168
Smith, Bessie BL: xv, xvi, xvii, xviii, *193,* **193–194;** JA: **182–183**
Louis Armstrong BL: 8
"Backwater Blues" BL: 11
blues lyrics BL: 20, 24
Clarksdale, Mississippi BL: 137
classic blues BL: 42
"Downhearted Blues" BL: 54
John Hammond, Sr. BL: 71
Fletcher Henderson JA: 89
Billie Holiday JA: 91
Alberta Hunter BL: 83; JA: 95
jazz BL: 92
Janis Joplin RR: 122
music business BL: 143, 146

"Nobody Knows You When You're Down and Out" BL: 154
piano BL: 161
Ma Rainey BL: 177; JA: 161
Don Redman JA: 163
"St. Louis Blues" BL: 187
saxophone, trombone, trumpet, and clarinet BL: 189
social history BL: 201
vocal styles BL: 229–230
Frank Walker BL: 235
Fats Waller JA: 209
Clarence Williams BL: 243–244
Smith, Bobbie RB: 244
Smith, Carl CO: 26, 94, 95, 99, **187**
Smith, Chester CO: 88
Smith, Clarence "Pinetop" BL: 27, 114, 158, 161, **195**
Smith, Connie CO: **187–188,** 194
Smith, Don CO: 14
Smith, Fiddlin' Arthur FO: 38, 110, 137, **189**
Smith, George "Harmonica" BL: 163, **194**
Smith, Glen FO: 210
Smith, Harry BL: 64, 232; FO: 7, 170, **189–190**
Smith, Hobart BL: 189; FO: 36, **190**
Smith, Huey "Piano" BL: **194;** RB: 165, 174
Smith, Jerry Lee "Smoochee" RB: 175
Smith, Jimmy JA: 51, 148, **183,** 200
Smith, Joe BL: 92, 189, 194; RR: 95
Smith, Leo JA: 7
Smith, Lonnie Liston JA: 135
Smith, Mabel Louise. *See* Big Maybelle
Smith, Mamie BL: xvii, xxi; JA: xxx, **183–184**
classic blues BL: 42
"Crazy Blues" BL: 46
Coleman Hawkins JA: 87
jazz firsts JA: 116
Ralph Peer BL: 156
record labels BL: 176
Bessie Smith JA: 183
Smith, Neal RR: 43
Smith, Odell FO: 159
Smith, Patti RR: 203
Smith, Pinetop. *See* Smith, Clarence "Pinetop"
Smith, Russell CO: 216
Smith, Sammi CO: 98, 118
Smith, Stuff JA: **184,** 207
Smith, Tommy JA: 26, **185**
Smith, Trixie BL: 165
Smith, Warren RR: 165
Smith, Will RB: **242–243**
Smith, Willie "The Lion" JA: 28, 45, 184; RB: 262
Smither, Chris BL: **195,** 234
Smithereens, The RR: 178
Smithsonian Institution BL: 9, 64; FO: 7, 144, 164, 170–171
"Smoke! Smoke! Smoke! (That Cigarette)" CO: **188,** 200
Smooth Bee RB: 195
smooth jazz JA: 125–126, **185,** 187; RB: 29, **243**
Smothers Brothers Comedy Hour, The CO: 116; FO: 209
Smyth, "Curley" Joe CO: 183
SNCC (Student Non-Violent Coordinating Committee) BL: 249
Snoop Doggy Dogg RB: **243,** 288
Snow, Hank CO: **188**
Ray Charles CO: 36
Ted Daffan CO: 51
Drifting Cowboys CO: 63
Stuart Hamblen CO: 93
"I'm Moving On" CO: 107–108
Eddie Noack CO: 152
Chubby Wise FO: 216
Snow, Kilby FO: 181
Snowden, Elmer BL: 95; JA: 60
social commentary RR: 221. *See also* protest songs
social history and the blues BL: **195–204,** *196, 198, 200*
Society Blues (Elijah Wald) BL: 168, 242
Society for American Music CL: 7, **210,** 211–212
Soft Cell RR: 158
"Soldier's Joy" CO: **189**
Solitaires, The RB: **243–244**
solo JA: 19, 22, 162, **185**
soloist CL: xvi
"So Long, It's Been Good to Know You (Dusty Old Dust)" FO: **190,** 212
Solti, Sir Georg CL: xxiv, 50, 63, **210–211**
Solzhenitsyn, Aleksandr CL: 192
sonata CL: xvi
Sondheim, Stephen CL: 27
song cycle CL: 8
song form JA: 1, 23, 27, 33
Song for My Father (Horace Silver) JA: **185–186**
songster BL: xviii; CO: xvii
Song Swappers FO: 157
songwriting credits RR: 113
Sonics, The RR: 41, 97
Sonic Youth RR: 160
Sonneck, Oscar CL: 160, 210, **211–212**

Sonnier, Lennis FO: 89
Sonny and Cher RB: 11; RR: 36
Sons of the Mountaineers CO: 131; FO: 132
Sons of the Pioneers CO: 46, 179, **189,** 204
Sony Walkman RR: 174
Sopkin, Henry CL: 13
soprano saxophone. *See* saxophone; *specific soprano saxophonists*
Sorrell, Jeannette CL: 12
Sorrels, Jim FO: 190–191
Sorrels, Rosalie FO: **190–191**
S.O.S. Band, The RB: **244**
Soul Assassins RB: 98
Soul Children, The RB: **244**
Soul Clan, The RB: 51, 207, 256
soul jazz JA: 200
Soulsonic Force RB: 10
Soul Stirrers, The RB: 48, 254
Soul Survivors, The RB: **244**
Soundgarden RR: 98, 167
soundies JA: **185**
sound systems RR: 200
Sousa, John Philip CL: **212**
South, Eddie JA: 207
South, Joe CO: 84
South Africa RB: 178; RR: 52
South African jazz JA: 97, 129, **186–187**
South by Southwest conference CO: 24
South Central (Los Angeles) RB: 129, 130
Southern Comfort RR: 122
Southern Fiddlers Convention (Union Grove) FO: 81
Southern Folklife Collection CO: 245
Southern rock CO: 53; RR: 3–6, *5,* 117, 127, 207
Southern Syncopated Orchestra JA: 12, 64
South Side (Chicago) BL: 20, 33, 40, 90
Sovine, Red CO: 9, 163; FO: 45
Sowerby, Leo CL: 43, **212**
Spacek, Sissy CO: 39
Spalding, Albert CL: **212**
Spampinato, Joey CO: 55
Spand, Charley BL: **204–205**
Spaniels, The RB: 36, 270
Spanish-American War FO: 179
Spanish guitar CO: 89; FO: 84
Spann, Otis BL: **205**
  Big Maceo BL: 17
  Fleetwood Mac BL: 63
  Forest City Joe BL: 65
  Louis Myers BL: 149
  Pinetop Perkins BL: 158
  Muddy Waters BL: 239
Spano, Robert CL: 13, 38, **212**
Spargur, John CL: 204
Sparks, Larry CO: 191; FO: 193
Sparks, Randy FO: 146
Sparrow, The RR: 228
Speaking of Now (Pat Metheny) JA: 20, 134
Speckled Red BL: 53, **205**
Spector, Phil RR: **221–223,** *222*
  Harold Battiste RB: 11
  Beatles RR: 21–22
  Blossoms, The RB: 21
  Crystals, The RB: 52
  Dixie Cups, The RB: 62
  girl groups RB: 106; RR: 91
  Goldstar Studio RB: 107
  Righteous Brothers RR: 204
  Righteous Brothers, The RB: 225
  Ronettes, The RB: 229
  Ike and Tina Turner RB: 263
Spector, Ronnie. *See* Bennett, Veronica
Speculum Musicae CL: 166, 169, **212**
speed metal RR: 145, 146
Speeer, George Thomas FO: 191
Speer Family, The FO: **191**
Speilberg, Steven CL: 239
Speir, H. C. BL: xxi, 138, 157, **205,** 211
Spellman, Benny RB: 150
Spence, Andy FO: 191
Spence, Bill FO: 56, **191–192**
Spence, Joseph BL: 38
Spence, Skip RR: 119
Spencer, Jeremy BL: 62; RR: 81, 82
Spencer, Tim CO: 189
Spencer Davis Group RR: 201
Spielberg, Steven FO: 8
"Spike Driver Blues" BL: **205**
Spinderella RB: 233, 234
Spinners, The RB: 187, **244–245**
spirituals CL: vii; BL: xv, xvii, 77–78, 133, 197
Spitzer, Nick BL: 175
Spivak, Charlie JA: 55
Spivey, Victoria BL: 96, 144, 153, **206,** 237, 245
Spoelstra, Mark BL: **206;** FO: 95, **192**
Spoleto Festival CL: 21, 77, 124, 152, **213**
"Spoonful" BL: 46, 89
Spottswood, Richard K. FO: 144
Sprague, Carl T. CO: **189;** FO: 98
Spratlan, Lewis CL: 138, **213,** *213*
Springsteen, Bruce JA: 169; RB: 23; RR: 166, **223–226,** *225*
Sproule, Daithi FO: 29
square dance FO: 5, 101, 133, 192, **192,** 209

Squire, Chris RR: 184
Squires, The RR: 253
Sri Chinmoy RR: 214
Stackhouse, Houston BL: 153–154, **206**
Stackolee BL: 103
Stafford, Jim CO: 13, 80
Stafford, Jo CO: 217
Stafford, Tom RB: 115
"Stagger Lee" BL: 103, 164
"Stairway to Heaven" BL: 113; RR: 133, 135, 137
Staley, Layne RR: 98
Stampfel, Peter FO: 98
Stampley, Joe CO: 11, 99
Stamps, Virgil O. CO: 26, 85; FO: 22
Stamps-Baxter Publishing Company CO: 14, 15, 26, 85, 86
standards RR: 59, 156
"Stand by Your Man" CO: **189–190,** 221
Standing in the Shadows of Motown (documentary) BL: 182; RR: 153
Stanley, Carter CO: 190, 191; FO: 193
Stanley, Paul RR: 130, 131
Stanley, Ralph CO: *190*
  gospel music CO: 86
  "I Am a Man of Constant Sorrow" CO: 107
  Ricky Skaggs CO: 186
  Stanley Brothers FO: 193, 194
  Stanley Brothers, The CO: 190, 191
  Keith Whitley CO: 214–215
Stanley, Roba FO: **192–193,** 215
Stanley Brothers, The CO: **190–191;** FO: **193–194**
  Emry Arthur FO: 6
  bluegrass music CO: 15, 16
  Albert E. Brumley FO: 22
  Flatt and Scruggs CO: 73
  Goins Brothers FO: 78
  Newport Folk Festival FO: 149
  shape-note singing FO: 184
  Keith Whitley CO: 214
Staples, Roebuck "Pop" BL: 79; RB: 245
Staple Singers, The BL: 79; RB: 81, **245,** 247
Stargard RB: **245–246**
Stark, John BL: 176
Starker, Janos CL: **213**
Starling, John FO: 183
Starnes, Jack CO: 51–52, 169
Starr, Edwin RB: **246**
Starr, Kay CO: **191–192**
Starr, Maurice RB: 194
Starr, Ringo
  "Act Naturally" CO: 1
  Beatles, The RR: 19, 22
  country rock CO: 45
  Pete Drake CO: 62
  drums RR: 68
  Electric Light Orchestra RR: 77
  Buddy Harman CO: 94
  Buck Owens CO: 156
Star Search CO: 99, 183
State Department, U.S. FO: 100; JA: 75
"Statesboro Blues" BL: 6, 130, **206**
Statler Brothers CO: **192**
Staton, Candi RB: **246**
Stax Records (Stax-Volt Records) BL: **180;** RB: **246–247**. *See also* Axton, Estelle; Stewart, Jim
Steel, John RR: 9
Steele, Davy FO: 13
Steele, Pete FO: 7, 13, 182
Steeleye Span FO: 30, 71, 102, **194**
steel guitar. *See* pedal steel guitar
"Steel Guitar Rag" BL: 240; CO: 218; FO: 134
steel-stringed guitar CO: 89–90
Steely Dan JA: 185; RR: **226–228,** *227*
Stegall, Keith CO: 38
Stein, Chris RR: 26–28
Stein, Gertrude CL: 224
Steinbeck John FO: 109
Steinberg, Lewis RB: 23
Steinberg, William CL: 30, 40, 179, **213–214**
Steiner, John BL: 178
Steinway, Betty CL: 48
Stelling Banjo company FO: 61
Stephney, Bill RB: 212
Steppenwolf RR: 41, 105, **228–229**
Steps Ahead JA: 22
Sterban, Richard CO: 153
Stereo MC's, The RB: 3
Stereos, The RB: **247**
Sterling, Corey BL: 190
Sterling, Scott RB: 157, 158
Stern, Isaac CL: 17, 45, 112, 113, 191, **214–215**
Steve Allen Show, The CO: 122; RR: 180
Stevens, Michael CO: 24
Stevens, Ray CO: 86
Stevens, Roger L. CL: 125
Stevie B. RB: **247–248**
Stewart, Amii RB: **248**
Stewart, Andy FO: 184, 185
Stewart, Billy RB: **248**
Stewart, Dave RR: 158, 178
Stewart, Ian RR: 208

Stewart, Jim BL: 131, 180; RB: 246
Stewart, John FO: 117; RR: 151
Stewart, Redd CO: 117, 197
Stewart, Reginald CL: 16
Stewart, Rod BL: 11
Stewart, Slam JA: 194
Stewart, Sylvester (Sly Stone) RB: 241–242
Stewart, Wynn CO: 91, 105, 191
Stilettos RR: 27
"Still" CO: 4, **192**
Still, William Grant CL: **215**
Still Life Talking (Pat Metheny) JA: 134, **187**
Stills, Stephen CO: 75; FO: 73; RR: 34, 35, 149, 254
Sting
  Chieftains FO: 33
  Gil Evans JA: 68
  Kenny Garrett JA: 74
  Toby Keith CO: 115
  Branford Marsalis JA: 127; RB: 176
  Maria Schneider JA: 171
Stipe, Michael RR: 201, 202
Stitt, Sonny JA: 85, 86, **187–188**
Stock, Frederick CL: 49, **215**
Stockhausen, Karlheinz JA: 21
Stokes, Frank BL: **206–207**
Stokes, Lowe FO: 187
Stokowski, Leopold CL: xxiv, **215–217**
  American Symphony Orchestra CL: 8
  George Antheil CL: 12
  Daniel Barenboim CL: 19
  Marion Bauer CL: 22
  Cincinnati Symphony Orchestra CL: 51
  Morton Gould CL: 92
  Alan Hovhaness CL: 108
  Eugene Ormandy CL: 169
  Philadelphia Orchestra CL: 176
  Wallingford Riegger CL: 189
  Artur Rodzinski CL: 190
  Oscar Shumsky CL: 208
  Ellen Taafe Zwilich CL: 246
Stoller, Mike. *See* Leiber, Jerry, and Mike Stoller
Stoltzman, Richard CL: **217,** 221
"Stompin' at the Savoy" JA: **188**
Stone, Cliffie CO: 76, 106
Stone, Curtis CO: 32
Stone, Harry CO: 87
Stone, Jesse JA: 87
Stone, Jessie RB: 19, 49, 83
Stone, Oliver (director) RR: 64
Stone, Oliver (fiddle player) FO: 86
Stone, Oscar CO: 12
Stone, Sly. *See* Stewart, Sylvester
Stone Canyon Band CO: 26, 44; FO: 22
Stoneman, Ernest "Pop" CO: 6; FO: 92, **194–195**
Stoneman, Roni FO: 194, 195
Stoneman, Scotty FO: 81, 115, 194, 195
Stoneman Family Band FO: 194–195
Stone Temple Pilots RR: 98
Stooges, The RR: 31, 188
Stookey, Noel Paul FO: 17, 83, 157
"Stormy Monday" BL: **207,** 236
Story, Carl FO: **195**
Storyville BL: 218; JA: **188**
Stovepipe, Daddy BL: 185
Stover, Don FO: 37, 83, 126
Strachwitz, Chris BL: **207;** FO: **195–196**
  Arhoolie Records BL: 7
  Clifton Chenier BL: 39
  Mance Lipscomb BL: 115
  music business and the blues BL: 145
  recording FO: 164
  San Francisco Bay Area BL: 35
  Mercy Dee Walton BL: 235
"Straight, No Chaser" JA: **188**
Straight Outta Compton (N.W.A.) RB: 78, 130, 196
Strait, George CO: **193,** *193*
  "All My Ex's Live in Texas" CO: 3
  Mark Chesnutt CO: 37
  Tommy Collins CO: 41
  Harold "Pappy" Daily CO: 52
  Johnny Gimble CO: 83; FO: 77
Strange Creek Singers, The FO: 76, 148, 181
"Strange Fruit" BL: 76; JA: 92
Stratocaster (Fender) RR: 111
Straus, Noel CL: 19–20
Strausbaugh, John RR: 182
Strauss, Richard CL: 223
Stravinsky, Igor CL: 13, 25, 63
Strawbs, The FO: 51
Stray Cats RR: 42, 158, 206
Strayhorn, Billy JA: 4–5, **188–189,** 193
Street, Mel CO: **193–194**
street singers BL: 49, 57, 89, 115
Strehli, Angela BL: 12, **207–208**
Strickland, Napoleon BL: 139
Stricklin, Al CO: 219
stride piano JA: 107–108, **189,** 209, 210
string bands BL: 7–8, 14, 61, **208,** 247
string bass. *See* double bass
Stringbean CO: **194;** FO: 180

Stringmusic (Morton Gould) CL: **217**
Striplin, Steve RB: 192
Stripling, Charlie FO: 196
Stripling, Ira FO: 196
Stripling Brothers, The FO: **196**
stritch JA: 114
Stroll, The (dance) RB: 280
Strong, Barrett RB: 188, 246
Strothers, Jimmy BL: 12; RR: 120
Strube, Gustav CL: 16, **217**
Stuart, Marty CO: 187, **194–195,** 202; FO: 197
Stuart, Mindy FO: 175
Stubbs, Eddie FO: 111
Stubbs, Joe RB: 87
Stubbs, Levi RB: 94, 95
Stucken, Frank von der CL: 51
Stuckey, Henry BL: 90, 137
Stucky, Steven CL: **217–218**
Student Non-Violent Coordinating Committee (SNCC) BL: 249; FO: 33
styles. *See* jazz styles, evolution of
Stylistics, The RB: **248–249**
Subotnick, Morton CL: **218**
Sudano, Bruce RB: 250
Sugar Hill RB: 108, *109,* **249**
Sugarhill Gang RB: xvii, 122, 217, 229, 249
Sugar Hill (San Francisco club) BL: 35
Sugar Shaft RB: 287
Suggs, Doug BL: 161
suicide RR: 161
Sullivan, Ed RR: 180. *See also The Ed Sullivan Show*
Sullivan, Enoch and Emmett FO: 196–197
Sullivan, Ira JA: 152
Sullivan, Jerry FO: 197
Sullivan, Margie FO: 197
Sullivan, Nikki RR: 113
Sullivan, Tammy FO: 197
Sullivan Family, The FO: **196–197**
Sumlin, Hubert BL: 82, **208**
Summer, Donna RB: 61, 62, **249–250,** *250*
Summer of Love RR: 119, 145–146
Summers, Bill JA: 88
Summers, John "Dick" FO: 176
Sumner, J. D. CO: 15
Sundance FO: 15, 46
Sunny and the Sunglows RB: **250**
Sunnyland Slim BL: 184, **208–209**
Sunny Mountain Boys FO: 134
Sun Ra JA: xxiv, 169, **189–191,** *190,* 192
Sun Records BL: 131, 179, **209;** CO: 170, 176–177; RR: 205–206. *See also* Phillips, Sam
Sunshine, Adrian CL: 198
Sun Studios
  "Blue Moon of Kentucky" CO: 16
  Memphis BL: 132
  Sam Phillips RR: 172
  Elvis Presley BL: 162; RB: 209
  Ike and Tina Turner RB: 262
  U2 RR: 237
  Yardbirds, The RR: 251
SUNY-Buffalo JA: 177
supergroups RR: xi
Super Nature RB: 233
Supernaw, Doug CO: **195**
Supremes, The RB: *230,* 230–231, 256; RR: 153, 154
Surfaris RR: 229
surf rock RR: xix, **229–230**
Surman, John JA: 92, 131, **191,** 208
Susskind, Walter CL: 51
Sutcliffe, Stuart RR: 18, 19
Sutherland, Joan CL: 106
Sutton, R. Glenn CO: 4
Svanoe, Bill BL: 236
Swaggart, Jimmy CO: 122
Swallow, Steve JA: 26, 152, **191–192**
swamp blues BL: 74, 111, 115, 120, 240
Swamp Dogg BL: **209–210**
Swanoe, Bill FO: 175
Swarbrick, Dave FO: 30, 64
Sweat, Keith RB: 72, 108
Sweat P RB: 197
Sweden BL: 17, 251
Sweeney, J. W. FO: 12, 138
Sweeney's Men FO: 107
Sweet, Matthew RR: 178
Sweetheart of the Rodeo (the Byrds)
  Byrds FO: 25; RR: 37
  country rock CO: 44–45; RR: 43, 45
  Flying Burrito Brothers CO: 75
  Kentucky Colonels FO: 115
"Sweet Home Chicago" BL: 8, **210**
Sweet Honey in the Rock BL: 249; FO: **197**
the Sweet Inspirations RB: 125
Sweet LD RB: 197
swing JA: xxiii, 14, 85, **192,** 252*t*. *See also specific swing era musicians*
swingbeat RB: 247–248, **250**
"Swingin'" CO: **195**

Switch RB: **251**
Switched-On Bach (Wendy Carlos) CL: 43, **218**
SWV RB: **251**
Sykes, Roosevelt BL: 155, 160, 161, **210,** 211, 221
Sykes, Roy, and the Blue Ridge Boys CO: 190; FO: 193
symphony CL: xvi
Symphony for Improvisers (Don Cherry) JA: 16, 31–32
Symphony Hall CL: 35, 182, **218**
syncopation JA: 161, 192, **192**
synthesizer JA: xxvi, 78, **192**
Szabo, Gabor JA: 80
Szell, George CL: xxiv, **218–219**
  Cleveland Orchestra CL: 52
  Dean Dixon CL: 69
  James Levine CL: 136
  Mannes College of Music CL: 147
  George Rochberg CL: 189
  Peter Serkin CL: 204
  Robert Shaw CL: 208
Szigeti, Joseph CL: **219–220**
Szymczyk, Bill BL: 105, 220, 250

T

Tabackin, Lew JA: 4
Tabano, Ray RR: 1
Tabuchi, Shoji CO: 22
Taggart, Blind Joe BL: 18, **211,** 242
Tairrie B RB: **253**
Taj Mahal. *See* Mahal, Taj
take JA: **193**
"Take Five" JA: 25, 197
"Take the 'A' Train" JA: 189, **193**
"Take This Job and Shove It" CO: 40, 159, **197**
talent scouts BL: xxi, 71, 120–121, 205, **211–212,** 223, 244
"Talk about Me" CO: **197**
talking blues BL: 232
Talking Heads RR: **231–232**
Tallent, Gary RR: 225
Talmadge, Art CO: 52
Tampa Red BL: xix–xx, **212;** RB: **253**
  acoustic guitar BL: 2
  aliases BL: 5
  Big Maceo BL: 17
  Chicago BL: 40, 41
  Blind John Davis BL: 49
  Thomas A. Dorsey BL: 54
  Memphis Minnie BL: 133
  protest songs BL: 167
  Ma Rainey BL: 177; JA: 161
  "Sittin' on Top of the World" BL: 191
  slide guitar BL: 192
  Speckled Red BL: 205
  talent scouts BL: 211
  vocal styles BL: 232
  Junior Wells BL: 241
Tams, John FO: 102
Tams, The (the Magnificents) RB: 174
Tandy, Richard RR: 76
Tanglewood Music Center CL: **221**
tango JA: 76
Tannen, Holly FO: 56
Tanner, Gid CO: 167, 180; FO: 161–162, 187
Tanner, Nora Belle FO: 87
tape recorder FO: 163
tapers RR: 53, 94, 117
Tarheel Slim BL: **212–213**
Tarleton, Jimmy FO: 49, 53
Tarlton, Jimmie BL: **213,** 231
Tarras, Dave FO: 118
Tarriers, The FO: 175
Tashi CL: 138, 205, 217, **221**
Tashian, Barry and Holly FO: **199–200**
Tasty Licks FO: 68
Tate, Baby BL: **213**
Tate, Tater FO: 195
Tatum, Art JA: **193–194**
  Dorothy Donegan JA: 55
  Charles Mingus JA: 136
  Oscar Peterson JA: 154
  piano JA: 155
  Bud Powell JA: 156
  "Tiger Rag" JA: 197
  Lennie Tristano JA: 199
  McCoy Tyner JA: 200
  Ben Webster JA: 213
Taub, Robert CL: **221**
Tausig, Carl CL: 76
Tavares RB: **253**
Taylor, Billy, Sr. JA: 18
Taylor, Cecil JA: **194–195,** *195*
  avant-garde JA: 7
  Andrew Cyrille JA: 46
  Leroy Jenkins JA: 107
  Steve Lacy JA: 119
  Michael Mantler JA: 126
  Archie Shepp JA: 177
  third stream jazz JA: 197
Taylor, Chad JA: 32
Taylor, Deems CL: **221–222**
Taylor, Dennis FO: 172–173
Taylor, Drew CO: 20
Taylor, Eddie BL: 182, **213;** RB: 221
Taylor, Gil CO: 103
Taylor, Graeme FO: 102, 117
Taylor, Hound Dog BL: 5, 85, **213**
Taylor, James "J.T." (Kool and the Gang) RB: 156

Taylor, James (singer-songwriter) FO: **200**
George Jones CO: 111
Newport Folk Festival FO: 149
Mark O'Connor FO: 152
singer/songwriter movement FO: 185
singer-songwriters RR: 220, 221
Taylor, Johnnie RB: 247, **254**
Taylor, Koko BL: **213–214**
Taylor, Lynne FO: 175
Taylor, Maddy FO: 185
Taylor, Mick BL: 127; RR: 208
Taylor, Montana BL: **214**
Taylor, Otis BL: 14, **214,** 233–234, 251, 253
Taylor, Roger RR: 191, 193
Taylor, Sam "the Man" RB: 119
Taylor, Susan CO: 215
Taylor, Ted RB: 33
Taylor, Tut FO: 16, 93, **200**
Taylor, Vince RR: 31
Tchaikovsky, Pyotr Ilich CL: xxiii, 44
Tchicai, John JA: 177
Teagarden, Jack JA: **195,** 214
Tears for Fears RB: 3
technique JA: 32, 33, 142, **195**
techno RB: xvii, 146, **254,** 260; RR: 201
technology RR: xi
Teddy Bears RR: 221
Tedeschi, Susan BL: **214**
Ted Mack Amateur Hour CO: 43, 122
Teena Marie RB: **254**
Teen Kings RR: 164
Tejano music BL: 7, 207
Television (band) RR: 188
Temirkanov, Yuri CL: 17, **222**
tempered scale CL: xix
Temple, Johnny BL: **215**
Temple of the Dog RR: 167, 168
tempo BL: 230; JA: **196**
Tempo Toppers RR: 141
Temptations, The RB: 151, **254–255,** *255;* RR: 154
Tench, Benmont RR: 177
Tenenbom, Steve CL: 221
Tennessee Barn Dance (radio show) CO: 81; FO: 111
Tennessee Cutups, The FO: 168
Tennessee Hillbillies CO: 212
Tennessee River Boys CO: 99
Tennessee Two CO: 35, 108
"Tennessee Waltz" CO: 43, 53, 117, **197**
tenor saxophone. *See* saxophone; *specific tenor players*
Terence Higgins Trust RR: 193
Terkel, Studs BL: 170; FO: 21
"Terraplane Blues" BL: 96, 97
Terrell, Jean RB: **256**
Terrell, Tammi RB: 277
territory bands JA: xxiii, 134, 141, 184, **196,** 197
Terry, Clark JA: 23, 81, 163, 192, **196,** 211
Terry, Lucy FO: 159
Terry, Sonny BL: *215,* **215–216;** FO: **200–201,** *201*
Champion Jack Dupree BL: 55
Blind Boy Fuller BL: 65
harmonica BL: 72, 73; FO: 92
J. B. Long BL: 120, 121
Brownie McGhee BL: 128, 129
Buddy Moss BL: 142
New York City BL: 153
Alec Seward BL: 189
Josh White BL: 242
Ralph Willis BL: 245
Tex, Joe RB: **256**
Texas BL: xix, 45, **216–217.** *See also specific cities, e.g.* Houston
Texas Playboys. *See also* Wills, Bob
Tommy Duncan CO: 66
Johnny Gimble CO: 82; FO: 77
Grand Ole Opry CO: 87
Leon McAuliffe FO: 134
"San Antonio Rose" CO: 183
Bob Wills CO: 218
Texas Tornados CO: 72
Texas Troubadors CO: 203
Tex-Mex music BL: 43, 187, 207; FO: 196, **201–202**
"T for Texas (Blue Yodel Number One)" CO: **197**
Thalberg, Sigismond CL: **222**
Tharpe, Sister Rosetta BL: 79, **217**
"That'll Be the Day" RR: 111, 112, 114
"That's All Right" BL: **217–218;** RR: x
Arthur "Big Boy" Crudup BL: 47; RB: 52
Elvis Presley BL: 164; RB: 209; RR: 179
rockabilly RR: 205
Sun Records BL: 209
Thayer, Tommy RR: 131
Thayil, Kim RR: 98
theater BL: xv, 145–146; FO: 165
Theater Owners' Booking Association (TOBA) BL: 10, 126; JA: 7, 182, 183
Thelonious Monk Institute of Jazz JA: 82

Them RR: 219
theme JA: 88
Theresa's (Chicago nightclub) BL: 40
Thibaud, Jacques CL: 182
Thibodeaux, Rufus CO: 150; FO: 148
Thiele, Bob JA: 158
Thiele, Chris CO: 150; FO: 149
Thiele, Scott CO: 150; FO: 149
Thigpen, Ben JA: 184
third stream jazz JA: xxiv, 171–172, **196–197,** 252*t*
13th Floor Elevators RR: 186
Thirty Seconds over Winterland (Jefferson Airplane) RR: 119, 120
"This Land Is Your Land" FO: 146, **202**
Thomas, Augusta Read CL: **222**
Thomas, Carla BL: 219; RB: 246, **256**
Thomas, Elmerlee BL: 249
Thomas, George BL: 218, 236, 237
Thomas, Henry BL: **218**
Thomas, Hersal BL: 218, 236, 237
Thomas, Hociel BL: **218–219**
Thomas, Irma BL: 238; CO: 184; RB: **257;** RR: 209
Thomas, Jesse (Babyface) BL: **219**
Thomas, Leon JA: 170
Thomas, Michael Tilson CL: 199, **222–223**
Thomas, Mickey RR: 121
Thomas, Rob RR: 214
Thomas, Rozonda "Chilli" RB: 259, *259*
Thomas, Rufus BL: **219;** RB: 15, 246, 247, 256
Thomas, Theodore CL: 49, 182, 215, **223**
Thomas, Timmy RB: **257**
Thomas, Willard (Rambling) BL: 167, **219**
Thompkins, Russell, Jr. RB: 248, 249
Thompson, Sir Charles JA: **197**
Thompson, Charles, and the Majestics RB: 186
Thompson, Danny FO: 109, 156
Thompson, Ernest FO: **202**
Thompson, Gail JA: 155
Thompson, Hank CO: 57, 102, **197–198,** 212, 215
Thompson, Joe, Nate, and Odell FO: **202–203**
Thompson, Les CO: 151
Thompson, Odell BL: 13
Thompson, Randall CL: 26, **224**
Thompson, Richard BL: 142; FO: 51, 64, 117
Thompson, Robert FO: 202
Thompson, Sonny RB: 154, **257–258**
Thompson, Sue CO: 81
Thompson, Tommy FO: 164, 165, *165*
Thompson, Tony RB: 41
Thompson, Uncle Jimmy CO: 86; FO: **203**
Thomson, Virgil CL: **224**
  Vladimir Horowitz CL: 107
  Louisiana Story CL: **142**
  Otto Luening CL: 143
  Leontyne Price CL: 184
  Ned Rorem CL: 191
  Carl Ruggles CL: 194–195
  social history and the blues BL: 204
Thorne, Francis CL: 7, **224–225**
Thornhill, Claude JA: 67
Thornton, Billy Bob CO: 195
Thornton, Willie Mae "Big Mama" BL: 158, **219–220;** RB: **258;** RR: 123, 138
Thorogood, George BL: 186, **220;** CO: 144
thrash metal RR: 145
Three Aces, The. *See* Aces, The
Thriller (Michael Jackson) JA: 109; RB: 137
"The Thrill Is Gone" BL: 105, **220**
Thurber, Jeanette CL: 71, 72, 161
Tibbett, Lawrence CL: **225**
Tiberi, Frank JA: 91
Ticketmaster RR: 167
Tierra RB: **258**
"Tiger Rag" JA: 193–194, **197**
Til, Sonny RB: *66,* 200; RR: 65. *See also* Orioles, The
Tillis, Mel CO: *198,* **198–199**
  Bobby Bare CO: 12
  Branson, Missouri CO: 22
  "Detroit City" CO: 56
  Lee Greenwood CO: 88
  Charlie McCoy CO: 136
  Pam Tillis CO: 199
Tillis, Pam CO: 199, **199**
Tillman, Floyd CO: 51, 100
Tillman, Jesse RB: 30
Tilton, Charlene CO: 122
'Til Tuesday RR: 178
Timbaland RB: **258**
timbales JA: 158; RR: 213
Time magazine JA: 24–25; RR: 199, 224, 236
Time Out (Dave Brubeck Quartet) JA: 24, 117, **197**
Time's Encomium (Charles Wuorinen) CL: **225,** 241
time signature JA: 25, 62, 197, **198;** RR: 174, 183

Timmons, Bobby JA: 137
Tin Angel (San Francisco) FO: 153
Tin Machine RR: 32
Tin Pan Alley CL: 86; BL: 176
Tinsley, Boyd RR: 52
Tipitina's (New Orleans) BL: 165
Tippin, Aaron CO: **199–200**
Titon, Jeff Todd BL: xxi, **220**
Tjader, Cal JA: 158
TLC RB: 199, **258–259,** *259*
TNN (The Nashville Network) CO: 12, 27, 109, 192; FO: 136
toasting RB: 18, 222; RR: 200
TOBA. *See* Theater Owners' Booking Association
Todd, Mazy FO: 73, 136
Tokens, The FO: 216
"To Know Him Is to Love Him" RR: 221, 222
Tokyo, Japan JA: 102
Toler, Dan RR: 6
Toll, Robert B. BL: 136
Tom and Jerry RR: 217
"Tom Dooley." *See* "(Hang Down Your Head) Tom Dooley"
Tommy Boy Records RB: **259**
Tommy (the Who) BL: 245; RR: 245
"Tomorrow Night" BL: 95, 107
Tom Tom Club RR: 232
tone cluster JA: 194, **198**
Tone Loc RB: 56, 289
Tonight Show, The JA: 127, 196; RB: 177
Too $hort RB: **260**
Toomey, Welby FO: 173
Topham, Top BL: 247; RR: 251
Tork, Peter RR: 149, 151
Torme, Mel JA: 130, **198**
Toronto Rock 'n' Roll Revival RR: 207
Toscanini, Arturo CL: xxiii, **225–226,** *226*
  Adagio for Strings (Barber) CL: 2
  Kurt Herbert Adler CL: 3
  Peter Herman Adler CL: 4
  Marian Anderson CL: 10
  Artur Balsam CL: 16
  Samuel Barber CL: 17
  Sir John Barbirolli CL: 18
  Leon Barzin CL: 20
  Giulio Gatti-Casazza CL: 86
  Erich Leinsdorf CL: 135
  Gustav Mahler CL: 147
  Willem Mengelberg CL: 151
  Metropolitan Opera CL: 155
  NBC Symphony Orchestra CL: 162
  New York Philharmonic Orchestra CL: 165
  Eugene Ormandy CL: 169
  Artur Rodzinski CL: 190
  Leonard Rose CL: 191
  Rudolf Serkin CL: 205
  Robert Shaw CL: 208
  Sir Georg Solti CL: 210
  William Steinberg CL: 214
  Richard Tucker CL: 227
  Earl Wild CL: 239
Tosh, Peter RB: 175; RR: 201
Totenberg, Roman CL: 35
"Touch of Grey" RR: 96, 187
Tourjee, Eben CL: 162
Toussaint, Allen BL: **220–221**
  Marcia Ball BL: 12
  Lee Dorsey RB: 70
  Snooks Eaglin BL: 57
  Ernie K-Doe RB: 150
  Smiley Lewis RB: 165
  Neville Brothers BL: 151–152
Tower, Joan CL: **226**
Towle, Phil RR: 147
Town Hall (New York) CL: **226;** FO: 56, 77; JA: 4
Town Hall Party CO: 19, 41, 78, 95, 133, 175
Townsend, Henry BL: 51, 98, 140, **221**
Townshend, Pete RR: 176, 243–246
Trachtenberg, Martha FO: 23
traders RR: 53, 94, 117
traditional jazz (classic jazz) JA: 190, **198,** 251*m*. *See also* Chicago jazz; New Orleans jazz (classic); recordings of early jazz; *specific musicians, e.g.* Beiderbecke, Leon "Bix"
trains BL: 23, 72. *See also* railroad songs
"Tramp" BL: 66, 128
trance RB: xvii, **260**
Transcendental Meditation RR: 17, 60, 61, 63
Traum, Artie BL: *221,* **221;** FO: 2, 186, *186,* **204**
Traum, Happy BL: **221;** FO: *186,* **204**
  Pat Alger FO: 2
  Mississippi John Hurt BL: 84
  Brownie McGhee BL: 129
  Sing Out! magazine FO: 186
travel BL: 23, 24, 103–104
Traveling Wilburys, The RR: 76–77, 166, 178
Travers, Fred FO: 183
Travers, Mary FO: 83, 157
Travis, Merle CO: **200**
  Delmore Brothers CO: 56
  "Divorce Me C.O.D." CO: 58
  Tennessee Ernie Ford CO: 76
  Grandpa Jones CO: 112

Travis, Merle (continued)
- Joe Maphis CO: 133
- "Sixteen Tons" CO: 185
- "Smoke! Smoke! Smoke! (That Cigarette)" CO: 188
- Hank Thompson CO: 197
- Doc Watson FO: 211

Travis, Randy CO: 154, 184, **201;** FO: 46
Travis picking CO: 200
Treemonisha (Scott Joplin) CL: 120, **227;** BL: 152, 176
tremolo JA: **198**
Trench Town (Kingston, Jamaica) RR: 200
Trent, Alphonso BL: 165; JA: 184
Tresvant, Ralph RB: 194
A Tribe Called Quest RB: 192, **260–261**
tribute bands RR: 131
Trickett, Ed FO: 17
Trick Pony CO: **201**
Trietsch brothers CO: 103
Trimble, Lester CL: **227**
Trischka, Tony FO: *188,* **204–205**
- five string banjo CO: 12
- bluegrass music CO: 16
- Bob Carlin FO: 28
- Country Cooking FO: 42, 43
- John McEuen FO: 136
- progressive bluegrass FO: 161
- Skyline FO: 188

Tristano, Lennie JA: 15, **198–199**
Tritt, Travis CO: 99, 194, **201–202**
Trivette, Al RB: 5
trombone BL: **189;** JA: xxvi, **199**. *See also specific trombonists*
Trone, Roland RB: 66
Trotter, Pat FO: 96
"Trouble in Mind" BL: **222**
Troyan, Joe CO: 112
"Truck Driver's Blues" CO: 51, 202
truck-driving songs CO: 65, 185, **202–203**
Trucks, Butch BL: 6, 222; RR: 4
Trucks, Derek BL: **222;** RR: 6
True Stories (movie) FO: 3; RB: 182
Trujillo, Rob RR: 148
Trumbauer, Frankie JA: 182, **199,** 214
trumpet BL: 8, **189;** JA: 142, **156, 199–200**. *See also* cornet; flugelhorn; pocket trumpet; *specific trumpeters*
Tse, Rono RB: 62
tsimbl FO: 117
TTF RB: **261**
tuba JA: xxvi, 56, 67
Tubb, Ernest CO: **203**
- Bill Cox FO: 45
- Thomas A. Dorsey BL: 54
- *Grand Ole Opry* CO: 87
- Jack Greene CO: 88
- Rex Griffin CO: 89
- guitar CO: 90
- Stuart Hamblen CO: 93
- Roger Miller CO: 140
- Eddie Noack CO: 152
- Hank Snow CO: 188
- "Walking the Floor over You" CO: 210

Tubb, Justin CO: 96, 203
Tucker, Maureen (Moe) RR: 240, 242
Tucker, Richard CL: **227**
Tucker, Sophie BL: 135; CO: 179
Tucker, Tanya CO: 31, 40, 201, **203–204,** 220
Tudor, David CL: **227–228**
Tuff Enuff (Fabulous Thunderbirds) BL: 61, 227
Tuft, Harry BL: 214
Tullock, Jake FO: 81
Tully, Alice CL: 5, 48, **228,** 235
Tulsa, Oklahoma BL: 17, 66, 135
"Tumbling Tumbleweeds" CO: 7, **204**
Tumbling Tumbleweeds (movie) CO: 179, 204
Tune Weavers, The RB: **261**
Tunica, Mississippi BL: **139**
tunings, guitar BL: xxii, 90, 157, 192, **222–223,** 224
Tupelo, Mississippi RR: 179
Turbans, The RB: **261**
Tureck, Rosalyn CL: **228,** 235
Turner, Big Joe BL: **223;** RB: **261–262;** RR: **232–233**
- boogie-woogie BL: 27
- Pete Johnson BL: 96
- Kansas City, Missouri BL: 140
- vocal styles BL: 231

Turner, Ike BL: 116, 137, 140, **223;** RB: 25; RR: 170
Turner, Ike and Tina RB: **262–263;** RR: 223
Turner, Lana JA: 176
Turner, Mary Lou CO: 4
Turner, Nat BL: 197
Turner, Othar BL: 139, **223–224**
Turner, Spyder RB: **263–364**
Turner, Tina BL: 140, 223; RB: **262–263;** RR: 223
turntable JA: 155
"Turn! Turn! Turn!" FO: 25, 183; RR: 36, 84

Turrentine, Stanley JA: 35, 174, 183, **200**
Tutwiler, Mississippi BL: **140**
Twain, Shania CO: 113, 118, 133, **204–205,** *205,* 214
12-bar structure JA: 19, **200**
12 New Etudes for Piano (William Bolcom) CL: 33, **228–229**
12-string guitar BL: **224–225**
  Atlanta BL: 9
  folk rock RR: 85
  Bob Gibson FO: 76
  guitar RR: 100
  Lead Belly BL: 112; FO: 123
  Blind Willie McTell BL: 130
  Pete Seeger FO: 183
  Mark Spoelstra BL: 206
12-tone composition CL: 15, 89, 129, 130, 175, 189
Twist, The RB: 39, 40, 60
Twista RB: **264**
Twitchell, Harmony CL: 114
Twitty, Conway CO: 21, 80, 98, 127, **205–206,** 210
2Pac. *See* Shakur, Tupac
two-tone bands RR: 158, 200
Tyler, John CL: 101
Tyler, Steven RB: 232; RR: 1–3
Tyner, McCoy JA: 40, 41, 124, 142, 163, **200–201**
Tyson, Ian FO: 105, *105,* 106
Tyson, Ronni RB: 233
Tyson, Sylvia Fricker FO: 105, *105,* 106

U

U2 CO: 39; RB: 133, 182; RR: **235–237**
UB-40 RR: 158
Uillean pipes FO: 10, 34–35, 61
U-Krew RB: **265**
Ulrich, Lars RR: 145, 147
"Uncle Pen" (song) CO: 141, 186, 191, **207;** FO: 193
Underground Railroad BL: 197
Underwood, Richard FO: 111
Undisputed Truth RB: **265–266**
Ungar, Jay FO: 19, 38, 43, 148
Ungar, Lynn FO: 148
Unifics, The RB: **266**
Union Station CO: 118; FO: 55
unison JA: **203**
United Distributors RB: 199
United Kingdom. *See also* Great Britain
  Blondie RR: 27
  blues rock RR: 28–29
  British invasion RR: 32–34
  Donovan RR: 60
  Electric Light Orchestra RR: 75–77
  folk rock RR: 85
  new wave RR: 156–158
  Oasis RR: **163–164**
  Roy Orbison RR: 165
  power pop RR: 176
  psychedelic rock RR: 185
  punk rock RR: 187
  Radiohead RR: 195
  Ramones RR: 198
Universal Music Group RB: 189, 193; RR: 154
upright bass. *See* double bass
Upsetters, The RB: 43, 168; RR: 140, 141
Upshaw, Dawn CL: **231**
Uptown Records RB: **266**
Urban, Keith CO: **207,** *211*
Urban, Michael BL: 204
urban blues BL: 20, 36, 57–59, 105, 231. *See also* Chicago blues
Urban Cowboy (movie) CO: 82, 122, 123, 146
Urban Dance Squad RB: **266**
urbanization CL: viii, xxi
Us3 JA: 3
U.S. Army
  Joe Henderson JA: 90
  Jimi Hendrix RR: 108
  Tom Paxton FO: 156
  Elvis Presley RR: 181
  John Prine FO: 160
  Wayne Shorter JA: 177–178
  Lester Young JA: 220
U.S. Marine Corps FO: 118; RB: 83–84
U.S. Navy CO: 65
U.S. Navy Band JA: 38, 176
USA for Africa FO: 14; RB: 224–225, 283
US Festival RR: 198, 207
Usher RB: *151,* **266–267,** *267*
Ussachevsky, Vladimir CL: 55, 143, **231**
Utah Symphony CL: **231**
U.T.F.O. RB: **267–268**

V

Valens, Ritchie RR: 113, *239,* **239–240**
Valentine, Gary RR: 27
Valentine, Hilton RR: 9
Valli, Frankie RR: 85–87
valve trombone JA: 130, 199
Vanderbilt, Gloria CL: 216
Vandiver, Pendleton CO: 207
Vandross, Luther RB: **269**
Van Eaton, J. M. RR: 67–68
Van Epps, Fred CO: 11; FO: 12
Vanessa (Samuel Barber) CL: 17, **233**
Van Halen RR: 106, 128, 153, 165
Van Halen, Eddie RR: 106
Vanilla Fudge RR: 41, 133, 152

Vanilla Ice RB: **269–270**
Vanity 6 RB: **270**
van Meter, Sally FO: 68, 79
Van Rijn, Guido BL: 165, 166, 171
Van Ronk, Dave BL: **227;** FO: *207,* **207–208**
  acoustic guitar BL: 4
  Animals, The BL: 7; RR: 9
  Frankie Armstrong FO: 6
  Rev. Gary Davis BL: 50
  New York City BL: 153
  "Spike Driver Blues" BL: 205
  "Statesboro Blues" BL: 206
  vocal styles BL: 233
  Elijah Wald BL: 235
Vänskä, Osmo CL: *233,* **233**
Van Vechten, Carl BL: 201
Van Vliet, Don (Captain Beefheart) RR: 257
Van Zandt, Miami Steve RR: 90, 225
Van Zandt, Townes CO: 67; FO: **208**
Varèse, Edgard CL: 215, **233–234;** RR: 257
variation JA: xxviii–xxix
vaudeville
  Allen Brothers FO: 4
  Carlisle Brothers CO: 31
  Michael Coleman FO: 39
  Uncle Dave Macon CO: 129
  Rouse Brothers FO: 176
  Roy Smeck FO: 189
  Bessie Smith JA: 182
  Mamie Smith JA: 184
Vaughan, James D. CO: 85
Vaughan, Jimmy BL: 25–26, 61, 208, **227,** 228
Vaughan, Stevie Ray BL: 25, 208, 227, **227–228;** RR: 32
Vaughn, Henry FO: 103
Vaughn, Sarah JA: 80, 109, *205,* **205–206**
V-Discs BL: 217
Vedder, Eddie RR: 97, 167–168
Vee, Bobby RR: 70, 114
Vee-Jay Records BL: **180;** RB: **270–271**
Vega, Suzanne FO: 185
Vega Instruments CO: 11; FO: 12, 13
Vega Tubaphone Banjo FO: 12, *13*
Velvet Underground, The RR: 8, 91, 188, **240–242,** *241*
Venom RR: 107
Ventures, The RR: 115
Venuti, Joe CO: 102; JA: 120, **206,** 207, 214
Verdi, Giuseppe CL: 154, 184
verse JA: **206**
verse-chorus song form JA: **206**
Vesey, Denmark BL: 197
VH1 CO: 174
vibraphone JA: **206**
  Gary Burton JA: 26
  Lionel Hampton JA: 81
  Red Norvo JA: 144–145
  Tito Puente JA: 158
  rhythm section JA: 164
Vibrations, The RB: 141
vibrato BL: 105, 229, 237; JA: 206, **207**
Vickers, Walter RB: 83
Vicksburg, Mississippi BL: 247
Vicktor Company CL: 182
Vietnam War
  Joan Baez FO: 9
  Archie Bell and the Drells RB: 14
  Country Joe McDonald FO: 135
  Pete Seeger FO: 183
  "Waist Deep in the Big Muddy" FO: 209
Vig, Butch RR: 160
Village Vanguard
  Richard Dyer-Bennett FO: 56
  Bertha "Chippie" Hill BL: 76
  Shirley Horn JA: 93
  Keith Jarrett JA: 104
  Thad Jones JA: 110
  Mel Lewis JA: 122
  Waltz for Debby JA: 210
  Weavers FO: 212
Vincent, Gene CO: 171; RR: 19, 42, 205
Vincent, Johnny BL: 138
Vincent, Vinnie RR: 130
Vinson, Eddie "Cleanhead" BL: **228;** JA: 38
Vinson, Walter BL: 140, 191, 208, **228–229**
violin JA: **207**. *See also* fiddle; *specific violinists*
violists CL: 138–139
Virginia Minstrels, The FO: 139
Visions of Terror and Wonder (Richard Wernick) CL: **234**
visual arts FO: 3
Vitaphone film shorts FO: 97, 189
Vita Trio, The FO: 189
Vito, Rick FO: 69; RR: 84
Vitous, Miroslav JA: *207,* **207–208**
vocalese JA: 29, 120, 126, 171, **208**
vocal styles BL: **229–234**
Voight, Andrew JA: 166
Voigt, Deborah CL: **234**
Volman, Mark RR: 258
Vonk, Hans CL: **234**
Von Schmidt, Eric BL: **234;** FO: 65

Vontastics, The RB: **271**
Vornbrock, Betty FO: 72
Voyager space probe BL: 94; RR: ix

W

W. W. and the Dixie Dancekings (movie) BL: 114; CO: 171, 216
"Wabash Cannonball" CO: 1, **209**
Wadsworth, Charles CL: 48, 213, **235**
Wagner, Linda CL: 55
Wagner, Richard CL: 25–26, 225
Wagner, Roger CL: 141, **235**
Wagoner, Porter CO: **209–210**
  "Whispering" Bill Anderson CO: 4
  Skeeter Davis CO: 55
  Freddie Hart CO: 95
  Norma Jean CO: 152
  Dolly Parton CO: 158
  Johnny Paycheck CO: 158
  "A Satisfied Mind" CO: 183
  "Uncle Pen" CO: 207
wah-wah pedal JA: 51, **209**
Wailers, The (reggae) RB: 175; RR: 199, 201
Wailers, The (rock) RR: 97
Wainwright, Loudon III FO: 136
"Waist Deep in the Big Muddy" FO: 183, **209**
Wakefield, David CL: 7
Wakefield, Frank FO: 3, 81
Wakely, Jimmy CO: 19, 42, 186
Wakeman, Rick RR: 116, 182, 184
Wald, Elijah BL: xvii, xxi, **235**
  boogie-woogie BL: 28
  "Dust My Broom" BL: 55
  protest songs BL: 168, 170
  "Sweet Home Chicago" BL: 210
  Dave Van Ronk FO: 208
Walden, Narada Michael RB: **273**
Walden, Phil BL: 209; RR: 4
Waldman, Wendy CO: 77
Waldron, Cliff FO: 61
Waldron, Mal JA: 19
Walker, Blind Willie BL: 89, **235,** 242; FO: 50
Walker, Charlie CO: 105
Walker, Clay CO: **210**
Walker, Dave RR: 82
Walker, Frank BL: xxi, **235**
  Allen Brothers FO: 3
  "Downhearted Blues" BL: 54
  Alberta Hunter BL: 83
  music business and the blues BL: 146
  Charlie Poole FO: 159
  vocal styles BL: 232
Walker, George CL: 138, **235**
Walker, Jerry Jeff FO: 36, **209**
Walker, Jimmy RR: 205
Walker, Joel CO: 11
Walker, Joe Louis BL: **235,** 252
Walker, Junior, & the All Stars RB: **273**
Walker, Owen FO: 172
Walker, Phillip BL: **235–236**
Walker, T-Bone BL: xx, **236**
  Clarence "Gatemouth" Brown BL: 30
  Pee Wee Crayton BL: 46
  Dallas, Texas BL: 216
  electric guitar BL: 58
  Blind Lemon Jefferson BL: 93
  B. B. King BL: 105
  "Stormy Monday" BL: 207
  Eddie "Cleanhead" Vinson BL: 228
  Jimmy Witherspoon BL: 245
walking bass BL: 160; JA: 56, **209;** RR: 15, 232
"Walking the Floor over You" CO: 203, **210**
"Walk on the Wild Side" RR: 91, 242
"Walk Right In" BL: 13, 36, 224, **236;** FO: 175
Wallace, Christopher. *See* the Notorious B. I. G.
Wallace, Henry FO: 185
Wallace, Hersal BL: 217
Wallace, Sippie BL: **236–237**
  classic blues BL: 42
  holy blues BL: 77
  Houston, Texas BL: 216–217
  Little Brother Montgomery BL: 141
  Bonnie Raitt BL: 177
  Hociel Thomas BL: 218
  "Women Be Wise" BL: 245
Wallenstein, Alfred CL: 141, **235**
Waller, Charlie FO: 43, 60, 122
Waller, Fats JA: **209–210**
  Count Basie JA: 10
  boogie-woogie BL: 27
  Benny Carter JA: 28
  James P. Johnson JA: 107
  music business and the blues BL: 147
  ragtime and the blues BL: 176
  recordings of early jazz JA: 162
  stride piano JA: 189
  Art Tatum JA: 193
"wall of sound" RB: 229; RR: 204, 221, 222, 224
Wall, The (Pink Floyd) RR: 172, 174, 175

Walls, Mississippi BL: **140**
Walls, Van "Piano Man" BL: **237;** RR: 126, 232
Walsh, Doc BL: 13, 193; FO: 29
Walsh, Joe RR: 75
Walter, Bruno CL: 27, 235, **235–236**
Walton, Mercy Dee BL: **237**
Walton, Staley CO: 12
Waltz for Debby (Bill Evans Trio) JA: **210**
War (band) RB: **273–274;** RR: 9
Ward, Bill RR: 106
Ward, Billy and the Dominoes RB: 181, 281
Ward, David Crockett FO: 210
Ward, Enoch FO: 210
Ward, Fields FO: 210
Ward, Robert CL: 61, **236;** BL: 123, **237**
Ward, Wade FO: 7, **210**
Wardlow, Gayle Dean BL: 139
Warhol, Andy RR: 240–242
Wariner, Steve CO: 207, **210–211,** *211,* 214
Warlocks, The RR: 93, 94
Warmack, Paul FO: 86
Warner, Anne and Frank FO: 160
Warner, Frank FO: 99, 160, 203–204, **210–211**
Warner, Gerrett and Jeff FO: 210
Warnes, Jennifer RR: 205
Warren, Baby Boy BL: **237**
Warren, Butch JA: 211
Warren, Diane CO: 173, 174, 223; RB: 161
Warwick, Dionne RB: **274**
Was, Don BL: 177; CO: 119, 150
Washboard Sam BL: 68, 167, **238**
Washington, Baby RB: **274**
Washington, Dinah BL: **238;** JA: 81, **211,** 223; RB: 16, **274–275**
Washington, Jackie BL: 249
Washington, Walter "Wolfman" BL: **238**
Wasn't That a Time? (documentary) FO: 124, 212
"Wasted Days and Wasted Nights" CO: 71, 72
Watanabe, Sadao JA: 80
Waterman, Dick BL: 47, 177, 217–218
"Watermelon Man" JA: 82, 88, 170, **211**
Waters, Ethel BL: **238;** JA: **211**
  Lovie Austin JA: 7
  Fletcher Henderson JA: 89
  recordings of early jazz JA: 162
  Don Redman JA: 163
  "St. Louis Blues" BL: 187
Waters, Muddy BL: xx, xxi, **238–240,** *239;* RR: ix
  acoustic guitar BL: 4
  bass and drums BL: 15, 16
  Carey Bell BL: 16
  Fred Below BL: 16
  Chuck Berry RB: 17; RR: 24
  Elvin Bishop BL: 17
  Michael Bloomfield BL: 20
  blues lyrics BL: 22
  Bumble Bee Slim BL: 32
  Chicago BL: 40, 41
  Clarksdale, Mississippi BL: 137
  James Cotton BL: 44
  Rory Gallagher BL: 67
  harmonica BL: 73
  Little Walter BL: 116
  Alan Lomax BL: 118
  Bob Margolin BL: 126
  Louis Myers BL: 149
  Robert Nighthawk BL: 154
  Paul Oscher BL: 155
  Pinetop Perkins BL: 158–159
  Robert Petway BL: 159
  Duke Robillard BL: 183
  Jimmy Rogers BL: 184
  Rolling Stones, The RR: 208
  slide guitar BL: 193
  George "Harmonica" Smith BL: 194
  Otis Spann BL: 205
  Hubert Sumlin BL: 208
  Sunnyland Slim BL: 209
  talent scouts BL: 212
  vocal styles BL: 231, 233
  Johnny Winter BL: 245
  ZZ Top BL: 255
Waters, Roger RR: 172, 174, 175
Waterson, Norma FO: 30
Watersons, The FO: 30, 42
Watkins, Doug JA: 180
Watkins, Sara CO: 150; FO: 149
Watkins, Shawn CO: 150; FO: 149
Watkins, Tionne "T-Boz" RB: 259, *259*
Watkins Glen festival RR: 5, 13, 207
Watson, Bobby JA: 185
Watson, Doc FO: **211**
  Tom Ashley FO: 8
  Manny Greenhill FO: 82
  Kentucky Colonels FO: 115
  Mark O'Connor FO: 152
  Ralph Rinzler FO: 170
  "Spike Driver Blues" BL: 205
  Mac Wiseman FO: 217
Watson, Gene FO: **211–212**
Watson, Jim FO: 164, 165, *165*
Watson, Johnny "Guitar" BL: **240;** RB: 18
Watson, Merle FO: 211

Watts (Los Angeles) BL: 155, 245
Watts, André CL: **236**
Watts, Charlie BL: 108, 185; RR: 68, 208
Watts, Noble "Thin Man" RB: 279
Wavy Gravy (Hugh Romney) RR: 249
Wa-Wan Press CL: 14, 23, 76, 88, **237**
Wayne, John CO: 31
WBAI (New York) FO: 209
WBLS (New York City) RB: 176
WBT (Charlotte, North Carolina) CO: 130; FO: 132
WDIA (Memphis) BL: 175
"We Are the World." *See* USA for Africa
Weather Report RB: **275**
  "Birdland" JA: **15**
  Bitches Brew JA: 16
  European jazz JA: 65
  Jaco Pastorius JA: 152
  Wayne Shorter JA: 178
  Miroslav Vitous JA: 207, 208
  Joe Zawinul JA: 223, 224
Weaver, Curley BL: 130, 142, **240**
Weaver, Sylvester BL: 1, **240**
Weaver Brothers and Elviry CO: 30
Weavers, The FO: **212**
  folk revival FO: 70
  "Goodnight, Irene" FO: 79
  Frank Hamilton FO: 90
  Lead Belly BL: 112; FO: 124
  Harold Leventhal FO: 124
  John Lomax BL: 120
  Pete Seeger FO: 182
  "So Long, It's Been Good to Know You" FO: 190
  "This Land Is Your Land" FO: 202
  "Wimoweh" FO: 215
  young black country blues artists BL: 248
Webb, Chick JA: **212**
  "A-Tisket A-Tasket" JA: 7
  Mario Bauzá JA: 11
  cutting contest JA: 45
  Ella Fitzgerald JA: 70; RB: 89
  Louis Jordan BL: 100; RB: 146
  Savoy Ballroom JA: 171
Webb, Jimmy CO: 31
Webb, Stan BL: 41
Weber, Steve FO: 98
Webster, Ben JA: **212–213,** *213*
  Cab Calloway JA: 27
  cutting contest JA: 45
  Duke Ellington JA: 61
  Groove Holmes JA: 92
  Bennie Moten JA: 141
  Archie Shepp JA: 177
  "Take the 'A' Train" JA: 193
Webster, Katie BL: **240**
weeper CO: **211–212,** 213
Weil, Cynthia RR: 204
Weiland, Scott RR: 98
Weill, Kurt CL: 1
Weill Recital Hall CL: 45, **237**
Wein, George FO: 83, 149; JA: 144
Weinberg, Max RR: 225
Weir, Bob RR: 93
Weisgall, Hugo CL: **237**
Weiss, Danny FO: 188, *188*
Weiss, George FO: 216
Weiss, Hy RB: 79, 243, 270
Weiss, Johnny CO: 43
Weiss, Julius CL: 120
Weissberg, Eric FO: 81, 114, 176
Welborn, Larry RR: 112
Welch, Gillian FO: **212–213**
"Welcome to My World" CO: **212**
Welding, Pete BL: 82, 173
Weldon, Casey Bill BL: 132, 192, **241**
Wells, Jean RB: **275–276**
Wells, Junior BL: 33, 69, 149, **241**
Wells, Kitty CO: **212–213**
  Everly Brothers CO: 70
  Don Gibson CO: 81
  "Hey Joe" CO: 99
  honky-tonk music CO: 102
  Harlan Howard CO: 105
  Jan Howard CO: 106
  "I Can't Stop Loving You" CO: 107
  Louisiana Hayride CO: 123
  Loretta Lynn CO: 127
  Benny Martin FO: 133
  weeper CO: 212
  "Wild Side of Life, The" CO: 215
Wells, Mary RB: 152, **276**
Welnick, Vince RR: 93
Welser-Möst, Franz CL: *237,* **237–238**
Welsh, Bob RR: 82
Werner, Joe FO: 89
Wernick, Pete CO: 16; FO: 42, 43, 100, 151, 161
Wernick, Richard CL: 234, **238**
Wertz, Kenny CO: 75; FO: 43
"We Shall Overcome" BL: 203; FO: 28, 33
Wesley, Fred, & the J.B.'s RB: **276**
West, Bill CO: 213
West, Dottie CO: 41, 79, 81, 178, 210, **213–214**
West, Hedy CO: 12

West, Kanye RB: **276–277**
West, Mae BL: 15
West, Speedy CO: 145, 160–161
Westbrook, Mike JA: 191
West Coast. *See* California
West Coast jazz JA: xxiv–xxv, 9, 24–25, 80, 142. *See also* cool jazz
West Coast Rap All-Stars RB: **277**
Westerberg, Paul RR: 177
Western Caravan, The CO: 43
Western Swing CO: **214;** FO: **213**. *See also specific artists*
  accordions FO: 2
  Cajun music FO: 27
  cowboy songs CO: 46
  drums RR: 67
Weston, Bob RR: 82
Weston, Kim RB: **277**
West Point, Mississippi BL: 82, **140**
West Side (Chicago) BL: 42, 51, 59, 123, 186, 213
Westside Connection RB: **277–278**
Wexler, Jerry
  Atlantic Records BL: 9
  Ahmet Ertegun RB: 83
  Aretha Franklin RB: 96
  Rick Hall RB: 115
  King Curtis BL: 106
  Memphis BL: 132
  Doug Sahm BL: 187
  Sam and Dave RB: 234
  Swamp Dogg BL: 209
Weymouth, Tina RR: 231, 232
WGN (Chicago) CO: 148
Wheatstraw, Peetie BL: 21, 22, 140, 153, 168, **241**
Wheeling Jamboree CO: 96; FO: 41, 44, 126, 154
Whelan, Mike FO: 18
"When the Levee Breaks" BL: 113, 133, 144
"When You Say Nothing At All" CO: 118, 215
Whetsol, Arthur JA: 60
"Which Side Are You On?" FO: **213–214**
While, Chris FO: 102
Whispers, The RB: **278**
Whitburn, Joel RB: 24, 30, 256
White, Barry RB: 251, **278**
White, Betsy. *See* Hood, Adelyne
White, Bryan CO: **214**
White, Buck FO: 214
White, Bukka BL: **241–242**
  blues lyrics BL: 22
  John Fahey BL: 61
  B. B. King BL: 105
  slide guitar BL: 192
  vocal styles BL: 230
  Washboard Sam BL: 238
White, Charles RR: 143
White, Clarence
  Byrds FO: 25; RR: 37
  Gene Clark FO: 36
  Richard Greene FO: 81
  David Grisman FO: 83
  Kentucky Colonels FO: 114, 115
  Muleskinner FO: 143, 144
White, Eric FO: 114
White, Jack CO: 127
White, Josh BL: **242;** FO: **214**
  aliases BL: 5
  Moses Asch FO: 7
  blind musicians and singers BL: 18
  Civil Rights movement FO: 34
  Lawrence Gellert BL: 67
  Manny Greenhill FO: 82
  holy blues BL: 77
  "Spider" John Koerner FO: 118
  Buddy Moss BL: 142
  New York City BL: 153
  protest songs BL: 168, 170
  record labels BL: 181
  Walter Roland BL: 185
  social history BL: 201–202
  Blind Joe Taggart BL: 211
  Elijah Wald BL: 235
  Blind Willie Walker BL: 235
  Weavers FO: 212
White, Josh, Jr. BL: 242, 249
White, Kevin FO: 25
White, Lenny JA: 15
White, Maurice RB: 77, 81, 165
White, Pat Goza FO: 214
White, Roland FO: 43, 114, 115, 145
White, Sharon CO: 186; FO: 214
white blues musicians. *See specific musicians*
Whiteman, Paul JA: **213–215,** *214*
  Bix Beiderbecke JA: 12
  Jimmy Dorsey JA: 55
  Tommy Dorsey JA: 56
  Ferde Grofé CL: 94
  Red Norvo JA: 144
  Don Redman JA: 163
  Jack Teagarden JA: 195
  third stream jazz JA: 197
  Frankie Trumbauer JA: 199
  Joe Venuti JA: 206
  violin JA: 207
"White Rabbit" RR: 118, 119
Whites, The FO: **214–215**
White Top, Virginia, folk festival FO: 190
Whitfield, Norman RB: 246, 265

Whitford, Brad RR: 1–3
Whiting, Margaret CO: 186, 192
Whitley, Keith CO: 143, 186, 191, **214–215;** FO: 47, 193
Whitley, Ray CO: 9; FO: 129
Whitlock, Billy FO: 139
Whitlock, Bob JA: 142
Whitman, Slim CO: **215**
Whittaker, Hudson. *See* Tampa Red
Whitter, Henry CO: 52, 167, 221; FO: 193, 202, **215**
Who, The RR: **243–246,** *244*
  classic rock RR: 41
  Eddie Cochran RR: 42
  Monterey Pop Festival RR: 151, 152
  Sonny Boy Williamson II BL: 245
  Woodstock RR: 248
"Whole Lotta Love" BL: 108, 113, 144; RR: 134
"Whole Lotta Shakin' Goin' On" BL: 17; CO: 122
WIBB (Macon, Georgia) RB: 26–27
Wiedlin, Jane CO: 207
Wiggins, Phil BL: 38, 73–74
Wilborn, Marshall FO: 111
Wilburn Brothers CO: 125
Wilcox, David BL: 223
Wild, Earl CL: *238,* **238–239**
"Wild Side of Life, The" CO: 102, 212, **215**
Wild Tchoupitoulas BL: 152
"Wild Women Don't Get the Blues" BL: 46, **242–243**
Wiley, Geechie BL: 3
Wilkerson, George FO: 73
Wilkerson, John FO: 170
Wilkins, Joe Willie BL: 206, **243**
Wilkins, Robert BL: 77, 89, **243**
Wilkinson, Kristin FO: 23
Willet, Slim CO: 79; FO: 214
Williams, Andre RB: 92, 199
Williams, Andy CO: 22, 140; FO: 145, 146
Williams, Audrey CO: 104, 216, 217
Williams, Bert BL: xv
Williams, Big Joe BL: **243**
  "Baby, Please Don't Go" BL: 11
  Michael Bloomfield BL: 20
  David "Honeyboy" Edwards BL: 57
  Forest City Joe BL: 65
  Larry Johnson BL: 95
  Doug Quattlebaum BL: 173
  Sonny Boy Williamson I BL: 244
Williams, Billy RB: **278**
Williams, Buster JA: 30, 83
Williams, Charles CO: 12
Williams, Clarence BL: 127, 162, **243–244;** JA: 209
Williams, Cootie BL: 228; JA: 61, 156
Williams, Dana CO: 56
Williams, Daniel Huggins FO: 59, 60
Williams, Deniece RB: **278**
Williams, Don CO: 39, **215–216**
Williams, Eddie RB: 143
Williams, Gloria RB: 177
Williams, Hank CO: viii, xvii, **216–217**
  Cajun music CO: 29
  Chuck Wagon Gang CO: 37
  "Cold, Cold Heart" CO: 40
  Drifting Cowboys CO: 63
  Bob Dylan RR: 69
  fiddle CO: 72
  Grand Ole Opry CO: 87
  Rex Griffin CO: 89
  honky-tonk music CO: 102
  Johnny Horton CO: 104
  Louisiana Hayride CO: 123
  "Lovesick Blues" CO: 125–126
  Benny Martin FO: 133
  Grady Martin CO: 134
  Emmett Miller FO: 138
  "Move It on Over" CO: 144
  pedal steel guitar CO: 160
  Ray Price CO: 163
  Fred Rose CO: 179
  Del Shannon RR: 215
  weeper CO: 212
  Hank Williams, Jr. CO: 217
  yodeling CO: 224
  "Your Cheatin' Heart" CO: 225
Williams, Hank, Jr. CO: viii, 3, 20, 116, **217**
Williams, Henry BL: 82
Williams, J. Mayo BL: 93, 178, 212, 239, **244**
Williams, Jerry. *See* Swamp Dogg
Williams, Joe BL: **244;** JA: 81
Williams, John CL: 5, 34, **239–240;** JA: 215
Williams, Lamar RR: 5, 6
Williams, Leona CO: 91–92
Williams, Lucinda CO: 32; FO: **215**
Williams, Mary Lou JA: xxx, *215,* **215–216**
  Lovie Austin JA: 7
  Barbara Carroll JA: 28
  Andrew Cyrille JA: 46
  Kansas City jazz JA: 111
  Mary Lou Williams Women in Jazz Festival JA: 129
Williams, Michelle RB: 59, *59*

Williams, Otis RB: 39, 254, 255
Williams, Paul RB: 254, 255, **279;** RR: 149
Williams, Pharrell RB: 193, 194
Williams, Robert Pete BL: 22, **244**
Williams, Susan CL: 26
Williams, Terry FO: 146
Williams, Tex CO: 43, 188, 200
Williams, Tony JA: **216**
 Cindy Blackman JA: 16
 Ron Carter JA: 30
 Miles Davis JA: 49
 "E.S.P." JA: 63
 fusion JA: 72
 Herbie Hancock JA: 82
 John McLaughlin JA: 131
 Diane Reeves JA: 163
 In a Silent Way JA: 98
 Larry Young JA: 219
Williamsburg Bridge (New York) JA: 165
Williamson, James. *See* Homesick James
Williamson, Lois LaVerne. *See* O'Day, Molly
Williamson, Narcissa CL: 34
Williamson, Robin FO: 106
Williamson, Skeets and Laverne CO: 9
Williamson, Sonny Boy I (John Lee Williamson) BL: **244;** RB: **279**
 James Cotton BL: 44
 Blind John Davis BL: 49
 harmonica BL: 72–73
 Lillian McMurry BL: 130
 mandolin BL: 125
 Yank Rachell BL: 175
 Joe Willie Wilkins BL: 243
Williamson, Sonny Boy II (Rice Miller) BL: **244–245;** RB: **279**
 Arkansas BL: 7
 blues rock RR: 28
 Eric Clapton RR: 39
 harmonica BL: 72–73
 Elmore James BL: 90
 Led Zeppelin RR: 134
 Little Walter BL: 116
 Robert Lockwood, Jr. BL: 116
 Alan Lomax BL: 118
 Pinetop Perkins BL: 158
 Jimmy Rogers BL: 184
 Houston Stackhouse BL: 206
 Yardbirds, The BL: 247; RR: 252
Williamson, Steve JA: **216–217**
Willie D RB: **279–280**
Willingham, Johnny "Gus" RB: 33, 34
Willis, Chuck RB: **280**
Willis, Ralph BL: **245**
Will Rogers Follies, The CO: 54, 79
Wills, Billy Jack CO: 219
Wills, Bob CO: *218,* **218–219**
 Milton Brown CO: 24
 cowboy songs CO: 46
 Tommy Duncan CO: 65–66
 Stoney Edwards CO: 68
 Johnny Gimble CO: 82; FO: 77
 Grand Ole Opry CO: 87
 Leon McAuliffe FO: 134
 Tiny Moore FO: 142
 Charlie Poole FO: 159
 "San Antonio Rose" CO: 183
 Sylvester Weaver BL: 240
 Western Swing FO: 213
 western swing CO: 214
 yodeling CO: 224
Wills, Johnny Lee CO: 219
Will the Circle Be Unbroken? (album: Nitty Gritty Dirt Band et al)
 Carter Family CO: 35
 Vassar Clements FO: 37
 Jimmy Martin FO: 134
 Nitty Gritty Dirt Band CO: 151
 Merle Travis CO: 200
 Doc Watson FO: 211
"Will the Circle Be Unbroken?" (song) CO: 34, **219**
"Will You Still Love Me Tomorrow" RR: 217, 221
Wilmington, Delaware BL: 220
Wilson, Al BL: 36, 82
Wilson, Brian RR: 15–18, 229–230
Wilson, Carl RR: 15, 17, 18
Wilson, Cassandra JA: 16, **217–218;** RB: **280–281**
Wilson, Dennis RR: 15, 16, 18
Wilson, Frank FO: 97
Wilson, Gretchen CO: viii–ix
Wilson, J. Frank RR: 168
Wilson, Jackie (R&B singer) RB: 48, 164, 188, **281;** RR: 153
Wilson, John RB: 239
Wilson, Kim BL: 61, 208, 227
Wilson, Mark FO: 72
Wilson, Mary RB: 256
Wilson, Murry RR: 15
Wilson, Nancy JA: 211, **218**
Wilson, Ron RR: 68
Wilson, Rossiere "Shadow" JA: 62–63, **218**
Wilson, Stan BL: 249
Wilson, Steve JA: 43
Wilson, Teddy JA: 76, 81, 213
Wilson, Tony RB: 124, 125
Wilson, Woodrow BL: 79
"Wimoweh" FO: 182, 212, **215–216**
Winburn, Anna Mae JA: 99
Winbush, Angela RB: **281**
Windows 95 RR: 210

Windows (Jacob Druckman) CL: **240**
Winograd, Arthur CL: 121
Winograd, Peter CL: 8
Winston, Winnie FO: 83
Winter, Edgar BL: 162–163, 245; RR: 116, 127
Winter, Johnny BL: 103, 216, 240, **245;** RR: 198
Winter Dance Party tour RR: 113, 239
Winwood, Stevie BL: 41, 233; RR: 39, 40, 125–126
Wire, The (magazine) JA: **218**
WIS (Columbia, South Carolina) FO: 110, 111
Wisconsin JA: 221
Wisconsin Chair Company BL: 178
Wise, Chubby CO: 15; FO: **216**
Wiseman, Mac FO: **216–217**
Wiseman, Scott FO: 127–128
WIS Hillbillies FO: 111
Wish You Were Here (Pink Floyd) RR: 172, 174
Withers, Bill RB: **281–282**
Witherspoon, Jimmy BL: 64, 130, **245**
Wittgenstein, Paul CL: **240**
Wiz, The (Broadway musical) JA: 23; RB: 184, 269
WLAC (Nashville) BL: 175
WLS (Chicago). *See also National Barn Dance*
  Arkie the Arkansas Woodchopper FO: 5
  Gene Autry CO: 7
  Duke of Paducah, The CO: 65
  Red Foley CO: 76
  harmonica BL: 72
  Hay, George D. CO: 96–97
  Hoosier Hot Shots CO: 103
  Bradley Kincaid FO: 116
  Lily May Ledford FO: 124
  Bill Monroe CO: 140
  National Barn Dance CO: 148
WLW (Cincinnati, Ohio) CO: 30
WMC (Memphis) CO: 96
WNOX (Knoxville, Tennessee) CO: 101, 124; FO: 126, 152, 153
WNYC (New York City) FO: 19
Wobblies FO: 158
WOBU (Charleston, West Virginia) FO: 45
Wolf, Peter BL: 94
Wolf, Richard RB: 162
Wolfe, Charles BL: 232
Wolff, Francis JA: 158
Wolff, Hugh CL: 163, 197, **240**
Wolfman Jack RR: 208
Wolf Trap CL: 27, **240–241**
Wolpe, Stefan CL: 207, **241**
Woltz, Da Costa, Southern Broadcasters FO: 110
Womack, Bobby RB: **282**
Womack, Lee Ann CO: 150, **219–220,** *220;* FO: 138
Woman Blue (Judy Roderick) BL: 184, 221
"Women Be Wise (Don't Advertise Your Man)" BL: 237, **245**
women blues singers BL: xvii, xix. *See also* classic blues; *specific artists*
women in jazz JA: xxix–xxxi. *See also specific artists*
women in rock RR: 187
Women's Philharmonic CL: 128, **241**
Wonder, Stevie RB: **282–283**
  Gary Byrd RB: 32
  Herbie Hancock JA: 83
  Kwamé RB: 159
  Motown RR: 154
  Minnie Riperton RB: 226
  David Sanborn JA: 169
  Spinners, The RB: 245
  Deniece Williams RB: 278
Wonder Who, The RR: 87
Wood, Andy RR: 167
Wood, Chris JA: 133
Wood, Randy CO: 170
Wood, Ron RR: 208
Wood, Roy RR: 75, 76
wood blocks JA: 54
Wooding, Sam BL: 92
Woodruff, Steve FO: 173
Woods, Gay and Terry FO: 194
Woods, Hosea BL: 236
Woods, Nick FO: 146
Woodstock '94 RR: 249–250
Woodstock '99 RR: 250
Woodstock Mountains Revue FO: 2
Woodstock (movie) RR: 245, 248
Woodstock music festival (1969) RR: **246–250**
  Arhoolie Records BL: 7
  Band, The RR: 13
  Creedence Clearwater Revival RR: 48
  Richie Havens FO: 93
  Jimi Hendrix BL: 75; RR: 108, 110
  Incredible String Band FO: 106
  Country Joe McDonald FO: 135
  psychedelic rock RR: 187
  rock festivals RR: 206

Woodstock music festival (*continued*)
rock revival RR: 207
Santana (band) RR: 213
singer-songwriters RR: 220
Who, The RR: 243, 245
"Woodstock" (song) RR: 220, 249, 254
woodwinds JA: 71, **218**. *See also specific woodwinds, e.g.* clarinet
Woody, Allen RR: 6
Wooley, Sheb CO: 139
Woolf, Virginia CL: 82
Woolweaver, Scott CL: 34
Work, John (folklorist) BL: 137
Work, John W. (composer) BL: 78
work camps BL: 27, 190
Workingman's Dead (Grateful Dead) CO: 45; RR: 95, 211
"Working on the Project" BL: 22, 168
Workman, Reggie JA: 40, 46
work songs BL: xvii
Works Project Administration. *See* WPA
World Hunger Year FO: 31
world music FO: ix–x, xvi; JA: xxvi, **218**
World War I CL: 160, 240; BL: 133–135, 200–201; FO: 150; JA: 63
World War II
Toshiko Akiyoshi JA: 3
and all-women big bands JA: xxx–xxxi
Gene Autry CO: 7
Leslie Bassett CL: 20–21
Ivy Benson JA: 14
Marc Blitzstein CL: 30–31
Jorge Bolet CL: 33
Philipe Brun JA: 25
Civil Rights movement FO: 33
Bill Cox FO: 45
Ernestine "Tiny" Davis JA: 47
Duke of Paducah, The CO: 65
Coleman Hawkins JA: 87
Hi Flyers FO: 96
Adolph Hofner CO: 101
Hot Club de France JA: 94
Cisco Houston FO: 100
Alberta Hunter BL: 83; JA: 95
International Sweethearts of Rhythm JA: 99
Japanese jazz JA: 103
Thor Johnson CL: 119
Pee Wee King CO: 117
Gail Kubik CL: 131
Leon McAuliffe FO: 134
Yehudi Menuhin CL: 153
migration BL: 133
Darius Milhaud CL: 155
Glenn Miller JA: 134
New Jersey Symphony Orchestra CL: 163
record labels BL: 178–179
Django Reinhardt JA: 164
"Reuben James" FO: 168
San Francisco Bay Area BL: 35
Artie Shaw JA: 176
social history BL: 202
Sir Georg Solti CL: 210
Isaac Stern CL: 214
Roosevelt Sykes BL: 210
Sister Rosetta Tharpe BL: 217
Weavers FO: 212
Earl Wild CL: 239
Jimmy Witherspoon BL: 245
Lester Young JA: 220
World Wide Web FO: 164
Worrell, Bernie RR: 232
"Would You Lay with Me (In a Field of Stone)" CO: 40, 204, **220**
WOWO (Fort Wayne, Indiana) CO: 103
WPA (Works Project Administration) BL: 22, 166, 199, 201; FO: 87
Wray, Link RR: 115
WRC (Washington, D. C.) FO: 97
Wrecking Crew, The RR: 68
"Wreck of the Old 97, The" CO: 52, 165, 167, 211–212, **220–221;** FO: 215
"Wreck on the Highway" CO: 1, **221**
Wright, Betty RB: 168, **283**
Wright, Billy RR: 141
Wright, Charley CO: 166
Wright, Chely CO: viii
Wright, Darlene (Darlene Love) RB: 21
Wright, Gary RR: 127
Wright, Gene JA: 24
Wright, Gil CO: 116
Wright, Harold Bell CO: 22
Wright, Johnny CO: 212
Wright, Norma Jean RB: 41
Wright, O. V. RB: 107, **283**
Wright, Richard BL: 201; RR: 172, 174
WROL (Knoxville, Tennessee) CO: 187
WRR (Dallas, Texas) CO: 20
WSB (Atlanta) CO: 33; FO: 53, 110, 192–193
WSM Barn Dance CO: 97, 129
WSM (Nashville) CO: vii
DeFord Bailey CO: 9
Owen Bradley CO: 21

Ralph Emery CO: 68
Grand Ole Opry CO: 86
Gully Jumpers FO: 86
harmonica BL: 72
Hay, George D. CO: 97
Robert Lunn FO: 128
Uncle Dave Macon CO: 129
Melba Montgomery CO: 142
Fred Rose CO: 179
Carl Smith CO: 187
Fiddlin' Arthur Smith FO: 189
Uncle Jimmy Thompson FO: 203
Ernest Tubb CO: 203
Wuorinen, Charles CL: 138, 143, 225, **241–242**
Wurlitzer electric piano RR: 126
Wu-Tang Clan RB: 110, **283–285**
WVON (Chicago) BL: 39, 175; RB: 271
WWOK (Alabama) CO: 84
WWVA (Wheeling, West Virginia) CO: 143, 157; FO: 41, 126, 154
Wyland, DeDe FO: 188, *188*
Wyman, Bill RR: 208
Wynans, Reese BL: 228
Wynette, Tammy CO: **221**
Harold "Pappy" Daily CO: 52
Gatlin Brothers CO: 79
George Jones CO: 111
Dolly Parton CO: 158
Johnny Paycheck CO: 158
"Stand by Your Man" CO: 189–190
weeper CO: 212

X

X-Clan RB: **287**
X-Ecutioners RB: **287**
XERA (Mexico) CO: 34, 83
xylophone JA: 144
Xzibit RB: **287–288**

Y

Yancey, Jimmy BL: 26, 85, 161, **247**
Yancey, Mama BL: 247
Yanofsky, Zal BL: 122
Yarbrough, Glen FO: 99
Yardbirds, The BL: **247;** RR: **251–253,** *252*
blues rock RR: 28
Eric Clapton BL: 41; RR: 39
John Lee Hooker BL: 80
Led Zeppelin BL: 113; RR: 133
Sonny Boy Williamson II (Rice Miller) BL: 245
Yarrow, Peter FO: 76, 83, 157
Yasgur, Max RR: 247
Yearwood, Trisha CO: 23, **223**
Yes RR: 184, 185
Yoakam, Dwight CO: **223–224**
"Always Late (With Your Kisses)" CO: 4
Bakersfield Sound CO: 10
Rosie Flores FO: 69
Buck Owens CO: 156
"T for Texas (Blue Yodel Number One)" CO: 197
yodeling CO: **224**
yoga CL: 153
York, John FO: 25; RR: 37
York, Paul FO: 53
Yorke, Thom RR: 195, 196
Yorkville, Toronto RR: 253
"You Are My Sunshine" CO: 54, **224–225**
Young, Andre. *See* Dr Dre
Young, Faron CO: 98, 140, 149, **225;** FO: 37
Young, Izzy FO: 57, **219**
Young, Johnny BL: 125, 148, **247**
Young, La Monte CL: **243**
Young, Larry JA: 15, 51–52, 131, 148, 216, **219**
Young, Lester JA: **219–221,** *220*
Count Basie JA: 10
Birdland JA: 15
cutting contest JA: 45
Stan Getz JA: 74
Dexter Gordon JA: 77
Chico Hamilton JA: 80
Billie Holiday BL: 76
Kansas City jazz JA: 111
Modern Jazz Quartet JA: 138
Charlie Parker JA: 152
Oscar Peterson JA: 153
saxophone JA: 171
Zoot Sims JA: 182
Sir Charles Thompson JA: 197
Lennie Tristano JA: 199
Frankie Trumbauer JA: 199
Ben Webster JA: 212
Young, Mighty Joe BL: **247–248**
Young, Neil RR: **253–255,** *254*
Buffalo Springfield RR: 34, 35
Rick James RB: 139
Pearl Jam RR: 168
singer-songwriters RR: 220
Young, Rusty CO: 45
young black country blues artists BL: 26, 204, 233, **248–253**
Youngblood, Lonnie RR: 108
Youngblood Brass Band JA: **221**
Youngbloods, The CO: 154
Young Hearts RB: **289**

Young M.C. RB: 56, **289**
Young People's Concerts (TV series) CL: 27, 59
Young Rascals, The. *See* Rascals, The
"Your Cheatin' Heart" CO: 212, 217, **225**
"You've Lost That Lovin' Feelin'" RR: 204, 223
Ysaÿe, Eugène CL: 20, 51, 152, **243**
Yule, Doug RR: 242

Z

Zager, Michael, & the Moon Band RB: 29, **291**
Zankel Hall CL: 45, **245**
Zappa, Frank RR: **257–259,** *258*
  Alice Cooper RR: 43
  jam bands RR: 117
  Jean Luc Ponty JA: 156
  rock revival RR: 207–208
  Velvet Underground, The RR: 241
Zawinul, Joe JA: **223–224**
  Cannonball Adderly JA: 3
  "Birdland" JA: **15**
  Bitches Brew JA: 15
  Richard Bona JA: 20
  Miles Davis JA: 49
  European jazz JA: 65
  Maynard Ferguson JA: 70
  Jaco Pastorius JA: 152
  piano JA: 155
  Wayne Shorter JA: 178
  In a Silent Way JA: 98
  Dinah Washington JA: 211
  Weather Report RB: 275
Zephyr BL: **253**
Zimbalist, Efrem CL: 209, **245**
Zoller, Attilla JA: **224**
Zorn, John JA: **224–225**
Zukerman, Pinchas CL: 43, 197
Zukofsky, Paul CL: **245**
Zwilich, Ellen Taafe CL: 7, **246**
zydeco BL: 38–39, 121, 183; CO: 29–30; FO: 27, 32
ZZ Top BL: 138, **254**

Editorial Board of Advisers

Richard Carlin, general editor, is the author of several books of music, including *Southern Exposure, The Big Book of Country Music, Classical Music: An Informal Guide,* and the five-volume *Worlds of Music.* He has also written and compiled several books of music instruction and songbooks and served as advisory editor on country music for the American National Biography. Carlin has contributed articles on traditional music to various journals, including the *Journal of Ethnomusicology, Sing Out!, Pickin', Frets,* and *Mugwumps.* He has also produced 10 albums of traditional music for Folkways Records. A longtime editor of books on music, dance, and the arts, Carlin is currently executive editor of music and dance at Routledge Publishers. He previously spent six years as executive editor at Schirmer Books and was the founding editor at A Cappella Books, an imprint of the Chicago Review Press.

Barbara Ching, Ph.D., is an associate professor of English at the University of Memphis. She obtained a graduate certificate in women's studies and her doctorate in literature from Duke University. Dr. Ching has written extensively on country music and rural identity, and she is the author of *Wrong's What I Do Best: Hard Country Music and Contemporary Culture* (Oxford University Press) and *Knowing Your Place: Rural Identity and Cultural Hierarchy* (Routledge). She has also contributed articles and chapters to numerous other works on the subject and has presented papers at meetings of the International Association for the Study of Popular Music.

Ronald D. Cohen, Ph.D., is professor emeritus of history at Indiana University–Northwest (Gary). He obtained a doctorate in history from the University of Minnesota–Minneapolis. Dr. Cohen has written extensively on the folk music revival and is the coproducer, with Jeff Place, of *The Best of Broadside: 1962–1988: Anthems of the American Underground from the Pages of Broadside Magazine* (five-CD boxed set with illustrated book, Smithsonian Folkways Recordings, 2000), which was nominated for a Grammy Award in 2001. He is also the author of *Rainbow Quest: The Folk Music Revival and American Society, 1940–1970* (University of Massachusetts Press) and the editor of *Alan Lomax: Selected Writings, 1934–1997* (Routledge). He is also the editor of the Scarecrow Press book series American Folk Music and Musicians.

William Duckworth is the composer of more than 100 pieces of music and the author of six books and numerous articles, the most recent of which is "Making Music on the Web" (*Leonardo Music Journal,* vol. 9, December 1999). In the mid-1990s he and codirector Nora Farrell began *Cathedral,* a multiyear work of music and art for the Web that went online June 10, 1997. Incorporating acoustic and computer music, live Web casts by its own band, and newly created virtual instruments, *Cathedral* is one of the first interactive works of music and art on the Web. Recently, Duckworth and Farrell created Cathedral 2001, a 48-hour World Wide Web event, with 34 events streamed live from five continents.

Duckworth is currently a professor of music at Bucknell University in Pennsylvania.

Kevin Holm-Hudson, Ph.D., received his doctorate of musical arts (composition with ethnomusicology concentration) from the University of Illinois at Urbana-Champaign. He is an assistant professor of music at the University of Kentucky and is an editor/contributor to *Progressive Rock Reconsidered* (Routledge). Dr. Holm-Hudson is also the author of numerous articles that have appeared in such publications as *Genre* and *Ex Tempore* and has presented papers on a wide variety of topics at conferences, including "'Come Sail Away' and the Commodification of Prog Lite," at the inaugural Conference on Popular Music and American Culture in 2002.

Nadine Hubbs, Ph.D., is associate professor of music and women's studies at the University of Michigan (Ann Arbor). She has written extensively on classical and popular music, particularly in relation to gender and sexuality. Dr. Hubbs is the author of *The Queer Composition of America's Sound: Gay Modernists, American Music, and National Identity* (University of California Press) and various essays, including "The Imagination of Pop-Rock Criticism" in *Expression in Pop-Rock Music* (Garland Publications) and "Music of the 'Fourth Gender': Morrissey and the Sexual Politics of Melodic Contour," featured in the journal Genders.

Craig Morrison, Ph.D., holds a doctorate in humanities with a concentration in music from Concordia University (Montreal, Quebec). He is currently a professor of music at Concordia, where he teaches a course titled "Rock and Roll and Its Roots." Dr. Morrison is the author of *Go Cat Go! Rockabilly Music and Its Makers* (University of Illinois Press) and contributed to *The Encyclopedia of the Blues* (Routledge). He has presented many papers on elements of rock and roll.

Albin J. Zak III, Ph.D., earned a doctorate in musicology from the Graduate Center of the City University of New York and is currently chairman of the music department at the University at Albany (SUNY). His publications include *The Velvet Underground Companion* (Schirmer Books) and *The Poetics of Rock: Cutting Tracks, Making Records* (University of California Press). Dr. Zak is also a songwriter, recording engineer, and record producer.